WITHDRAWN

Bad News

The Double-Edged Sword: How Character Makes and Ruins Presidents from Washington to Clinton

Fate of the Union: America's Rocky Road to Political Stalemate

Hard Bargain: How FDR Twisted Churchill's Arm, Evaded the Law, and Changed the Role of the American Presidency

Riddle of Power: Presidential Leadership from Truman to Bush

None of the Above: Why Presidents Fail and What Can Be Done About It

Promises to Keep: Carter's First 100 Days

A Question of Judgment: The Fortas Case and the Struggle for the Supreme Court

The Detroit Race Riot: A Study in Violence (with Tom Craig)

BAD NEWS

Where the Press Goes Wrong
in the Making of the President

ROBERT SHOGAN

Ivan R. Dee

CHICAGO   2001

Library of Congress Cataloging-in-Publication Data:
Shogan, Robert.
    Bad news : where the press goes wrong in the making of the president /
Robert Shogan.
        p.   cm.
    ISBN 1-56663-346-X
    1. Press and politics—United States. 2. Presidents—United States—
Election. I. Title.

PN4888.P6 S53 2001
070.4'49324973—dc21   00-050434

To Ellen, Cindy, and Amy

Contents

Preface

POLITICIANS AND THE PRESS have been blaming each other for most of the problems of our election process since the first presidential campaign, with some merit on each side. For their sins, politicians are answerable to the electorate every two or four years. Journalistic accountability is a much less structured affair. Fortunately, though, most reporters, at least the ones I have known, seem to be both ambitious and conscientious, a combination that produces a good deal of individual and collective soul searching for ways to improve their performance. My hope is that this book will contribute to that process as well as aiding concerned citizens who happen not to be directly involved in either politics or journalism, by providing them with a sort of self-defense manual against the excesses and errors of the practitioners of both trades.

I myself owe a great deal for whatever I have been able to accomplish in journalism to scores of colleagues who over four decades have been patient enough to make suggestions that have helped me to cover the news. They are too many to mention all of them. But I want to give special thanks to one old friend from my first newspaper job, Tom Allen, at the *Bridgeport Herald;* to one newer friend who helped guide me through my years at the *Los Angeles Times,* Don Frederick; and to my best friend and life partner, Ellen Shrewsbury Shogan, who helped edit this manuscript with an understanding heart and a clear head. I also wish to express my appreciation to Ben Ginsberg, David Samuels, and Warren Mitofsky who read portions of the manuscript, and to my publisher, Ivan Dee, for his belief that older reporters should not just fade away.

R. S.

Chevy Chase, Maryland
January 2001

Bad News

O N E

The Enablers

MONTHS BEFORE George W. Bush officially announced his candidacy for the presidency, I spent a day with him as he campaigned in his home state of Texas for reelection to the governor's office he had won four years earlier. We traveled in style in his sleek chartered jet, which, as Bush pointed out, "is what you get when you have $14 million in your war chest."

The rolling countryside stretching from Austin to San Antonio that the governor ranged across on this hot, dusty day is rich in Texas history. Hays County, his first stop, was named for Jack Hays, a legendary Texas Ranger captain who led a bloody rout of the Comanches a century and a half ago. San Marcos, the county seat, is home to Southwest Texas State College, alma mater of the first Texan president, Lyndon Baines Johnson. Next we visited Floresville, about one hundred miles south, the site of the two-hundred-acre ranch that used to belong to John B. Connally, another self-made Texas titan and another presidential aspirant—a domain to which Connally clung even after he went bankrupt.

But in his stump speeches Bush was less interested in the past than in writing new history of his own. Governor Bush is no more a spellbinder than was President Bush. But the eldest son's direct, informal manner created an impression of force and authenticity that his father rarely achieved. Although he was nominally only running for reelection as governor, Bush promised the admiring south Texas crowds that his candidacy would be the harbinger of nothing less than a fundamental shift in American culture to what he heralded as "the responsibility era."

"I'm worried about a culture that says, 'If it feels good, do it, if you've got a problem just go ahead and blame somebody else,'" Bush declared. "I see a more compassionate time which says that each and every one of us are responsible for the decisions we make in life."

By then it was no secret that Bush had been something of a hellion as a young man. "George had a good time, and there were a lot of gin and tonics and a lot of fun and a lot of wise-guy remarks," his cousin and friend since childhood, John Ellis, a TV journalist, told me. And down deep, Bush remains a smart aleck. "If someone agreed with me 100 percent of the time, one of us wouldn't be necessary," he remarked, trying to demonstrate his willingness to accept different viewpoints. Then he added: "That's a funny line, you ought to get it in the paper."

But the years have altered his mores and his way of life. On his fortieth birthday, Bush—reputedly with some prompting from his wife—decided that alcohol was "interfering with my energy level," and quit drinking cold. That did not turn him into an advocate for prohibition. But during our travels that day he did urge young people not to drop out of school, not to use drugs and alcohol, and, in particular, not to have children out of wedlock. He spoke highly of a Baptist program called "True Love Waits," which advocates sexual abstinence before marriage.

"Do you think a presidential candidate needs to practice what he preaches?" I asked him after the speechmaking, when we chatted aboard his campaign jet.

Bush gave me a look that would curdle milk in an ice-cold bottle. "I have never committed adultery, if that's what you're asking," he snapped. Then, still glaring at me, he said, "Now there's a question that I'd like to ask you."

"Sure, go ahead," I told him.

"How does it feel to belong to a profession where you have to ask people questions like that?"

"That's what I do for a living," I said. But I knew that was not

4

much of an answer. And for a long time afterward I thought about Bush's question.

I had been a newspaperman for more than forty years. I had covered national politics for more than thirty years. Still, I had no easy answer to Bush's question. What sort of profession is journalism that required me to ask a candidate for president about his sex life? And what sort of a profession is politics that the candidate felt compelled to answer?

Obviously political journalism is an intrusive and exasperating trade. More important, it bears the burden of power—power to do good and also harm. Or so many people believe. But how much of the power is real, and how much just perception? And what is the basis of this power? The more I thought about Bush's question, and the other questions it generated, the more I realized there are no simple answers. The trade of journalism had changed a lot since I started working on newspapers. And presidential politics had changed at least that much. In fact they had each forced changes on the other. And to understand how all this had happened I realized I needed to go back in time, to the year I started covering presidential politics, to the year that politics and journalism both began to change dramatically, back to 1968.

"The Democratic National Convention is as good as over," Democratic National Chairman John Bailey declared in January of that year. "It will be Lyndon Johnson, and that's that."

This assessment voiced by Bailey and almost universally shared by the political and journalistic establishment of that day would turn out to be one of the monumental miscalculations in American history. Fewer than three months after Bailey's confident prediction, Lyndon Johnson, landslide victor over Barry Goldwater in 1964, architect of the most sweeping program of social and economic reform since the New Deal, master manipulator of political power, would be forced to abandon his plans to seek another term in the White House. Even more important, the events of 1968 would touch off a wave of change that would engulf not only LBJ's Democrats but the opposition Republicans as well and lay the foundation for a new order in American politics.

This new order would be marked by the domination of personality and technology, the self-selection of candidates and the self-promotion of candidacies, the fragmentation of constituencies, the shifting of voter loyalties, and, most conspicuous of all, the thrust of the media to the forefront of the political scene. Indeed, the enhanced prominence of the media in the new political system that resulted from the turmoil of 1968 gave rise to the widely accepted notion that journalists had shouldered aside the established political leadership to assume command of the quadrennial making of the president. This view has taken hold not only among media consumers, the readers and viewers of political journalism, but also among a fair number of respected scholars, as witness a proliferation of books with titles such as *The Mass Media Election, Media Power in Politics,* and *Channels of Power.*

On closer inspection, based on what I have learned covering presidential campaigns, the concept of media hegemony turns out to be a substantial oversimplification and exaggeration. Instead of conquering the political hierarchy, the media merely moved into the void created by its implosion, and then had to contend with many of the same problems that had wrecked the old power structure. No one can deny that the media have helped shape the course of American politics for the past generation. But more frequently they have been acted upon rather than acted in their own right. Lacking a common agenda or the will to exercise power, the press and television have served mainly as a conduit for events and as potent instruments in the hands of others.

As became evident in the presidential campaign just concluded, a new hierarchy has emerged, building on the rubble of the old to rule the new political order and to define the role of the media. The new establishment differs from the old not only in makeup but also in tactics, reflecting the erosion of both political parties and the heavier weight of money and technology in the balance of political power. Prominent on its membership rolls are fund-raisers, lobbyists, interest-group panjandrums, and assorted technocrats skilled in the arts of polling and imagery. Unable to depend as much as they once could on party apparatus, the new leadership has learned to rely more and more on its ability to exploit the media to reach the electorate. Although this formula does not guarantee success, it worked well enough in the early months of the 2000 campaign in each party to help the established favorites suppress energetic insurgencies and secure their party's presidential nominations for Republican George W. Bush and Democrat Al Gore.

The new reality of the campaign trail boils down to this: the media all too often have been reduced to filling the role of enablers. Without fully realizing it or intending it, they allow and sometimes abet the abuse of the political process by the candidates and their handlers.

None of this is to excuse the sins of omission and commission committed by the media, both the electronic and print branches. The chapters that follow will reveal their all-too-willing acceptance of the slick offerings of the packagers of candidates, who, like the Shadow in the old radio show, seem to wield "the power to cloud men's minds." But it is not just the machinations of the competing campaigns that are to blame. The innate weaknesses and limitations of the press corps are also a large part of the problem. In their coverage of campaigns the media at one time or another have been guilty of just about every one of the seven deadly sins—pride, greed, lust, anger, envy, sloth, and, finally, as anyone who has watched reporters swarming around a press room buffet can testify, gluttony.

Of these failings, probably the most common and most injurious are sloth and pride. Too often journalists, myself included, have been unwilling to make the effort to learn what they do not know, and to make the information they do possess relevant and significant for their audiences. Too many of us, eager for attention, have been too willing to create stories that are larger than life and reality, and too impressed with our own importance to benefit from the criticism leveled against our work.

Don't the media do anything right? Of course they do. They provide fast and relatively accurate accounts of day-to-day events, without which the political system cannot function. They excel at probing wrongdoing, such as the fund-raising abuses perpetrated by both parties in the 1996 presidential campaign. What political journalism too often fails to provide, though, is a context for these events and revelations that would help readers and viewers understand why this reportage matters. Of course some journalists have the imagination and fortitude to break out of formulaic patterns and provide coverage that illuminates. But these exceptions serve to demonstrate the standards for political coverage that others should strive to meet.

Whatever the performance of the press, the outcome of presidential elections is usually shaped by the state of the union—whether it is at war or peace, enjoying a boom or struggling through a bust. In the orchestration of presidential campaigns, the press plays second fiddle. The candidates wield the baton and set the tone, for better and often for worse. The media could not elevate the discourse of the 1980 presidential campaign above the stunted level set by Ronald Reagan and Jimmy Carter. When Michael Dukakis could not defend himself against George Bush's irrelevant indictments, reporters could not exonerate him. If Bob Dole could not find a good reason for unseating Bill Clinton, the press could not discover it for him.

Still, the media have the potential for significant impact. While the national condition generally dictates the fate of the incumbent, whether he ultimately wins or loses, the media can help to decide who the challenger will be. They also can influence how voters view the nation's problems, and in assessing the solutions offered by the opposing candidates, can help shape the nature of governance until the next election. Yet the performance of political journalism cannot be weighed in isolation. The most important thing I have learned during more than three decades of covering elections is that presidential campaigns bind together the strengths and faults of political journalism with the strengths and faults of the political system itself. As this book will demonstrate, understanding the journalistic coverage of presidential campaigns depends on understanding the forces that influence the decisions of politicians. This book will show how in each election from 1968 through 2000, from Nixon's narrow victory over Humphrey to the Bush-Gore competition, the interaction of politics and journalism has defined the nature of the campaign. It will show where the press went wrong and where it went right, and what difference that made. And it will also show where, because of the nature of the campaign and the candidates, the press was sometimes helpless to make any difference at all.

This linkage between politics and journalism is rooted in history. The two institutions have grown up together in this country, locked in an often awkward symbiosis. In the nation's infancy, journalism possessed nothing like the reach and resources it now has. Yet political leaders even then sought to take advantage of the influence of the press, meanwhile nurturing the resentment and suspicion of its practitioners.

While the Founding Fathers generally paid lip service on patriotic occasions to the notion of a free press as a bulwark of liberty, they resisted concrete measures to guard that freedom. In the only substantial reference to the notion of legal protections for the press in the Federalist papers, Alexander Hamilton, the great proselytizer for constitutional ratification, dismissed the idea as "impracticable." Rather than insert any language in the nation's charter, Hamilton advised that the security of the press "must altogether depend on public opinion, and on the general spirit of the people and the government"—which of course are precisely the forces against which the press needs to be protected if it is to be free.

The political leadership of the time conceived of the First Amendment, like the rest of the Bill of Rights, as an afterthought, a promise offered and kept to aid ratification of the Constitution. And the adoption of the First Amendment did not reduce the tension between the political establishment and the press.

His two terms in office so embittered Washington against the press that Hamilton thought it prudent to excise from the first president's draft of his Farewell Address his vitriolic condemnation of the political journalists of the time. The coverage of his governance,

Washington had complained, displayed "all the invective that disappointment, ignorance of facts, and malicious falsehoods could invent to misrepresent my policies."

If the Founders were quick to criticize the press, they had even harsher words for political parties. On leaving office Washington warned his countrymen that parties were likely to foster a spirit that "agitates the community with ill-founded and false alarms; kindles the animosity of one part against another; foments occasionally riot and insurrection," and "opens the door to foreign influence and corruption." This view drew support from all sides. Hamilton contended that the spirit of "faction," a term then used interchangeably with party, "is apt to mingle its poison in the deliberations of all bodies of men." Hamilton's bitter adversary, Jefferson, declared: "If I could not go to heaven but with a party, I would not go at all."

So much for heaven. Here on earth, Hamilton, Jefferson, and most of their colleagues soon became fierce partisans who organized political parties in order to gain and maintain power. And being intensely practical men, they found the press—for all its shortcomings—an essential tool for furthering their partisan enterprises. Outraged at what he considered the libels perpetrated against him by the Federalist press supported by Hamilton and his allies, Jefferson set up the poet and journalist Philip Freneau as editor of the *National Gazette* as a counterforce. As part of the bargain, Jefferson, then Washington's secretary of state, secured a job for Freneau at the State Department and promised to award him government printing contracts.

A pioneer in manipulating the press to undermine his adversaries, Jefferson was more than paid back in kind by the Sally Hemings scandal, which erupted during his second term in the White House. Jefferson's nemesis in this affair was James Thompson Callender, a journalistic hatchet man who began his career as a Jeffersonian acolyte, turning his venom against Jefferson's enemies, often with Jefferson's encouragement. Callender struck first at Hamilton, exposing his adulterous affair with a Philadelphia housewife, which had made him the victim of a blackmailing husband. Next the resourceful Callender smeared another Jefferson foe, President John Adams, as "the corrupt and despotic monarch of Braintree," in a pamphlet which Jefferson helped subsidize.

But when Jefferson himself reached the White House and rejected Callender's demands for a postmaster's job, the infuriated scribe subjected Jefferson to the same treatment he had meted out to the Virginian's foes. First Callender put out the word that Jefferson had subsidized his efforts against Hamilton, Adams, and other Federalist targets, Washington among them. Even more damaging was Callender's claim that Jefferson had fathered several children by one of his slaves, a young woman named Sally Hemings. The ensuing public controversy took an even uglier turn when Chief Justice John Marshall, a bitter Jefferson adversary, publicly praised Callender's journalism. That led a pro-Jefferson editor to warn the slave-owning Marshall that his appreciation of the Sally Hemings story should be tempered by the supposed fact that, as the editor not so subtly put it, "upon this point his character is not invulnerable."

The political damage to Jefferson from this furor was limited because of the decrepitude of the Federalists, who were soon to expire as a political party. But the experience left its mark on the sage of Monticello, who personified the ambivalent attitude of the new nation's best and brightest toward the press. It was, after all, Jefferson who had famously said, "If it were left to me to decide whether we should have a government without newspapers, or newspapers without a government, I should not hesitate a moment to prefer the latter."

But that was in 1787 when Jefferson was a private citizen. Some twenty years later, nearing the end of his second term in the White House, with the memory of the Sally Hemings affair still painfully fresh, Jefferson wrote that "the man who never looks into a newspaper is better informed that he who reads them, inasmuch as he who knows nothing is nearer the truth than he whose mind is filled with falsehoods and errors." To make things easier for readers, Jefferson proposed—presumably with tongue firmly in cheek—that newspapers be organized into four sections—truth, probabilities, possibilities, and lies—adding that he expected the first of these divisions to be disproportionately short.

Despite Jefferson's misgivings, the growing popularity of the press had made the citizens of the nation he helped to found the largest newspaper-reading public in the world. And thanks in good measure to the efforts of Jefferson, his rivals, and his allies, the press had assumed the role it has continued to play over two centuries of American political history: a nettlesome but indispensable presence.

In the 1790s newspaper circulation in the young nation doubled. By the early nineteenth century, politicians counted on journalists not only to report their speeches but first to improve them, transforming the rough notes of their delivered talks into a polished oration. The politicians and the journalists generally contrived to delay publication, making it less likely that an alert rival would note the discrepancy between the original utterance and the published version.

To grease the system's wheels, a national political press flourished in the new capital. The thirty-four senators of the Eighth Congress, convening in 1801, had ninety-five subscriptions spread among twenty-three newspapers, most of them national newspapers such as the *National Intelligencer*, the leading Jeffersonian organ, and the *Washington Federalist*, the voice of that party. Only eleven of the senators bothered to order a newspaper from their home states.

Yet newspapers proliferated around the country too. By the time Tocqueville made his memorable visit in 1831, Americans could choose from among seven hundred papers, including sixty-five dailies. By 1850 the number had increased to two thousand, of which two hundred were dailies. "The number of periodical and occasional publications which appear in the United States surpasses belief," Tocqueville marveled. He added that "the most enlightened Americans" believed that the number undermined the potential influence of the press, citing as "an axiom of political science" the theory "that the only way to neutralize the effect of public journalism is to multiply them indefinitely."

Whatever the merits of that hypothesis, the rapid increase in towns and cities created a more direct and pragmatic spur to the spread of newspapers. The communities' governing bodies generated printing contracts that supported the local papers and generally bought the loyalty of their editors. The local ties between politicians and journalists were matched on the national level where, during the country's first half-century, most major papers verged on being subsidiaries of political parties, their bonds bolstered by patronage. Andrew Jackson, who forged the modern Democratic party, named nearly sixty journalists to high office. Old Hickory did not disguise his expectation that these scribes would repay his generosity by fending off the torrent of contumely unleashed by opposition journalists.

Around the time of the Civil War, the press's overt partisanship began to recede. The creation of the Government Printing Office in 1861 took away the printing contracts that had helped to subsidize papers loyal to the incumbent administration. Lincoln, the first president elected by the new Republican party, ended the custom of chief executives maintaining a semi-official voice among the capital's press. And finally, but certainly not least, the penny press arrived on the journalistic scene. Sheets such as James Gordon Bennett's *New York Herald* and Horace Greeley's *New York Tribune,* by selling for a nickel less than the prevailing rate, gained mass circulations and enough advertising revenue to free themselves from dependence on partisan largesse.

Still, the press continued to make its influence felt in politics, and Lincoln was not above catering to this strength. Convinced that the support of the *Philadelphia Press* for Stephen A. Douglas in the 1860 election widened a rift among Pennsylvania Democrats which had eased his path to the White House, the grateful president helped the paper's editor gain appointment as secretary of the Senate. For good measure Lincoln secured a Marine Corps commission for the editor's son.

Lincoln's interest in cementing friendships in the press was understandable, for he had felt the sting of his journalistic foes. He blamed Republican losses in the 1862 elections in part on newspapers, which, "by vilifying and disparaging the administration," furnished the Democrats the weapons for victory. In the face of vicious press attacks throughout his presidency, Lincoln tried to take such abuse in stride. "I have endured a great deal of ridicule without much malice and have received a great deal of kindness, not quite free from ridicule," he wrote a friend who had expressed sympathy about a journalistic brickbat aimed at the chief executive. "I am used to it."

As newspapers grew more independent and more important, presidents sought new ways to influence their coverage. Theodore Roosevelt blazed the trail. Grateful reporters noticed his sensitivity to their deadlines and the special interests of their readers. What the gentlemen of the press may not have noticed was how effectively this considerate chief executive used them to float trial balloons, a tactic TR invented to test the public reaction to his ambitious schemes for busting trusts at home and swinging a big stick abroad.

Determined to control the public's perception of himself, the hero of San Juan Hill was happy to have reporters cover his hikes and hunting forays. But no photo was ever taken of this proponent of the strenuous life swinging a tennis racket, a pastime he thought too sissified. And he advised William Howard Taft, his successor, not to allow coverage of himself on the golf links, considered by Roosevelt also to appear insufficiently manly. In the 1920s the increase in mass-circulation newspapers and national magazines fostered the rise of a new profession, press agentry, whose practitioners found a fertile field in politics. Among their most enthusiastic early clients was Florence Harding, who helped Republicans win the presidency in 1920 by her vigorous promotion of herself and her husband Warren as "just folks." "I love the newspaper fraternity," the future First Lady confessed. "I'd tell them where to get a story and they'd get it and never mention me." The Hardings both had additional reason to be grateful for the discretion of political reporters, who never reported a word about the president's widespread womanizing.

Franklin Roosevelt, like his distant cousin after whose career he modeled his own, brought with him to the White House a keen appreciation of newspaper clout. A bargain with the press had in fact opened his road to the presidency. This was not a deal with a humble scrivener but with one of the barons of the fourth estate, the publisher William Randolph Hearst. As the 1932 campaign approached, Hearst, though past his prime, still wielded plenty of power—his newspapers reached sixteen million readers in every large city across the land; his magazines sold thirty million copies—and he still dreamed imperial dreams. Convinced that thanks to the Great Depression the Democrats were bound to win the White House, isolationist Hearst determined to ensure that their candidate would not rekindle efforts to enlist the United States in Woodrow Wilson's League of Nations, which he detested.

Hearst knew that Roosevelt, the early front-runner in the Democratic race, had ardently supported the League in the past, so the publisher ordered a barrage of editorials denouncing the New York governor as a hopeless internationalist. In Georgia, Roosevelt supporters sent word to the New York governor that Hearst had instructed his local staffers "to get up interviews against Roosevelt" with a particular eye on appealing to "the old Tom Watson element" in the party, whose hearts still beat in tune to the xenophobia of nineteenth-century Southern populism.

Roosevelt tried to dispose of the problem quietly, dispatching an aide to assure the editor of Hearst's flagship paper in the East, the *New York American,* that the charges of internationalism against him were false. Hearst would have none of it. "If Mr. Roosevelt has any statement to make about his not now being an internationalist, he should make it to the public publicly, and not to me privately," he insisted in a page-one editorial.

FDR soon caved and delivered a speech which, as critics pointed out, gave Hearst exactly what he wanted. Liberal commentator Elmer Davis called Roosevelt "a man who thinks that the shortest distance between two points is not a straight line but a corkscrew."

Roosevelt could afford to put up with such criticism. His reversal on the League not only silenced Hearst but gained support for his candidacy for the nomination among Democrats in the South and West. They provided the base that prevented any other rival from seriously challenging him.

As he took office and prepared to tackle the Great Depression, FDR had a threshold problem of his own which required a deft hand with the media—his paralysis. Before his inauguration his longtime political operative, Louis Howe, inspected the hallways and doorways of the White House with an eye for locations where the president in his wheelchair might be exposed to view by visitors and to photographs by the press. Howe's precautions helped ensure that most Americans had no more than a dim idea of the severity of the president's condition, that he actually spent most of his life in a wheelchair, that even with his braces he could not stand erect without support, and that even with assistance he could walk only a few yards. A complaisant press corps submitted to the White House ban on pictures of the president in a wheelchair, being lifted out of an auto, or being carried up stairs. When Roosevelt fell in the mud behind the speaker's platform at Philadelphia's Franklin Field as he was about to deliver his address accepting renomination in 1936, Secret Service agents and aides quickly surrounded him, shielding his sprawling figure from the 100,000 onlookers. Pool reporters knew about the incident but never reported it.

In the same spirit that ignored Warren Harding's philandering, the press chose to look the other way when an old flame, Lucy Mercer, came back into Roosevelt's life. FDR's romance with Mercer, when he was Wilson's assistant secretary of the navy during World War I, nearly destroyed his marriage when Eleanor Roosevelt learned of the affair. But decades after the romance ended, the two began seeing each other again, without Eleanor's knowledge and without the press taking public notice. Lucy Mercer Rutherfurd, as she was then known, was with FDR in Warm Springs, Georgia, when he died.

FDR arrived in the White House just as radio was gaining political effect. During his four terms as president, most notably through his celebrated fireside chats, Roosevelt made radio a key medium for expounding his policies, in the process achieving unprecedented personal rapport with the citizenry, whom he invariably addressed as "my friends."

After his resonant voice fell silent forever on April 12, 1945, many in the press had trouble mustering much respect for his plainspoken successor, Harry Truman. Reporters regarded the man from Missouri as drab and pedestrian. "To err is Truman," some wiseacres jeered. A bitter jest summed up the difference between the squire of Hyde Park and the son of the Middle Border: "For years we had the champion of the common man in the White House. Now we have the common man." Truman had to fend off criticism not only for alleged policy blunders, foreign and domestic, but even for minor notions that seized his fancy. When he proposed to build a new balcony on the White House, the *New York Herald Tribune* upbraided him "for meddling with a historic structure which the nation prefers as it is."

The press corps's low estimate of Truman leadership ability was reinforced by the Democratic debacle in the first postwar congressional elections in 1946, which put Capitol Hill under Republican control for the first time since Herbert Hoover's election in 1928. Then, to make matters worse, as the presidential campaign approached, the Democratic party fell apart. On the left, Henry Wallace, FDR's erstwhile vice president, recruited liberals and blacks for his new Progressive party, while on the right, Southerners bolted the party and rallied behind Strom Thurmond, the candidate of the States' Rights party, more popularly known as the Dixiecrats. By the time the nominating conventions concluded and Truman faced the challenge of the GOP's formidable standard-bearer, New York governor Thomas E. Dewey, journalists of every leaning and experience regarded FDR's successor as a gone goose. "The cold facts are in many ways unjust to Harry Truman, but they cannot be removed by personal pluck," Ernest K. Lindley, *Newsweek's* Washington bureau chief wrote with an evident attempt at compassion shortly before the Democratic convention that summer. "The best service Truman could render his party right now is to step aside."

The major pollsters who had correctly predicted the outcome of the two previous presidential elections since 1936 all forecast a Dewey victory. Two months before election day, Elmo Roper blandly announced that "my whole inclination is to predict the election of Thomas E. Dewey by a heavy margin and devote my time and effort to other things. Unless some major convulsion takes place in the next month and a half, Mr. Dewey is as good as elected."

It was hard to find a dissenting opinion. Of American newspapers, 65 percent, representing nearly 80 percent of the nation's total circulation, supported Dewey, and their editors and correspondents were confident they were backing a winner. In its October 11 issue *Newsweek* published the results of a poll of fifty top political reporters, every one of whom predicted that Dewey would be the next president.

So convinced were the reporters of the inevitability of Dewey's victory that they ignored the evidence of their own eyes: the large crowds that were gathering to hear Truman wherever he spoke, far outnumbering the audiences that Dewey attracted. Some mentioned this puzzling phenomenon in their stories, but most discounted the significance of Truman's audiences, concluding that they were drawn by the prestige of the office rather than what Truman stood for politically.

Having nothing to lose, Truman seized the initiative. As he toured the country on his campaign train he attacked the Republicans furiously, from start to finish, giving rise to the shouts of "Give 'em hell, Harry" which became the battle cry of his candidacy. For his part Dewey, certain of victory, chose to ignore Truman, delivering speeches filled with smug generalizations and creating the impression that he was conducting not an election campaign but rather a triumphant goodwill tour.

While Truman was whistle-stopping around the country, I was starting my sophomore year at Syracuse University, working on the student newspaper, the *Daily Orange*. Like nearly everyone else I was sure that Dewey would win. At dinner on election night, another student offered 20 to 1 odds if I would bet on Truman. I told him my parents had worked too hard to help me get through college for me to throw money away like that.

Later that night I was at the *Daily Orange* offices when I heard the incredible returns that showed Truman actually leading Dewey. Since no one had thought beforehand that there would be any interest in an election story, I volunteered to write one at the last minute. Even as I listened to the vote come in on the radio, I could hardly believe what I was typing on my Royal portable: "According to late returns Tuesday President Harry S. Truman is threatening a stunning upset of pre-election predictions." It was the first election story I had ever written, and probably the most memorable.

Truman's victory taught me and other journalists never to take any election for granted. But that was 1948. By 1968 that lesson had been all but forgotten by the media. It took the shocks of one of the most tumultuous years in American history to awaken our memories and remind us to test predictions against reality.

TWO

1968:
"The Omnipotent Eye"

IN 1960, as John Kennedy closed in on the Democratic presidential nomination, Harry Truman, eight years removed from the White House but still a force in his party, raised his voice to object. "Senator, are you certain that you are quite ready for the country, or that the country is ready for you in the role of president?" Truman asked pointedly. "May I urge you to be patient."

Truman had in mind Kennedy's youth and his Catholic faith, both of which he and other Democratic elders regarded as probably fatal obstacles to Kennedy's chances for the presidency. The testy old campaigner had a point, yet his criticism missed the mark. In ways that did not occur to most of his fellow Democrats, Kennedy's timing could not have been better. Hindsight makes clear that he had correctly assessed the nation's growing restlessness and the shifts in the political power structure, notably the increasing impact of television. By appreciating and exploiting this new dynamic, Kennedy was able to overcome considerable handicaps, capture the nomination of his party, and regain the White House for the Democrats. In the process he helped to change the nature of presidential politics. By demonstrating the ebbing of the old regime, Kennedy accelerated its demise and paved the way for the birth of the new order, with its salient role for the media.

The political changes wrought in the country in the aftermath of World War II made possible Kennedy's success. Before that epochal conflict, "in each major party some 50 to 100 men—state leaders, local bosses, elder statesmen, big contributors—decided nominations," presidential scholar Richard E. Neustadt wrote. They held this power because they could deliver voters to the polls to support the candidates they had chosen. This system was far from perfect; it had to struggle against the separation of powers written into the Constitution by the Founders as impediments to the political parties they despised. Yet at its best the boss-run party system served as a crude mechanism for the electorate to make claims upon the government. For all its limitations, inertial forces had kept this machinery running throughout the nineteenth century and well into the twentieth.

Victory over the Axis shattered the inertia. During the postwar decades Americans became a nation on the move, in several directions at once—upward in educational as well as economic status, outward from the cities to the suburbs, and westward and southward to the inviting climes of the Sunbelt states. Between 1940 and 1960 the population jumped by more than one-third, from 132 million to 179 million, nearly all of it in the metropolitan areas of big cities. During the same twenty-year period the gross national product increased fivefold, from $100 billion to more than $500 billion, and family income soared. Educational levels advanced: more Americans completed high school and more went on to college, and even to graduate school.

Inevitably this metamorphosis eroded traditional partisan allegiances and undermined the authority of the once-potent party bosses. Changing constituencies with increasingly complex interests made it harder for the party leaders to define and dominate political debate. Voters with better educations and more leisure time to find out things for themselves declared themselves independent. Compounding the other difficulties of the old bosses, the mass media, riding a wave of technology, took control of political communication. "Men still talk to each other," the social scientists Joseph Bensman and Bernard Rosenberg observed. "But what we say to each other is very often no more than an extension of facts and feelings relayed to us by the mass media."

Politicians had always had to reckon with journalists but never regarded them as playing more than a subordinate role. Now the press began to move to center stage, to become an integral part of the theater of presidential politics. And the star of the show was television.

The magic box had emerged as a pervasive and intrusive force, at once enlightening and confusing, informing and distracting. Between 1950, when Congressman John Kennedy was a junior member of the House of Representatives, and 1960, when Senator Kennedy was preparing to run for president, the number of American families owning television sets increased tenfold, to more than 45 million, or nearly 90 percent of the population. The medium's capacity for instant projection of ideas and personalities into living rooms everywhere created a voice that drowned out the traditional political chain of command.

Party leaders clung to their old titles and struggled to preserve their traditional influence, but they waged a losing battle. Kennedy's candidacy foreshadowed their ultimate defeat. With his emphasis on his own compelling personality rather than on the fading strength of his party, Kennedy tapped into the potential of the media to gain his party's nomination.

He aimed at waging and winning campaigns in a few key primary states, and by doing so bringing pressure on party leaders through the media. The media, Kennedy calculated, could be relied upon to give his anticipated victories an importance well beyond the literal arithmetic of the convention delegates he gained. His key victory came in tiny West Virginia, where he upset Hubert Humphrey with an impassioned appeal to that state's mostly Protestant voters to prove they were not bigots by voting for a Roman Catholic for president. In the general election Kennedy's skill in projecting his cool self-assurance in television debates galvanized his supporters, contributing to his narrow victory over Vice President Richard Nixon.

Theodore White, in his narrative of the 1960 battle for the presidency, recalled "the quantum jump" in the size of the crowds that gathered for Kennedy's campaign stops. "They seethed with enthusiasm," White wrote, "and multiplied in numbers as if the sight of him, in their homes on the video box, had given him a 'star quality' reserved only for television and movie idols."

Victory gave Kennedy the opportunity to deploy his talent for media manipulation on a grander scale. He had not been president for long before his voice and his face, his manner and his habits, his staff and his family seemed one and indivisible with the office he held. It was a phenomenon unmatched since Franklin Roosevelt's tenure. What it had taken Roosevelt years to achieve, Kennedy accomplished figuratively overnight with the great help of television. His quick wit, virile good looks, and crisp manner were ideally suited to the camera. The first president to risk having his press conferences televised live, he converted the reporters in attendance into a cast of supporting players who complimented his starring performance. "We couldn't survive without television," he once acknowledged to an aide.

Not that Kennedy neglected the "pencil press." As powerful as it was in itself, television also served as the key to the other media. Kennedy's televised news conferences became news events. One survey showed that his press conferences received more coverage in the print press than those of any of his predecessors, including Franklin Roosevelt. This despite the fact that FDR had conducted his press conferences three or four times more often than Kennedy and against the backdrop of the Great Depression and World War II.

During his campaign for the White House, Kennedy had learned the value of making himself accessible to the press and of cultivating the most influential journalists. In the presidency he stepped up this courtship. His use of the perquisites of the White House to charm the press prompted the *New York Times*'s venerable Washington columnist Arthur Krock to complain of "news management" in the form of "social flattery of Washington reporters and commentators on an unprecedented scale."

But it was not solely Kennedy's invitations to luncheons or dinners or the occasional confidences that captivated the press corps. More broadly, the air of urgency created by Kennedy and his associates as they involved themselves and the country in one crisis after another, from the battle against the price hike in steel to the Cuban missile confrontation, gave journalists covering the White House a vicarious sense of importance. The sovereign of the latter-day Camelot also created an elevated atmosphere in his court. By entertaining and consulting the luminaries of the arts and academe, Kennedy linked his administration to the world of culture and ideas. "The glow of the White House was lighting up the whole city," exulted White House historian-in-residence Arthur Schlesinger, Jr., of the New Frontier's heyday. "It was a golden interlude." And the press corps basked in the reflected radiance.

The mystique Kennedy generated around himself, with the considerable help of the media, only grew larger after his death, adding to the burdens facing his successor, Lyndon Johnson. The new president had learned from watching Kennedy to respect the growing importance of the media in the political process. But that knowledge failed to provide the grace, poise, and self-assurance that had helped Kennedy exploit the media's power.

The anxieties and resentment Johnson felt toward Kennedy heightened LBJ's own insecurities rooted in his childhood, when he was buffeted by conflicts between his parents and humiliated by his father's business reverses. These experiences drove Johnson to seek power, enough to give him control over his life and protect him against further traumas.

As a ten-year-old he became enamored of money, so much so that he consented to let other boys grab one of his ear lobes and yank it—ear popping, as it was called, being then a popular pastime—in return for a payoff. The going rate was a nickel for five pulls, and Johnson, who even then had very large ears, made a choice victim. Later his friends would remember young Lyndon submitting to the yanking, with tears streaming down his face at the pain, determined to earn his five cents. It was not the last time Johnson's intensity would cause him pain.

Although growing up he seemed brighter and quicker than average, he was unwilling to rest on this natural superiority. Instead he pushed himself relentlessly to take full advantage of his talents. "Everything was competition with Lyndon," recalled one of his cousins. "He had to win."

Now, in the most powerful office on earth, he was still competing, this time against the ghost of an American hero, and he sensed he was waging a losing battle.

It was not only on television—where he almost invariably came across as unctuous or overbearing—that Johnson felt himself to be less than his predecessor, but also in print. "We are not equipped by experience, by tradition, by personality or financially to cope with this," Johnson complained to one of his aides. "I just do not believe that we know how to handle public relations and how to handle advertising agencies, how to handle manuscripts, how to handle book writers, so I think they're going to write history as they want it written."

Johnson's fundamental problem, though, was not the media but Vietnam, the trackless morass into which he had led the country by stealth, with the complicity of most of the media. With openness and candor during the 1964 presidential campaign, Johnson might have won public support for a consistent policy toward Vietnam. But he did not wish to risk diminishing his anticipated landslide in that campaign, or later the broad support he sought for his Great Society programs, with a full-dress debate on such a controversial issue as the war.

In the months following the election, despite his campaign pledge not to send American boys "to do what Asian boys ought to be doing," Johnson dispatched tens of thousands of young Americans to Vietnam. This he could do on his own, as commander-in-chief. But he was reluctant to ask Congress to approve the economic sacrifices needed to finance the war and to keep inflation under control. This would have touched off just the sort of debate on his policies that he sought to avoid. Instead his war policy was founded on secrecy and dissembling, as it had been from the beginning. In August 1964 he used the confused reports of a purported North Vietnamese attack on U.S. destroyers to push through a panicky Congress the Tonkin Gulf resolution, which gave him a blank check for military action in Indochina. The constitutional validity of this resolution was as hazy as its language. Nevertheless it allowed the president to run the war behind the country's back, all the while creating the impression that peace was just around the corner.

For the most part, the media failed to challenge that impression. During the 1964 presidential campaign the vast majority of political journalists, including staffers on such liberal papers as the *Washington Post,* accepted LBJ's depiction of himself as a moderate, seeking to stave off the alleged extremism of his much maligned Republican challenger Barry Goldwater while trying to prevent communism from sweeping across Southeast Asia. Much of the press backed him against rising criticism of his Vietnam policies from the left. Even the *New York Times,* whose editorials and correspondence from the field were often critical of the administration's policies, harbored influential hawks such as Hanson W. Baldwin, the paper's military editor. When soon after the election Johnson launched an air war against North Vietnam, Baldwin contended in a major article that a U.S. pullout from Indochina would be "disastrous." He offered this rationale for Johnson's policy: "Vietnam is a nasty place to fight. But . . . it is far better to fight in Vietnam—on China's doorstep—than fight some years hence in Hawaii, on our own frontiers."

In the months that followed, as a steady escalation of the bombing and of U.S. troop reinforcements failed to substantiate administration promises of a "light at the end of the tunnel," uneasiness spread through the press and the rest of the country. As 1968 began, one of the most prestigious of Johnson's Vietnam critics, the columnist Walter Lippmann, warned that the war would have a punishing impact on the Democratic party. "No one should ignore the depth of the revulsion which a large number of Americans—who are essential to a successful Democratic Party—feel at the spectacle of Vietnam," Lippmann wrote. Johnson's reelection, Lippmann predicted, "will not arrest but will force the disintegration of the party." If Robert Kennedy, brother of the slain president, intended to wait until 1972 before making his move for the White House, Lippmann chided, "He had better wonder what will be the condition of the party after four more years of distrust, division and dissent."

But few in the Democratic party or among the media shared Lippmann's view. Whatever the columnist might think about the urgency of his running for president, Robert Kennedy, whom the media had long portrayed as the inevitable heir to the Camelot legacy, had rejected pleas from the leaders of the nascent anti-war movement that he challenge Johnson for the presidency. Whereupon the movement's political strategists turned instead to a much lesser-known figure—Senator Eugene McCarthy of Minnesota.

Still convinced that Lyndon Johnson controlled his party, the media paid scant attention to the McCarthy challenge. In its first issue of 1968, in a preview of the forthcoming presidential election, *Newsweek* ignored the Democratic party altogether. Instead it focused on the GOP, offering an early analysis of the makeup of the delegations that would choose the Republican standard-bearer at the party's national convention in July. The front-runner, Richard Nixon, was only one hundred or so delegates short of the majority he needed for nomination. Two governors, from opposite ends of the continent as well as the GOP's ideological spectrum, the liberal Nelson Rockefeller of New York and the conservative Ronald Reagan of California, trailed the former vice president.

Only a few weeks later, though, the political world turned. As January 1968 ended with the Vietnamese Tet New Year, the Communists staged their boldest stroke of the war, an astonishingly well-coordinated guerrilla assault against South Vietnamese cities that had been depicted as secure bastions for the Saigon government. Before their attacks were finally repelled, the enemy had even penetrated the compound of the American embassy in Saigon.

The Tet offensive was the first milestone of the presidential campaign. And the impact of the media's saturation coverage of the fighting was the first measure of the influence they would wield in 1968's tumultuous struggle for the White House.

The media built a platform for the role it would play in the struggle over Vietnam policy by its coverage of the civil rights revolution in the South in the earlier years of the decade. That upheaval ultimately did more to wreck the once dominant electoral coalition forged by Franklin Roosevelt than even the war in Indochina. Journalism earned its enhanced prestige by the fortitude of individual reporters who penetrated the walls of bigotry and brutality that had long shielded racism in the Old Confederacy. "If the news media had not carried into American homes the scenes of black children, Freedom Riders, and other protesters being hosed, beaten, bitten by dogs, and stuck with cattle prods, the conscience of the nation might never have been massively stirred," wrote Harris Wofford, who was President Kennedy's liaison to the civil rights movement.

Television made its mark here, in particular through its coverage of the 1963 demonstrations in Birmingham, Alabama, where local police commissioner Eugene "Bull" Connor loosed police dogs against unarmed demonstrators. "The Birmingham riots were made for television," wrote Theodore White, "and the sight television brought the nation was unprecedented: official violence naked in the streets."

So too, in covering Tet, television led the charge. Even before the Tet attack, television news had made the Vietnam War its own, giving Americans at home, in their living rooms, an unprecedented, wrenching linkage with their sons in combat. But until Tet the conflict had consisted mainly of skirmishes and firefights scattered around the lush countryside, lacking pattern or direction. Now the Communist offensive defined the conflict in stark outline. The Tet story dominated the network news shows, most particularly NBC's "Huntley-Brinkley Report," whose vivid reports of the street fighting were climaxed by the on-camera execution in a battle-torn Saigon street of a Viet Cong prisoner by South Vietnamese General Nguyen Ngoc Loan.

Newspapers did not lag far behind. Editors splashed the grisly photo of the South Vietnamese general, pistol in hand, and his victim on front pages around the country. Typical of many papers, the *New York Times* in its headlines coupled the White House's statements on the fighting with news of the actual battles that seemed to belie Washington's claims: "Johnson Says Foe's Raids Are a Military Failure; Saigon, Hue Battles Go On." Tet commanded the covers of both *Time* and *Newsweek,* which featured color photos of the battle carnage along with such headlines as "Hanoi Attacks—And Scores a Major Psychological Blow."

That headline summed up the story of Tet. Although the Communists suffered terrible losses and failed to achieve their military goals in the cities of Vietnam, they scored a far-reaching political success in the United States. Despite Johnson's claims that the enemy had been turned back, Americans were shaken by what they read and especially by what they saw of Tet, which the media had faithfully transmitted. Further damage to the administration's reassuring outlook was sustained in mid-March, only a few weeks after Tet, when the *New York Times* disclosed that the high command in Vietnam wanted an additional 200,000 troops to carry on what many Americans had now come to regard as a hopeless fight.

Media disaffection reached from large metropolitan dailies to small-town weeklies, whose communities had come to feel the cost of the war. After two young men from the tiny Alabama hamlet of Brewton were lost in battle in Southeast Asia, the local weekly abandoned its support for the war. "If we had a reason to be there, that cause has long been forgotten," explained *Brewton Standard* editor Tom Gardner.

In the wake of Tet, public opposition to Johnson's Vietnam policy mounted sharply, and the anti-war movement benefited greatly. In the New Hampshire Democratic presidential primary, insurgent candidate McCarthy won 42 percent of the Democratic vote to Johnson's 50 percent. Here the media invoked a new principle that came to be known as the "rule of expectations," awarding McCarthy a "moral victory." Since McCarthy had done better than the polls suggested he would do, and better than most journalists thought he would do, the media reasoning went, he had in effect come out on top. To support this claim, journalists added the write-in votes cast for McCarthy on the Republican side and calculated a grand total that was only 230 votes short of Johnson's figure.

It is hard to quarrel about a moral victory, since no one can be sure what the term means. And the context of the times helps to explain the media's judgment—a powerful president, elected by a landslide fewer than four years earlier, up against an obscure senator in a state with a strong patriotic tradition. Even so, the media's view of the New Hampshire results suffered from the twin devils of news coverage—hyperbole and naiveté. While it was true Johnson was far better known than McCarthy, the president had not bothered to campaign in New Hampshire while McCarthy and his army of youthful supporters stumped the state constantly. The McCarthy forces were able to stir up whatever potential grievances against LBJ might exist in New Hampshire. Given the fact that Johnson was running a costly and dubious war, it is not surprising that they found sufficient resentment to allow McCarthy to make a strong showing.

Also overlooked by the media in the sudden enthusiasm for McCarthy and the anti-war movement were poll results suggesting that much of McCarthy's support came from voters who were less opposed to the war than to Johnson's conduct of it. These McCarthy backers wanted Johnson to be more hawkish, not to make peace. Had the media paid attention to this aspect of the New Hampshire vote, they would have helped prepare the public for the mountain of obstacles and frustrations that the peace movement would encounter in the campaign ahead.

In any event, the New Hampshire results demonstrated that the war could be a political liability for Lyndon Johnson, a reality that journalists should not have needed a primary election to grasp and communicate to their readers. Had the press been more alert and sensitive to the intensity of the McCarthy campaign in New Hampshire, the results of the vote would have been less surprising. Some reporters did venture into the Granite State and observed the energy of the anti-war campaigners and the positive reactions of the electorate. But, like the reporters on Truman's campaign train who discounted the size of the president's crowds, they dismissed the evidence of their own eyes because it contravened conventional wisdom.

As it was, the tendency of the media to overlook reality and then to make up for that neglect by exaggeration transformed the decision of fifty thousand Democrats in New Hampshire into a referendum on the Johnson presidency. More than that, as succeeding chapters will show, the rule of expectations first invoked in New Hampshire in 1968 would have a profound and often capricious impact on elections to come. But at the time neither journalists nor politicians had much interest in considering the future. They were all too caught up in the turbulence of the present.

Typical of the overall coverage of the New Hampshire primary, *Newsweek* labeled the results "an astonishing political upset" for McCarthy and breathlessly declared: "In the space of five days last week, a phenomenon that began as little more than a courageous exercise in political dissent was transformed into a convulsion that shook every corner of the American political landscape."

Spurred by such reportage, events did move swiftly, though not according to anyone's plan. Robert Kennedy, having reassessed his position in the light of the New Hampshire vote, announced his own candidacy for the Democratic nomination. "I do not run for the Presidency merely to oppose any man," said Kennedy. "I run because I am convinced that this country is on a perilous course."

Before the month was out, Lyndon Johnson withdrew from the race. "With America's sons in the fields far away," Johnson told a stunned nation over television, "with our hopes and the world's hopes for peace in the balance every day, I do not believe that I should devote an hour or a day of my life to any personal partisan causes."

Within a fortnight of Johnson's withdrawal, Martin Luther King, Jr., was assassinated in Memphis, where he had gone to lend his support to a garbage strike. The cities, including the nation's capital, exploded in violence as blacks vented their long pent-up fury. Dominating the media, the smoke billowing over Washington's historic landscape and the urban violence elsewhere cast another cloud over the political landscape.

Johnson's vice president, Hubert Humphrey, soon entered the race, more or less as Johnson's surrogate, and incongruously dedicated his candidacy to a restoration of "the politics of happiness and the politics of joy."

While Kennedy and McCarthy fought it out in the primaries, Humphrey stayed out of the fray, counting on the backing of the bosses. They were committed to support him regardless of the outcome of the primaries, which then selected only a minority of the delegates. The hopes of the anti-war movement for the McCarthy and Robert Kennedy candidacies rested on political symbolism tied to success in the presidential primaries, much the same formula John Kennedy had used in 1960.

The Kennedy-McCarthy primary duels throughout the country gained abundant media attention. But front-runner Humphrey's absence from these contests deprived them of much of the symbolic significance they had held in 1960. Their tangible importance was less than met the eye: the primaries did little to interfere with the control of the nomination by the party hierarchy.

By official count, sixteen states and the District of Columbia held some form of primary in 1968 and chose about 40 percent of both parties' convention delegates. But that figure was misleading; the sentiment of the voters in primaries was not necessarily reflected in the delegate support a presidential candidate received at the convention. In six primary states, delegates could run without letting voters know which presidential candidate they preferred; in one of these states, New York, delegates were actually prohibited from stating their preference beforehand.

In the nonprimary states, procedures often were even more arcane and the results more frustrating for the anti-war forces. The process of selecting convention delegates in many states was begun (and sometimes finished) a year or more before the convention. By the time Eugene McCarthy announced his candidacy on December 2, 1967, nearly a third of the convention delegates had already been selected, the vast majority of them firmly committed to whomever the local party organization favored. Most of these states either had no written rules at all governing the delegate selection procedure, or rules that were inaccessible to outsiders.

These circumstances probably made Humphrey's nomination inevitable. But the nature of the campaign had unintended consequences, and Humphrey's nomination turned out to be the last gasp of the old order. The exposure of the gross inequities of the system by which Humphrey won his delegates led the 1968 convention to set in motion a process of reform which would codify a new nominating process. More important to Humphrey in the short run, his triumph was tarnished by the tragedy and violence that marked the conclusion of the bitter battle for the Democratic nomination.

Even before the convention opened, the nation, which had yet to recover from the King assassination, was stunned again by the murder of Robert Kennedy. Intense media coverage, with its echoes of the reporting of the assassination of John Kennedy only five years previous, magnified the trauma of Robert Kennedy's slaying on the night of his victory in the California primary. Television crews that had been standing by in Los Angeles for the finale of the primary campaign on that June evening plunged directly into covering the shooting. ABC news cameras were still recording the Kennedy victory party in the Ambassador Hotel when the shots rang out. Within moments the network cameras were recording the chaos of the assassination. The sound track picked up cries of "Oh, goddam! Oh no! Oh no!" while the cameras caught Ethel Kennedy kneeling beside the prostrate figure of her husband.

Networks filled the airwaves with discussions of the causes of violence, but basically both the electronic and print media reflected bewilderment over who or what was to blame. In New York, WPIX-

TV encapsulated the widespread frustration and grief by transmitting over its silent screen the single word "Shame."

In sum, the powerful presentation of the tragedy by the media, particularly television, darkened the nation's mood. It also reinforced the growing, if often grudging, acceptance of the mass media as the dominant messenger for political information.

A few weeks after Kennedy's death, the messenger became part of the message amidst the chaos and rioting at the Democratic National Convention in Chicago. In simplest terms, the bedlam was produced by the clash between an impassioned force, the anti-war movement, and an implacable object, Chicago's iron-willed Mayor Richard J. Daley. The previous fall, leaders of the Vietnam protest had first discussed arranging "some sort of militant nonviolence" at the Democratic convention. Lyndon Johnson's withdrawal a few months later sidetracked their planning. But the assassination of Robert Kennedy and the defeat of the anti-war forces in the nominating contest sent the planners back into high gear.

As the anti-war forces organized for their demonstrations, Daley stood firm against what he declared to be a threat against the peace and safety of the city he governed. Refusing to grant permits for parades or demonstrations, he assigned all twelve thousand Chicago police to twelve-hour shifts and mobilized five thousand Illinois National Guardsmen. Some six thousand U.S. troops, including units of the 101st Airborne armed with flamethrowers and bazookas, stood by in the suburbs. The violence that inevitably erupted caught reporters right in the middle of the fray. And the protesters, who, fully mindful of the media's power, had made "The whole world is watching" their battle cry, wanted to make sure they paid attention. Understanding that, Daley and his cops lashed out not only at the protesters but at the media.

The police reacted to minor infractions of the law (such as violations of the curfew they had declared), symbolic acts (such as the lowering of the American flag), the hurling of insults, rocks, and sometimes bags of excrement, and sometimes to no direct provocations at all by charging, clubbing, gassing, and mauling the demonstrators and the press. "They bashed reporters so devotedly," observed anti-war activist Todd Gitlin, "that they assured themselves a bad press." The eagerness of Daley's brigades to rough up the press was not limited to the streets. The manhandling of CBS correspondents Dan Rather and Mike Wallace on the convention floor triggered a blast of condemnation of the mayor's "thugs" from Walter Cronkite himself.

"Not since the gangster days of a generation ago has the reputation of a city been so tarnished," the *New York Times* declared. Under the headline "The Iron Fist," the *Washington Post* editorialized: "The Chicago technique for keeping photographs of police brutality from public view is a very simple one: it is to club photographers, smash cameras and confiscate film."

As a consequence of television coverage of the violence, Daley and his riot squad assured a bad press not only for themselves but for the Democratic party. The depiction of the rioting in the streets, along with the bitter floor debate between the disillusioned McCarthy and Kennedy delegates and the dominant Humphrey forces within the convention hall, provided Americans the image of a party unable to control even its own deliberations, let alone lead the way out of the Vietnam quagmire.

Watching in his hotel suite, nominee-to-be Humphrey fumed at the television coverage. "I'm going to be president some day," he shouted at the television screen. "I'm going to appoint the FCC— we're going to look into all this." But the rioting in Chicago, like Tet, was the sort of dominant event that television could not disregard without abandoning the reasons for its existence.

Long after the final ballot was cast at the convention assuring Humphrey's nomination, the controversy over the role of the media continued. Mayor Daley issued a "white paper" which contended that had not the media been present to provide an audience, Chicago's streets would have escaped violence. The National Commission on the Causes and Prevention of Violence released its own report which labeled the clashes "a police riot."

The media responded with further accusations against the oppressiveness of the Chicago police. What the press failed to do in its self-absorption with the abuse inflicted upon reporters was to explore the reasons for the pandemonium in Chicago and what it portended for the nation's politics. As it turned out, the success of the protesters in dramatizing their cause in Chicago led others to follow their example. New violence and new tragedies followed, from the Days of Rage on the streets of Chicago to the campus protests at Kent State and Jackson State. At the same time the violence served to harden the resentment shared by millions of middle-class Americans toward the obstreperous youth of the sixties.

This intensified polarization of society seemed to victimize the media itself. The liberal columnist Joseph Kraft warned that much of Middle America—a term he coined—had come to regard journalists as pretentious phoneys. The left replicated this antagonism; leaders of the war protest viewed journalists as servants of the establishment they were challenging. By neglecting to explore these issues, the media denied the public the benefit of lessons that could have been learned from the turmoil at Chicago.

One journalist who did pause to probe beneath surface events was Theodore White, the veteran chronicler of American politics. Touring the streets outside the Democratic convention, White viewed the carnage and scribbled in his notebook: "The Democrats are finished." What was finished was not only the party's hopes in 1968 but the way the party had operated for most of its history.

Party bosses had been able to maintain control of the delegates who delivered the nomination to Humphrey. But as the campaign and election results would show, these delegates had little connection to the voters they were supposed to represent. While losing the battle over the nomination, the anti-war forces had forced the convention to approve a special commission to review the antiquated party nominating rules that had sustained the authority of the hierarchy. The party regulars had won the battle of Chicago. But they would learn in 1972 that they had lost control of their party.

Among those watching the televised turmoil in Chicago, no one was more interested than Richard Nixon, already anointed as the Republican nominee. Although Nixon had dispatched a team of aides to the scene to offer the press the GOP's view of the proceedings, he decided that the damage the Democrats had done to themselves needed no elaboration. "Just let it lie," he told his agents. "They're doing plenty to each other."

As Nixon well knew, the winds of change were sweeping through the musty corridors of Republican power too. While the Democrats in 1968 felt themselves to be victims of the media, Nixon's quest for the 1968 Republican nomination showed how a presidential contender could use the press, television, and the new technology to control his own destiny.

At the outset of his candidacy, Nixon realized that Barry Goldwater's capture of the 1964 nomination, based on grass-roots conservative support, had undermined the supremacy of his own party's establishment. Moderate in ideology, Eastern in orientation, these movers and shakers had nominated Wendell Willkie, Thomas E. Dewey, Dwight Eisenhower, and, in 1960, Richard Nixon. Looking ahead to 1964, they had seemed prepared to lend their support to Nelson A. Rockefeller, the governor of New York. But Rockefeller's liberal stewardship of the Empire State had persuaded many Republicans that either he or they were in the wrong party. Taking inspiration from John Kennedy's early drive for the 1960 nomination, GOP conservatives launched an insurgency of their own, on behalf of Goldwater. In their effort to replicate the Democratic insurgency, however, Goldwater's admirers overlooked the care that Kennedy had given to winning media attention and acceptance. As a result, Goldwater's effort in 1964 illustrated not only the waning strength of the old political order but the increasing potency of the media to harm as well as help a candidate.

Announcing his candidacy, Goldwater had promised that his campaign would be "an engagement of principles." But his principles were soon drowned out by press coverage of his ill-considered off-the-cuff remarks. In short order Goldwater proposed to make Social Security voluntary, to follow up the abortive 1961 Bay of Pigs operation with another exile invasion of Cuba—this time with U.S. air support, and to give NATO field commanders the discretion to use nuclear weapons. Goldwater had been saying such things most of his political life, but no one had paid much attention. Now that he was running for president, his remarks made network news shows and front pages around the country. It was not so much the substance of what Goldwater said—this was hard to sort out—that did him harm. More damaging was the general personal impression he created of being reckless and erratic, a stereotype he would struggle vainly to alter throughout the campaign.

Media treatment of Goldwater exemplified how new developments in politics and journalism were reinforcing each other, laying the groundwork for a change in the political order. With the help of the press, particularly television, John Kennedy in 1960 had greatly dramatized the primaries. Accordingly, the press intensified its coverage of the 1964 primaries, and its daily search for the item most likely to catch the eye of the viewer and the reader was most often satisfied by Goldwater's ramblings. The Arizona senator was an easy target, and that was the trouble. The press found it more convenient to depict the outspoken Republican challenger as a reckless warmonger than to scrutinize the Vietnam policies of the devious Democratic incumbent who in fact was escalating the war.

Theodore White's narrative of the 1960 campaign, the first in what would be a series of books on *The Making of the President*, also influenced press coverage of presidential politics. A former *Time* correspondent and a successful novelist, White contrived to transform the dreary routine of campaigning into a romantic spectacle, endowing hitherto overlooked actions and utterances with profound meaning. The 1964 campaign press corps, for whom White's 1960 book was required reading, seized upon Goldwater's ad libs as portents of his philosophy and his character, to the candidate's growing indignation.

The mammoth proportions of Goldwater's defeat at the hands of Lyndon Johnson in 1964 did not alter the significance of his bold seizure of the nomination. An entrepreneurial candidacy that got off to an early start and displayed determination and resourcefulness could overcome a somnolent regular party organization in the GOP as well as in the Democratic party. It was a lesson from which Richard Nixon profited in 1968. Nixon also benefited from another aspect of Goldwater's experience and of his own turbulent political career—the importance of the media's role in the political process. Learning from Kennedy and from Goldwater, Nixon saw that the decline of the old order had opened the system and the road to the White House to a new breed of operator, the independent political entrepreneur. Like an ambitious businessman, the political entrepreneur needed to raise his own capital, develop his own clientele, and establish his own goals. And the man who sixteen years earlier as GOP vice presidential nominee had nearly been forced off his party's ticket by a newspaper exposé certainly did not have to be reminded that such a candidate needed to be skillful in using the latest techniques of his trade to manipulate the media.

Remembering Nixon's past defeats—in his bids for the presidency in 1960 and for the governorship of California in 1962—many in the press dismissed his chances of comeback. "He still looks like a loser to me," *Newsweek* executive editor Kermit Lanser told me in early 1968 after candidate Nixon paid a call on the magazine. *Time*'s editors had so little regard for Nixon's prospects that they assigned their chief political reporter, Simmons Fentress, to cover Nelson Rockefeller at the start of the campaign and for months ignored his pleas to switch to Nixon. By the time some journalists discarded their biases against him, Nixon was well on the way to nailing down the nomination.

The lack of real competition contributed to the smooth functioning of Nixon's tightly organized campaign, whose managers sought to protect him against stumbling into the sort of controversy that had brought down the early front-runner, George Romney. In another demonstration of the power of the media to wreak damage, Romney's candidacy had been destroyed by his remark to a radio interviewer that he had been "brainwashed" on Vietnam. It was the sort of cautionary tale that hardened Nixon's determination to avoid such exposure.

To Richard Whalen, one of "the bright young men" the candidate had recruited as a speech writer and issues adviser, it seemed "as though Nixon were being assisted by a team hired in a package deal with IBM." Ultimately Nixon's computers would store his positions on sixty-seven different issues and spew out that information under the candidate's signature to voters around the country.

No foreseeable pitfall was overlooked. Even the elephants trotted out as party symbols at Nixon rallies were first given enemas to insure against the embarrassment of an act of nature. In the same spirit, Nixon's handlers carefully structured his public appearances, including his contacts with the press, to limit the possibility of impromptu complications.

Nixon's only declared opponent for the nomination, Rockefeller, had turned out—as Nixon expected—to be little of a threat. Because of his fame, his wealth, and his engaging personality, Rockefeller greatly impressed some journalists who viewed him, despite his defeat in 1964, as a serious rival to Nixon. As a *Newsweek* correspondent I was excited but apprehensive when the magazine assigned me to cover Rockefeller. After Syracuse University and the *Daily Orange*, I had spent the better part of two decades working for newspapers around the country. I had covered politics before, but this would be my first presidential campaign, and I was concerned about my lack of seasoning.

I need not have worried. Nothing could have prepared me for reporting on Rockefeller's candidacy; it was *sui generis,* the kind only a billionaire could indulge in. "Rocky" spent so lavishly that his staff joked about it. "Gentlemen," Leslie Slote, the governor's press secretary grandly announced to a group of reporters at one campaign stop, "my candidate will appear in two hours to address a huge crowd which is even now being expensively recruited." Most of Rockefeller's expenditures went to finance his trips around the country, during which he hoped to convince party leaders that Nixon was a loser and that only Rockefeller could win the White House for the GOP. The success of this effort depended on the public being influenced by media coverage of Rockefeller's campaign, and their rising support showing up in opinion polls. Or so Rockefeller hoped.

That strategy was punctured just before the Republican convention, when the Gallup Poll, which Rockefeller had counted on to prove that the party needed him to win, instead showed Nixon beating Democratic standard-bearer Humphrey while Rockefeller only ran even with him. That finished Rockefeller and assured Nixon of the nomination.

Still, the general election campaign was bound to be rougher going for Nixon than the struggle to become his party's nominee. He had to contend not only against Hubert Humphrey and the Democrats but against the third-party candidacy of Alabama governor George Wallace. Born of racial hostility and working-class discontent, Wallace's drive for the White House broadened its appeal as the pugnacious candidate won backing in the suburbs of the North as well as in the South.

For the media, in a campaign marked by the unexpected and the unprecedented, Wallace was another new wrinkle. At first most journalists were unwilling to take the candidate and his raucous rhetoric seriously, behaving, as a team of London *Times* reporters wrote in *American Melodrama,* "like parents who refuse to look when their child is doing something naughty for fear it might encourage him." But by the fall of that year they more than made up for their early neglect by swarming all over Wallace's rallies. "Don't forget we are in the bad news business," one television producer explained.

This was a fact of media life no one had to explain to Wallace. He realized that the press was drawn irresistibly to conflict, and he supplied plenty of it by literally shaking his fist at the political establishment and "the pointy headed bureaucrats" who served it. As passionate as he was on the stump, Wallace was canny enough not to take himself all that seriously, a trait that made it difficult for journalists to dislike him personally, whatever contempt and disapproval they may have felt for his beliefs. On one occasion, when phoning a prominent newspaper editor to get more sympathetic editorial treatment, Wallace explained: "I just called up to kiss your ass some more."

Through it all Nixon stuck to his overall media strategy, which was to deprive political journalists of most of their potency by relying on television commercials and other means of communication over which he could maintain complete command. The rationale for this approach had been laid out early in the campaign by H. R. Haldeman, Nixon's ranking advance man and later his White House chief of staff, in a memo to the candidate: "The time has come for political campaigning—its techniques and strategies—to move out of the dark ages and into the brave new world of the omnipotent eye."

The gist of Haldeman's message was that a candidate could reach a much larger audience, with greater ease, via television commercials than through the traditional frantic schedule of personal appearances. Just as important, he could exercise greater control over the message. The same notion had occurred to other politicians, but it was the Nixon campaign that had the resources and foresight to take maximum advantage of it.

Nixon went through the customary routine of speeches and interviews, structured and paced in his case to limit the possibility of impromptu complications. And he had learned to make the most of such occasions. While reserving the main thrust of his message for his commercials, Nixon was glad to keep reporters content by caring for the details that he knew made their jobs easier. For wire services and afternoon papers, he made sure to provide enough new quotes to help them write a fresh lead. He advised television crews when to set up their cameras, and correspondents what part of his speech texts they could skip. "Just be ready for the last five minutes," he told NBC's Herb Kaplow, who was trying to digest a twenty-four-page speech text. "You'll be fine."

Remarkably, such minor accommodations on Nixon's part were enough to impress some of journalism's supposedly hardest-boiled practitioners. CBS's Mike Wallace, the epitome of the relentless interrogator, who remembered being cold-shouldered by Nixon when he tried to interview him in the 1960 campaign, said of the 1964 edition of Nixon: "He's more relaxed. He's more fun."

When the veteran political correspondent Jules Witcover interviewed Nixon early in the campaign, the candidate answered Witcover's first question, then without interruption proceeded with his discourse until he had covered the second, third, fourth, and fifth questions that Witcover had prepared. Amazed, Witcover told Nixon that he had answered all the questions Witcover had written down without his having to ask them. "You must have peeked at my notes," Witcover suggested facetiously. Nixon, never quick to take a joke, especially when the point might have something to do with his deviousness, seemed stricken. "Oh no," he protested with obvious sincerity, "I wouldn't do that."

Nixon did not have to deal with such contretemps in his television commercials, in which he answered questions from local voters. This advertising held far more significance than the output of the reporters who covered his campaign, because they were seen by a vastly larger audience. Nixon's aides carefully designed the commercials not to seem designed. His advisers had concluded, Nixon said, "that the more spontaneous the situation, the better I come across."

Some spontaneity. Nixon's aides handpicked the questioners and edited their responses.

Sample exchange: A well-dressed, middle-aged black man asks Nixon about one of the key slogans of his campaign, law and order— a theme designed to appeal to white fears of black crime and violence. "What does law and order mean to you?" the questioner wants to know.

"To me law and order must be combined with justice," Nixon replies. "Now that's what I want for America. I want the kind of law and order that deserves respect."

There was no follow-up.

The important point to such appearances, as Nixon media adviser William Gavin explained, was not what Nixon said but how he was perceived. "Reason requires a high degree of discipline of concentration; impression is easier," Gavin wrote in a memo. In a TV film, Gavin pointed out, "the candidate can be shown better than he can be shown in person because it can be edited so only the best moments are shown."

Against the hazy backdrop created by his squad of obfuscators, Nixon deftly avoided explaining how he would keep his promise to end the war in Vietnam. He marched on to the nomination and victory over Humphrey and Wallace in the fall.

In 1968 the media served mainly to witness and transmit events— the fighting abroad, the anguish over the war at home, the upheaval among the Democrats—whose deeper meaning was well beyond the grasp of most reporters, and most politicians too, for that matter. But the drama and significance of these events, the aggressive response of the media, and the torpor of the political establishment combined to give the press an importance far exceeding its previous status. As the campaign year advanced, some journalists began to realize that their role was changing. What few yet understood was that this alteration reflected not just political turmoil but broader shifts in American society and in power relationships in government. By the time the next presidential campaign was under way, the media would come to realize that these changes were making over the face of presidential politics and of political journalism.

THREE

1972: *"The Greatest Goddam Change"*

FOUR YEARS AFTER the collapse of the old political order gave political journalists a breakthrough opportunity, they dropped the ball—not once but twice. They missed the two biggest stories of the 1972 campaign, events of historic importance—the reforms of party rules that paved the way for George McGovern's totally unforeseen nomination, and the web of deceit and corruption that undergirded Richard Nixon's landslide reelection.

The media neglected both stories for much the same reason: they were complex events that fell outside the traditional lines of news coverage. On the surface, neither compelled public attention, and reporters saw little reason to believe that perception would change in the long run. Because of the lack of coverage, Watergate, for all its ultimate significance, had little impact on the campaign itself. The Democrats' rules changes, though, not only influenced the contest for the Democratic nomination in 1972 but set in motion events that altered the future of presidential campaigns.

The creation of a special party commission to reform the nominating process—intended to placate the anti-war delegates—had been obscured by the cloud of blood and angst generated by the 1968 Democratic convention. Too distracted by the chaos that surrounded them to consider the full import of the proposal, the party regulars promptly forgot about it. So did the media.

The anti-war forces did not forget. Still infuriated by the tyranny of the old nominating system, and feeling vindicated by their party's loss of the presidency, they lost no time in pressing the Democratic leadership to make good on the Chicago convention's promise of reform. Under the chairmanship of George McGovern, then a little-known senator from South Dakota, the newly created Commission on Party Structure and Delegation Selection laid down a set of laws and standards to govern Democratic parties in every state and territory in selecting delegates to the 1972 national convention. The new rules struck directly at the confusion and arbitrariness of the delegate selection process which in 1968 had frustrated the anti-war forces. They mandated the selection of delegates within the year of the convention, and public notice of delegate selection procedures. And they all but eliminated the power of party officials to appoint delegates. After his first look at the new rules, Lawrence O'Brien, newly installed as the Democratic National Chairman, hailed them as "the greatest goddam change since the two-party system."

The media yawned. Reporters have always regarded the internal activities of national parties as a no-man's-land. And the inquiries of a commission, headed by an obscure senator, into arcane procedures certainly seemed no exception to that rule of thumb. What, reporters asked themselves (if they thought about the subject at all), could such an enterprise possibly accomplish?

A great deal, as it turned out. The new rules opened up the nominating process. By doing so, they made presidential campaigns harder to predict and harder to control. This gave structural impetus to the growing influence of the press—endowing its judgment and information with greater weight. But the press was slow to grasp this new reality, which became clear as the campaign developed.

Fresh from his work on the commission, McGovern announced that he would run for president. The goal of his candidacy, he declared, would be to end the war in Vietnam, which had created more passionate divisions in the country than any event since World War II. The press and most of the rest of the political world ignored him.

McGovern had drawn only a flicker of national attention in 1968 when he announced for the presidency a fortnight before the convention and sought to rally the anti-war supporters of the slain Robert Kennedy to his own candidacy. Afterward he returned to the twilight zone to which most senators from small states are consigned, a situation which his role on the reform commission did nothing to alter.

When the widely respected journalist and novelist Richard Dougherty left his post as New York bureau chief of the *Los Angeles Times* to become McGovern's press secretary in the fall of 1971, he told Dick Wald, an old friend and an executive of NBC News: "I need an adventure. I need to set the blood racing." Said Wald, expressing the collective wisdom of national political journalism: "You need a sanity pill." Still another negative judgment came from Jack Germond, the political columnist. "He's not going anywhere," Germond said of McGovern. "He can't make news. He's too auto-lib, too predictable. Press a button and that's what McGovern would say."

One reason political journalists found it so easy to shrug off McGovern was that most of them already knew the identity of the next Democratic presidential nominee, and most likely the next president—Senator Edmund Muskie of Maine. Only three years earlier, Muskie had been, like McGovern, just another senator from a small state. But running for vice president in 1968, by contrast with the other national candidates (Humphrey, Wallace, Nixon, and Spiro Agnew), Muskie had comported himself with dignity and self-confidence. Early on he displayed a wry New England sense of humor. He claimed in his acceptance speech that when a reporter asked his mother whether she intended to vote for him, the good woman replied, "Well, if no one offers any better, I suppose I will."

That fall, as Muskie stumped in Pennsylvania, he was beset by hecklers protesting the war. Unable to make himself heard, he invited the loudest of the bunch to share the platform with him. The hecklers were disarmed. More important, the rest of the country, and certainly the press corps, was impressed. The media made much of the incident. At a time when the country seemed out of control, here was one politician who could keep a steady hand. A new hero, steady Ed Muskie—"trusty Muskie" as his admirers called him—was born.

Then, on midterm election eve in 1970, Muskie, appearing on behalf of Democratic congressional candidates, delivered a powerful television address, shaming Republicans for their campaign rhetoric. Speaking from the kitchen of his Maine home, more in sorrow than anger, Muskie said of Republican claims that Democrats were soft on crime: "How dare they tell us that this party is less devoted or less courageous in maintaining American principles than they are themselves. What contempt they must have for the American people to talk to them that way." The speech enhanced Muskie's image of strength and solidity. *Newsweek* put him on its cover under a headline declaring: "Democrats Shape Up." The Maine senator became the indisputable front-runner for his party's 1972 presidential nomination and won a flock of endorsements from party leaders. The press not only failed to question the value of this support but enhanced and exaggerated Muskie's strength.

"You were giving him credit for delegates in states where delegates hadn't been selected yet," Jack Chestnut, one of the managers for Hubert Humphrey, who tried to make a comeback after his 1968 defeat, complained to reporters after the campaign. In other words, the press overlooked the changes wrought by the delegate reform commission and assumed that, as in the past, the choice of delegates and the delegates' choice of candidates could be dictated far in advance by the party leaders who backed Muskie.

By exaggerating Muskie's strength, the press did him a disservice, creating expectations for his candidacy that he could not possibly meet. As Chestnut put it: "The press had put him so far out ahead as the leader that they were giving him a measure that was far too high in the eyes of the public."

But Muskie and his advisers made the mistake of believing their own press clippings and, like the press, overlooking the impact of the changes wrought by the Democratic party's new nominating rules. Muskie set about running for the nomination as if the traditional procedures were still in effect and he was the functional equivalent of the incumbent president.

The press treated him that way. This meant that Muskie did not have to face the chief worry of most candidates—getting attention. But Muskie's role as overdog had a downside too: the press was watching him, waiting for him to make a mistake. All candidates make mistakes, but a dark horse's mistakes usually are ignored while a front-runner's may have disastrous consequences. As it turned out in Muskie's case, a front-runner could get in trouble even if he did not make a mistake—if he just did nothing to make himself seem exciting.

As Ed Muskie appeared to be cruising to the nomination, concerned mainly not to make waves, just that standpat quality created difficulties. Muskie faced fundamental problems that the press failed at first to perceive. He was running as a man of the center who would pull the nation's disparate social and political forces toward some ill-defined midpoint on the ideological spectrum where most voters supposedly congregate. This was something like the strategy Lyndon Johnson used in 1964 when he ran against the extremism of Barry Goldwater.

But America as the 1972 campaign approached was a very different place from what it had been in 1964. Under Richard Nixon's stewardship, the discontent of the 1960s had deepened and the divisions multiplied. In *State of the Nation,* a survey of the American mood in 1971 and 1972, William Watts and Lloyd Free found that while most Americans pronounced themselves satisfied with the material circumstances of their personal lives, "an air of uneasiness is abroad in the land." Little more than one-third of the public approved of the way the nation was being governed; more than half agreed with the proposition that "What you think doesn't count very much"; and half felt that "The people running the country don't really care what happens to people like yourself."

Every public issue of consequence contributed to disharmony. Weariness with the Vietnam War was widespread, but Americans were sharply split over the way the war should be ended. Many young people supported amnesty for draft violators, but most other Americans opposed it. A majority of blacks and whites resisted the idea of forced busing as a remedy for segregated schools. But twice as many blacks as whites believed that some form of busing, mandatory or voluntary, was needed to give their children a chance at a better education.

This splintering of old alliances and proliferation of new interest groups ran directly counter to the basic premise of Muskie's candidacy and assured its failure. Muskie wanted to find the middle ground and hold it. This is a strategy better designed for general election campaigns when the attention of the entire electorate is focused on two major party candidates. But the competition for the presidential nomination within the Democratic party in 1972 had no center, only a cluster of fragmented constituencies, many of them at war with one another. By trying to position himself in the middle, Muskie failed to appeal strongly to any of the various groups fastened on their own particular interests. And by his occasional shifts from left to right and back again on such issues as Vietnam, Muskie succeeded mainly in creating an impression of vacillation and opportunism.

Patrick Caddell, polling for McGovern's campaign, noticed a change in attitudes toward front-runner Muskie in 1971 as the campaign took form. "A lot of people who had perceived him after the 1970 speech as being a very decisive individual, a person who had some substance, began to get the feeling that there wasn't much there—that he was not taking stands and was all over the place," Caddell said later. "Our feeling by late December of 1971 was that he was in serious trouble."

But this shift in the way voters looked at the Democratic party's front-runner escaped most reporters, who failed to comprehend the connections that were shaping presidential politics. Certainly journalists recognized the troubled national mood. But few stopped to think about the link between the electorate's angst and anger and the way voters looked at presidential candidates. In mid-January 1972 a CBS News nationwide survey of political reporters and local politicians showed that most believed Muskie would go to Miami within a few hundred delegates of clinching the nomination.

A few exceptions to this journalistic lack of perception stood out. One was R. W. Apple, the indefatigable chief political correspondent of the *New York Times.* From covering Nelson Rockefeller and the Vietnam War, Apple had learned to mistrust the conventional wisdom and was probably the first to report that all was not well with Muskie. His editors buried his story in the back of the paper, but still it made its mark. "Muskie Campaign Lacks Spark," the headline read. The burden of Apple's tale, published in the late fall of 1971, was that Muskie had "failed to generate any sense of excitement" within the party. "In the long run," Apple added ominously, "many politicians across the country believe that because of the lack of deep-rooted enthusiasm for Muskie's candidacy (which also shows up in interviews with voters in many states), if he starts slipping, he will slip rapidly."

Fairly vague stuff. But over the long run it would contribute to Muskie's undoing. Reading the story in New York, Dick Dougherty immediately fired off a memo to McGovern, urging him to plan a "speedy and effective response" to a sudden withdrawal by Muskie from the campaign.

Dougherty was more than a little bit premature. But as he anticipated, Apple's story carried considerable weight with other reporters. The reasons for this have to do with the unique role of the *Times* in American journalism in general and political journalism in particular. "The *New York Times* is not the hometown newspaper of New York, but it is the hometown newspaper of all men of government, all men of great affairs, all men and women who try to think," Theodore White observed. "In the sociology of information it is assumed that any telephone call made between nine and noon anywhere in the executive belt between Boston and Washington is made between two parties, both of whom have already seen the *New York Times* and are speaking from the same shared body of information. The *Times* is the bulletin board not just for the city but for the entire nation's idea and executive system. . . . It is the first paper read in the White House and the first paper read in any newsroom in the country after the local papers have been read."

With the not-so-gentle nudge from the *Times,* more and more reporters began to look for chinks in Muskie's armor. No one wants to get caught sticking with a losing candidate. And no one wants to miss one of the best stories in political journalism—the fall of the mighty. Reporters quickly fastened on the Achilles' heel of Muskie's candidacy: the high expectations his front-runner status had created. To demonstrate his invincibility and his national appeal, Muskie pledged he would campaign in every primary in every state in the country, thus setting himself up for an upset somewhere. He enjoyed a big lead in the polls, but that too exacerbated the expectations problem. Early polls gave him 65 percent of the vote in New Hampshire, an enormous margin. As the press saw it, that figure became a minimum for Muskie's performance.

"Senator, if you get only 60 percent of the vote in New Hampshire, will you consider that a defeat?" Questions like that began to burn Muskie's naturally short fuse.

Because the importance of New Hampshire was the cornerstone of conventional wisdom about presidential campaigns, it was unfortunate for Muskie that in New Hampshire the Maine senator had a particularly grievous problem with the press. While the *New York Times* may have reigned supreme over political journalism in most places in the world, in New Hampshire it took a back seat to a newspaper called the *Manchester Union Leader.* The *Union Leader*'s publisher, William Loeb, a strident conservative and a practitioner of knife-and-kill journalism, pounded away at Muskie day after day, then took off after his outspoken wife, Jane, mocking her for some flip remarks she supposedly made.

Muskie, as he said later, was "just goddamned mad and choked up over my anger." Flying back to New Hampshire from Florida where he had been campaigning, he hired a flatbed truck, had it hauled in front of the Union Leader office, and stood upon it to denounce Loeb as "a liar" and "a gutless coward."

In short, Muskie blew his cool. But it was not just his language that seemed unpresidential, it was the tears that came to his eyes as he raged at Loeb for attacking his wife. Wait a minute—were they really tears? In the media a great debate ensued over that question. Some reported that Muskie had wept as he stood on the truck in the February snowfall. Others concluded that the moisture in his eyes was just the result of the falling snow. In any case, Muskie's display of emotion—whether tears or merely a sob—was the wrong thing for people to see. Now the media, having shaped the image of Muskie as a pillar of strength, tore that pillar down, and with it the temple of his front-running candidacy. "It changed people's minds about me, about what kind of guy I was," Muskie said later. "They were looking for a strong steady man, and here I was weak."

The damage from that episode, and from Muskie's whole lackluster performance in his front-runner role, left its mark on the New Hampshire returns. Muskie won with 46 percent of the vote to 37 percent for George McGovern. He had beaten McGovern by nine points, almost double digits, a solid victory in anyone's book. But not in this case.

By the perverse new rules of politics and journalism—the standards that had made Eugene McCarthy a New Hampshire winner even when he had finished second four years earlier—Muskie lost, and McGovern won. *Newsweek,* in a much-quoted demonstration of damning with faint praise, called Muskie's triumph "underwhelming." The reaction to the vote damaged Muskie's prestige and shook his confidence. After his poor fourth-place finish in the Florida primary, where Alabama governor George Wallace rode a tide of anti-busing sentiment to victory, Muskie lost his front-runner status and his temper too. He lashed out bitterly at Wallace and his supporters, whom he condemned as "racists."

A few weeks later in the Wisconsin primary, Muskie finished

fourth behind McGovern, Wallace, and Humphrey, in that order, and a reporter asked, "Senator Muskie, are you finished?" He was, whether he wanted to admit or not.

Meanwhile McGovern, having less to lose, had been much more adroit than Muskie in taking the hard blows of the campaign. In Florida, where he had made only a minimal effort and finished sixth, he was far more restrained than Muskie in his response. He labeled Wallace an "extremist" but added that many who voted for him "did so because they are deeply frustrated and disgusted with the way their government is ignoring their concerns and interests."

McGovern had shown himself to be a good loser. And the press was beginning to pay attention to him, a moment that his staff had long awaited through the frustrating weeks while they chafed at the lack of coverage their candidate received. Not only were his early campaign activities ignored by the press, but he was even excluded from the early public opinion polls of attitudes toward Democratic candidates. As his executive assistant and chief troubleshooter Gordon Weil complained afterward, Gallup and other pollsters said McGovern had been excluded because his name recognition was low, because he did not get press coverage. And one reason the press didn't cover him was that he was not even mentioned in the polls. "It was a vicious circle," lamented Weil.

Early in 1972, Dick Stout, a colleague of mine in Newsweek's Washington bureau, after inspecting McGovern's grass-roots organization in key states around the country, wrote an impassioned memo to the magazine's editors, urging that they give McGovern more coverage. "He has more real support at the local level than anyone else," Stout, a veteran of the 1968 McCarthy campaign, wrote. He wanted more time to cover McGovern instead of Muskie. But Newsweek's editors, in the tradition of the journalists who covered the election of President Thomas E. Dewey in 1968, and of the Time editors who insisted that Simmons Fentress cover Governor Rockefeller, knew better than their reporter. "Stick with Muskie," they ordered.

McGovern's lack of renown—or name identification, to use the term favored by the pollsters—had its advantages. It helped him with an electorate mistrustful of the more familiar political crowd. And because they were ignored by the national press, McGovern's aides worked to establish a network of contacts among local journalists who did not share the narrow-minded view of the national pundits. "I soon learned that the local media were better respected than the national press and would have a far greater impact on the electorate," Gordon Weil recalled. These local journalists proved to be a strong asset for McGovern in the primaries.

As underdogs, McGovern's staff had to make the most of any asset. And in their low-key way they soon began to break new ground in press manipulation. Led by Gary Hart, McGovern's campaign manager (later a U.S. senator and a twice-failed presidential candidate), they became early practitioners of the art of "spin" as it might have been taught by the Actors Studio. Although the early returns from the Iowa caucuses—the delegate contest that was decided the week before New Hampshire's primary—showed Muskie defeating McGovern by a margin of three to two, Hart instructed the McGovern aides "to look as happy as possible." The ploy worked, as Hart later boasted. "The jollier the McGovern people began to look, the more solemn the Muskie staffers appeared."

It also helped that later returns showed McGovern narrowing Muskie's victory margin. The next morning Hart claimed a "moral victory" for his candidate and then "hot-footed it out of the state," leaving Muskie's aides to explain the confusing Iowa numbers to reporters. That night Hart had the satisfaction of hearing Bill Lawrence, ABC News' political correspondent, report to millions of viewers, "The Muskie bandwagon slid off an icy road in Iowa last night." As Hart and his colleagues raised their glasses in celebration of their "moral victory," he remarked: "We sweated blood for that sentence."

After Iowa and New Hampshire, reporters began to look for virtues in McGovern's candidacy and inevitably discovered them. The first demonstration of this tendency was the Wisconsin primary, four weeks after New Hampshire. McGovern won there with only 30 percent of the vote, and by some estimates about one-third of that support came from Republican crossovers. Yet the Wisconsin primary established McGovern as the front-runner for the Democratic nomination. The press, as if seeking to make up for the shabby treatment given McGovern in the early stages of the campaign, now treated him as a rising new star in the political firmament. Hitherto regarded as a one-issue candidate, McGovern "tapped deep wells of economic discontent" in Wisconsin, *Time* reported. "His support was astonishingly broad, bracketing liberals, conservatives, blue-collar workers, farmers, suburbanites and the young." *Newsweek* wrote: "McGovern's past failure to make a splash now lends his candidacy an unusual freshness."

Still, McGovern, like the other candidates, had not found a way to reconcile the racial resentments and harsh feelings that infused the hard core of George Wallace voters in 1972, as they had four years earlier. But when Wallace was shot and seriously wounded in May, on the eve of the Maryland and Michigan primaries, which he won handsomely, his wounds eliminated him as a force in the 1972 campaign.

McGovern's media honeymoon did not last long. As his prominence grew, his freshness wore off, and the press responded to him much as they had to Muskie. During McGovern's surge to the front of the Democratic field, the press had written positive stories that portrayed him as an idealistic insurgent, challenging the party establishment and the long odds against his candidacy. When McGovern took the lead, the press gave him the same treatment it had given Muskie. And it hurt.

The press did not invent things. It simply concentrated on criticism of McGovern and on his controversial statements; since he was the leader of the pack, that is what made news. McGovern's opposition to the war, the centerpiece of his candidacy, had considerable potential appeal to voters. But the press had already covered McGovern's objections to the war. Reporters needed something new. And McGovern had the misfortune to provide them with a new angle by likening Nixon to Hitler, because of his Vietnam policies, and by proclaiming that the U.S. Senate chamber "reeks of blood"—outbursts which to millions of patriotic Americans made him seem wild-eyed and dangerous.

This sort of coverage soured the favorable rapport between the press and the McGovern campaign and exacerbated the natural tensions that prevail between candidates and reporters in any campaign. McGovern began more and more to see himself as a victim, and the press to view him as a sorehead.

Reporters stressed the unpopularity of McGovern's call for an unconditional amnesty for draft violators. That proposal reflected McGovern's own convictions and his need for support on college campuses. But polls showed that only about 20 percent of the voters accepted the idea. His advisers tried to persuade the press to give McGovern credit for having the courage of his convictions, even when they were unpopular. Instead journalists played upon examples of McGovern's inconsistency. He said he was opposed to criminal penalties for marijuana but not in favor of legalizing it. He personally believed in a woman's right to abortion but did not support abortion on demand as federal policy. As he seemed to say one thing, then another, his foes and the press portrayed him as guilty of extremism, or shiftiness, or both.

The proposal most damaging to his candidacy was his scheme for welfare reform, which provided a government grant to every American, regardless of economic status. The upper and middle classes would return all or part of their "demogrants" to the government in taxes; poor people would keep the entire amount to supplement their earnings. Because the economic ramifications of the plan were difficult to calculate, McGovern's advisers warned him to stick to its broad principles in explaining it.

Nevertheless McGovern began using the figure of $1,000 as the sum of a demogrant. By going into details, he trapped himself. During the California primary campaign, in a televised debate with Humphrey who had become his chief opponent, McGovern was inevitably challenged to say how much his plan would cost. The embarrassed candidate had to admit that he could not tell, nor could anyone else. After the debate, when Gary Hart mentioned the $1,000 plan, McGovern snapped: "I wish I had never heard of the goddam idea." The press depicted the whole affair as an example of McGovern's muddled thinking.

Instead of contributing to the confusion of the Democratic contest, the press could have helped avoid some of it. Had political reporters paid more attention to the new nominating rules and explained their significance, the nature of the campaign probably would have been different. Muskie would not have been such a heavy favorite at the start, and he would have had a better chance of surviving his "underwhelming" victory in New Hampshire. McGovern might still have won the nomination. But if the press had been alert and diligent from the start, reporters would have anticipated McGovern's potential strength. His candidacy would not have had to endure the roller-coaster ride of expectations that took him from total obscurity to the top of the Democratic heap and then, as the general election began, back down to the status of hopeless underdog.

Even allowing for confusion over the demogrant plan, McGovern, far more than most modern presidential candidates, seemed willing, even eager to offer explicit answers to the major questions before the public. He was trying to adhere to the justifiably high standard that the media sets for presidential candidates.

He pledged to end the war and bring home all American troops within ninety days of his assuming the presidency. He vowed to cut billions from the defense budget and save billions more by closing a variety of tax loopholes. He promised to spend these savings on creating new jobs, expanding Social Security benefits, and offering tax relief to homeowners. He called for new ethical standards to guard against the corruption and abuse of federal authority.

Whether or not these proposals had great merit, they deserved attention and debate during the general election campaign in the fall, when McGovern took on Nixon. But McGovern's message, whatever its strengths and shortcomings, was drowned out by the press concentration on his blunders.

His biggest error was the selection of Missouri senator Thomas

Eagleton as his running mate. McGovern scarcely knew the man, having met him only briefly on two occasions. But Eagleton was a Catholic from a border state, and he enjoyed good connections to the labor movement—all areas where McGovern himself was weak.

Eagleton quickly accepted, "before you change your mind," he told McGovern, a wry comment that Freudians would suggest McGovern might have taken as a warning signal. Hard on the heels of Eagleton's nomination came the disclosure that the senator had a past history of mental illness for which he had received electroshock therapy, an episode Eagleton acknowledged to McGovern only after it had been unearthed by the Knight newspapers.

The Eagleton affair became a multi-dimensional story. First, his mental illness allowed newspapers and television to invoke two powerful clichés. Here was evidence of past instability in a man who would be, the press reminded voters, "only a heartbeat away" from the Oval Office, whose occupant "had his finger on the nuclear trigger." Beyond Eagleton's emotional or mental difficulties, his failure to be forthcoming with McGovern did not speak well for his integrity and dependability.

These issues were legitimate subjects for journalistic inquiry. Indeed, the press had an obligation to pursue the story. The "heartbeat" and "nuclear trigger" metaphors, though timeworn, were valid, based on the Constitution and the realities of the cold war. But the press, already zealous to expose McGovern's foibles, used the Eagleton affair to raise doubts not just about the Missouri senator but about McGovern. What did it say about McGovern's judgment that he picked Eagleton in the first place? Then, how did McGovern's handling of the disclosure reflect on *his* character? At first McGovern stuck by Eagleton, saying he supported him "1,000 percent." Did that make him stubborn and rigid? Then McGovern in effect fired Eagleton off the ticket. Was he then two-faced and a hypocrite?

One line of attack asserted that by waiting for public reaction before forcing Eagleton from the ticket, McGovern demonstrated that he was no more high-minded than traditional politicians. "In the 'old politics' this sort of maneuvering was an accepted technique for approaching tough decisions, euphemistically known as 'keeping your options open,'" William Greider wrote scornfully in the *Washington Post.* "The 'new politics' of the McGovern campaign . . . will have to think of something different to call it." The Eagleton affair, claimed the *New York Times,* had damaged McGovern's "image" as "an unusually candid Presidential candidate."

But what was the so-called new politics supposed to mean? McGovern himself, as Greider wrote, "has always insisted that he is above all a pragmatic politician." His claim to being different, so far as it went, was based mainly on his professed willingness to deal frankly with issues that other politicians ducked, and on his positions on those issues. The Eagleton affair had nothing to do with substantive issues. The case turned on public attitudes toward Eagleton's medical history and toward his deception of McGovern. For his own sake and Eagleton's, McGovern tried to sway opinion in Eagleton's favor and overdid it. When that effort failed, McGovern had no choice—under the "new politics" or the old—but to find another running mate.

While some critics in the press were exposing McGovern as duplicitous, others were depicting him as incompetent. Acknowledging that McGovern had had "bad luck," the *New York Times'* James Reston nevertheless argued that "he has also misjudged the problem of picking a Vice President" and "overrated the efficiency of his new young staff." The columnist Joseph Kraft contended that "the Senator from South Dakota has not shown the one thing a Presidential candidate must show—the capacity to govern."

The Eagleton affair was certainly a dismal chapter in the McGovern saga, reflecting no credit on anyone involved. But the press overdid its barrage against McGovern. The view that McGovern's choice of his running mate demonstrated his unfitness to manage the country's affairs does not stand the test of comparison with other instances of vice presidential selection. The discussions leading to McGovern's selection of Eagleton were terribly confused, but no more so than the conversations preceding John Kennedy's 1960 offer of the vice presidency to Lyndon Johnson in the hope and belief that he would not accept it. After that imbroglio, which created resentments that endured for years, Robert Kennedy confided to a friend: "My God, this wouldn't have happened except that we were all too tired last night."

McGovern's aides were not as assiduous as they might have been in examining Eagleton's background. But how carefully had the staff of McGovern's Republican opponent, Richard Nixon, in 1968 looked into the background of Maryland governor Spiro Agnew in a state whose politics was famous for its nonchalance about ethical standards? No one thought to raise that question until the summer of 1973, when Agnew was plea bargaining with federal prosecutors to avoid imprisonment for bribery and tax evasion.

Reporters did not employ such perspective in writing about the Eagleton affair. In the wake of that fiasco, the Democratic ticket of McGovern and his ultimate choice for vice president, R. Sargent Shriver, seemed to the press like the *Titanic* after it struck the iceberg—floundering and about to sink. "We were no longer McGovern, presidential nominee," Richard Dougherty, the candidate's press secretary, wrote of the post-Eagleton atmosphere. "We were McGovern in trouble." Dougherty imagined journalists around the country saying to their colleagues, "What went wrong today? What's he done now?"

The press did not set out to wreck McGovern's candidacy; it was not guilty of malice in the 1972 campaign. Instead it committed on a grand scale one of its most habitual sins—exaggeration. The press perceived the Eagleton affair and what it purportedly revealed about McGovern's personality as an event of great significance, and this perception was transformed into a reality that overshadowed all else.

The 1972 campaign also provided evidence of another relatively recent development in press coverage: "pack journalism." Reporters assigned to follow a single candidate for weeks or months are like hounds chasing a fox, Timothy Crouse observed in *The Boys on the Bus*, his vivid portrayal of 1972 campaign coverage. "Trapped on the same bus or plane, they ate, drank, and compared notes with the same bunch of colleagues. After a while they begin to believe the same rumors, support the same theories, and write much the same stories."

Everyone denounces pack journalism, but it is hard to avoid, given competitive pressures. Perhaps the best antidote for it is another phenomenon of the trade—the countertrend story. Reporters who can break away from the pack and find something fresh or innovative to say will boost their reputations—and if they can do it often enough, their paychecks. This takes imagination, initiative, and a bit of gumption. But political journalists, when they are not being lazy, are an ambitious lot. And usually there are at least a few who are willing to challenge the conventional wisdom, as R. W. Apple demonstrated in the fall of 1971 when his story questioned the inevitability of Muskie's nomination.

Regardless of the foibles of the press, George McGovern would have had trouble catching Richard Nixon. With the economy apparently sound and Nixon seemingly in control of events in Indochina, the odds in his favor were long. Yet McGovern trailed Nixon by only twelve points in the polls in June, after his victory in the California primary. And by the normal rhythms of politics he should have reduced the margin, particularly with the favorable publicity he could reasonably have expected from his party's nominating convention. Instead, after the convention and the Eagleton fiasco with its hyperbolic coverage, Nixon's margin almost doubled, depriving McGovern of the chance to pull together the major elements of his party and force Nixon to confront him and defend his administration.

Nixon had no desire to do that and, as it turned out, no need to. The president and his allies, who had long complained of being unfairly abused by the press, found it hard to conceal their delight and surprise at what seemed to them a reversal of form. Victor Gold, veteran of countless battles with the media as press secretary to Spiro Agnew in 1972 and before that as a press aide to Barry Goldwater in 1964, told me: "I used to think that you guys were out for our blood. But I can see now that you're out for anybody's blood."

The media would gladly have taken a few shots at Nixon too. But they saw little opportunity—and the opportunity that did develop, the Watergate scandal, they failed to recognize.

Reporters found it easier to cover the conventional trappings and processes of the campaign, which meant mainly the struggles of Mc-Govern. As for Nixon, he had concluded that he did not need to campaign in the conventional sense. Early in his presidency he had established a political base by going over the heads of the press and presenting himself as a champion of middle-class voters, a natural role for him. Although he had been raised in California, the town he grew up in, Whittier, resembled the sort of small town in Ohio where Nixon's father, Frank, had been raised late in the nineteenth century. "Three words describe my life in Whittier: family, church, and school," Nixon later recalled.

As a politician Nixon took pains to strengthen his bonds to the middle class. Perhaps the most memorable instance occurred in the 1952 campaign when, answering charges of suspect fund-raising in the famous "Checkers" speech, he declared: "Pat doesn't have a mink coat. But she does have a respectable Republican cloth coat. And I always tell her that she'd look good in anything." And he had dramatized his role as a defender of the middle class throughout his career by leading the charge against communism. The Vietnam War protest movement made another convenient target. In his "Silent Majority" speech in 1969, Nixon used the threat of anti-war demonstrators to win the backing of his middle-class constituents for winding down the war in Vietnam in his own way and at his own pace.

Then, just as Democratic infighting for the nomination was at its height, Nixon made his breakthrough trip to China. Voters viewed the two competing parties in 1972 as if they were on a split television screen. On one side of the screen they could see the Democrats battering each other in the early stages of their nominating campaign; but most of the screen was taken up with Nixon arriving at the Great Wall and meeting with Chinese leaders in Beijing. Later, as Humphrey and McGovern debated in California, the nation watched Nixon and Brezhnev in Moscow, reaching agreement on a strategic arms treaty. This was Nixon's real campaign, and the Democrats, to say the least, were overmatched.

His overseas triumphs behind him, Nixon let Agnew and other surrogates carry the burden of the battle against McGovern. The president cut back sharply on press conferences. Previous chief executives had met with the press on average about thirty times a year. But in the election year of 1972 Nixon held only seven press conferences. Instead he delivered fourteen radio addresses in which he could offer his side of an issue without having to deal with questions.

On the few occasions that Nixon ventured into the hustings, those reporters who chose to accompany him had little to show for their pains. Only a handful were fortunate enough to be part of the press pool chosen to travel on Air Force One. And even these lucky ones rarely caught more than a glimpse of his person. The rest of the press were relegated to buses at the rear of a long motorcade, which put miles between them and the president. Often the only evidence they had of his presence was the sound of his voice on the public-address system.

Most major publications dutifully sent reporters to cover these excursions. But left to their own devices, many journalists chose to stay home and follow the president on television, which was the forum he had chosen to wage his reelection campaign. And of course Nixon had by now mastered the medium, even when on the road. When on rare occasions unfriendly hecklers got through the tight security cordoning off his events, Nixon would say: "I have a message for the television crews. Besides these few over *here*," he said pointing to the hecklers, "let's show these thousands over *there*," gesturing at the thousands of schoolchildren who were regularly transported to presidential events.

After the campaign was over, some members of the press analyzed their frustration. "We couldn't cover Nixon, so we all rushed out and covered Agnew," said Jim Perry of the *Wall Street Journal*. "I think a lot of reporters believe that covering a campaign means to jump on the campaign plane and go along with the candidate and listen to the same speech and measure the crowd he had that day. That's the kind of thing we were doing—going along and saying how wonderful the crowds were."

The press's greatest sin in the general election campaign was a sin of omission—its failure to cover Watergate. After the campaign George McGovern complained: "I was subjected to the close, critical reporting that is a tradition in American politics. Yet Mr. Nixon escaped a similar scrutiny. Not a single reporter could gather the courage to ask a question about the bugging and burglary of the Democratic National Committee."

True, the media had reported that the June 1972 break-in at Democratic party headquarters in Washington's Watergate complex had been linked to Nixon's campaign committee aides. And McGovern had hammered away at this disclosure from the stump, charging that it was a sign of pervasive corruption within the Nixon administration. But details were hard to come by.

When Nixon finally held a press conference more than two months after the burglary, reporters seemed to accept his assurance that no one at the White House had any connection with the crime. No one asked a follow-up question. To Dick Stewart, Muskie's press secretary, the press conference seemed little more than a jocular give-and-take between the president and the press. "It was a helluva press conference from the president's point of view," Stewart said.

CBS offered a fifteen-minute special report on Watergate, but it did not run until October 27, less than two weeks before the election. Among the print media, *Newsweek, Time,* the *Los Angeles Times,* and the *New York Times* also worked the story hard, but the collective impact was not strong enough to make a dent on the campaign.

Why did the press not do a better job in covering Watergate? It was a hard story to get at. No one was handing out press releases with inside information on what the White House dismissed as "a third-rate burglary." And traditional political sources in both parties were not much help; most were as baffled by the Watergate "caper," as it was often called early on, as were the media. This was a story that required hard digging in offbeat areas. As some reporters found out, they could spend a lot of time digging and get nowhere. "This is the kind of story that may take ten people to move a couple of inches," complained Max Frankel, Washington bureau chief of the *New York Times,* as his paper struggled to catch up with the *Washington Post.*

The press had little incentive to go after the story because the public, intensely cynical about the nature of politics and particularly of political parties, did not seem to care. And editors were reluctant to commit resources to coverage that was not likely to attract viewers or readers. "I think most people took the view that there was nothing exceptional about the Watergate incident except that the perpetrators got caught," Rick Stearns of the McGovern campaign said afterward. "Most Americans seem to believe that political parties engage in this kind of activity as a matter of course. Political parties as institutions are in such disrepute that sabotage directed at a party fails to arouse the average American."

For all of that, the media should have tried harder to find out about Watergate during the 1972 campaign, a conclusion I believe many reporters now share. One clue that should have served as an incentive for me and for other reporters to dig harder at Watergate was the anxiety of the Nixon administration over the episode. One summer night a few weeks after the break-in, I received a call at home from Robert Mardian, who had been in charge of the internal security division at the Justice Department and then had moved to the Committee to Re-Elect the President, or CREEP, the singularly appropriate acronym for Nixon's campaign organization.

Mardian told me he had "something important" to tell me about Watergate and urged me to come to his apartment, coincidentally located in the Watergate complex. I had known Mardian since Nixon's 1968 campaign. He had been a helpful source on politics and also on the operations of the Justice Department under John Mitchell, Nixon's attorney general. But he had never asked me to his home before, nor had I ever heard him sound so troubled.

I was certainly not prepared for what he had to tell me in a conversation that lasted several hours and did not end until well after midnight. Mardian, it turned out, wanted to offer me the *real* explanation for Watergate. It had nothing to do with Nixon or his reelection committee. Instead, he said, propounding a theory that others close to Nixon were trying to promote, it was some sort of CIA operation. To prove his point, Mardian told me that some of the Cubans involved in the burglary had also been linked to plots by Robert Kennedy, when he was attorney general, to assassinate Fidel Castro. Mardian claimed that he had come across evidence of the anti-Castro plots in the files of the internal security division at Justice. These schemes had obviously not succeeded, and Mardian contended that the result was a vendetta involving the Cubans and the CIA which had somehow led to the Watergate break-in.

All of this Mardian confided to me off the record, telling me I was free to use the information as I saw fit but making me swear that I would keep his identity a secret. As fantastic as his story seemed to me then, it later turned out to have some basis in fact. A Senate investigating committee did turn up evidence of anti-Castro plotting by the Kennedy administration and of CIA links to some of the Watergate burglars. But I had a hard time finding proof of this back in 1972, and without being able to attribute it to Mardian, I could not write a story.

It took me a while to grasp what I should have sensed right away. The whole story about Kennedy, Castro, and the Cubans, even though it was not entirely fiction, was an elaborate smokescreen put out by Mardian to distract me from possibly following the trail of the Watergate burglary to the Nixon White House. Later I found that Mardian had planted the same semi-bogus information with other reporters. All of us should have realized that if Nixon's team was so distraught as to employ such measures to divert the press from Watergate, they must have had something very serious to hide.

By following up more aggressively on leads provided by the *Washington Post* coverage led by Bob Woodward and Carl Bernstein, the press could have made Watergate into a bigger issue and forced Nixon on the defensive. The Democratic-controlled Congress might well have jumped into the fray by subpoenaing witnesses, which would have led to more disclosures, more leads, and more stories.

That sort of coverage would surely have had an impact on the campaign. Even if disclosures about Watergate had not changed the outcome, they would almost certainly have forced a closer and more productive contest. McGovern would have had an audience for the issues he wanted to raise. Even Nixon might have benefited. Early disclosures about Watergate might have led him to abandon his cover-up, perhaps staving off the threat of impeachment and saving his presidency. As it was, the post-election Watergate disclosures, apart from driving Nixon from the White House, heightened the media's awareness of their deficiencies in covering the 1972 campaign and gave journalists a new sense of mission as they prepared to cover the 1976 battle for the White House.

FOUR

1976: *The Talent Scouts*

⚑ WHEN THE SEEDS of Jimmy Carter's implausible run for the White House were still germinating, his principal strategist, Hamilton Jordan, urged Carter to bend every effort to "generate favorable stories in the national press. Stories in the *New York Times* and the *Washington Post* do not just happen," Jordan argued in a memo written as the 1972 campaign was drawing to a close. "They have to be carefully planned and planted." He listed eighteen journalists whom Carter should cultivate, adding that some, like *New York Times* columnist Tom Wicker and Katherine Graham, publisher of the *Washington Post,* "are significant enough to spend an evening or leisurely weekend with."

Jordan's advice, though somewhat naive, reflected the altered state of presidential politics, a shift so glaring it had captured the attention even of such outsiders as Jimmy Carter and his advisers. The transformation had been building all through the 1960s, spurred by John Kennedy, the politician and the legend. Then came the earthquake of 1968, rocking the existing system off its foundations. In 1972 the reforms in the nominating rules provided the final touch, ratifying and reinforcing all that had gone before.

The astute political scientist Nelson Polsby summed it all up in scholarly trappings: "The fundamental effect of changes in the rules of the game has been to weaken the influence of parties and party elites on presidential nominations and to strengthen elites who have access to the devices and the channels of mass publicity." And who

69

were these new elites? Polsby mentioned public relations consultants and media technicians, and even rock performers and movie stars. Indeed, the day would soon come when the glitterati of show business would move in on presidential campaigns in a huge way, helping their favored candidates lap up the mother's milk of politics in quantities never before imagined. But for the time being, Polsby made clear, the greatest benefits of this power shift in the political game were the players who had the most direct access to the information network—professional journalists.

No wonder then, despite the deficiencies they had demonstrated in the 1972 campaign, in 1976 political reporters attracted more attention than ever before. And most of them minded not at all. Some began thinking of themselves, in the phrase of one veteran reporter, as "talent scouts," searching out and evaluating presidential prospects, replacing the networks of the old-fashioned machines, thus living up to such generous assessments of their importance as put forth in Hamilton Jordan's memo to Carter.

Whatever the precise merits of Jordan's counsel, the former Georgia governor took the advice to heart and expanded upon it. Although my name did not make Jordan's list of eighteen influentials, the first time I interviewed Carter for the *Los Angeles Times,* in the summer of 1974, he urged me to pay a weekend visit to his farm in Plains, where he raised peanuts. When I asked him what I would do there he told me we could look for old arrowheads. I declined.

Events would show that Jordan's memo was off the mark. While recognizing the growing significance of journalists, he misconstrued how best to influence their reports. Carter's early efforts at ingratiation gained him little in the way of coverage. Of course, as Jordan argued, stories in the *New York Times* and the *Washington Post* did not "just happen." But they did happen when Carter won first the Iowa caucuses and then the New Hampshire primary; the press, true to form, reacted to events and gave Carter a boost on his road to the White House. Nevertheless Carter's early efforts to impress individual reporters reflected the growing realization among presidential candidates—in the wake of the upheavals of 1968 and 1972—of the importance of scoring points with political journalists.

For their part, the media too had tried to learn from past battles. Stung by criticisms of their treatment of the McGovern-Nixon contest, major news organizations drew up plans for more intensive coverage in 1976. They would place greater emphasis on the candidates and the issues and less on the horse-race aspects of the campaign—or so they promised themselves. CBS, NBC, and several newspapers also planned wider use of what they liked to call "precision journalism"—polling on the issues as well as for voter preferences on candidates. A few newspapers set up separate election desks or assigned specialists to cover such campaign features as the raising and spending of money. And many journalists resolved to avoid being duped by contrived "media events," aspects of the campaign that had no purpose except to attract television cameras.

Half a dozen news organizations, including the *New York Times,* the *Wall Street Journal,* and the Knight-Ridder papers, assigned reporters to a campaign "media watch," monitoring the performance of their colleagues. Even before the primary season opened, some of these monitors hastened to write stories warning of the dangers of inflating the significance of early primaries and measuring the results against artificial "media expectations"—cautionary lessons of 1972. "We all did a little soul-searching after '72," said Walter J. Pfister, Jr., an ABC news executive. "I think this year we wanted to make sure we didn't interfere with the process by our predictions."

Now too, a troop of academic researchers—some with generous subsidies from the Social Science Research Council—took to the field to grade the media's efforts to learn from their past blunders. All this was a bit too much for some journalists. "They're three deep this year," wisecracked the *Wall Street Journal's* managing editor Fred Taylor as the campaign began. "There's the reporter covering the campaign, the reporter covering the reporter covering the campaign, and the sociologist watching the whole damn mess."

For all these good intentions, once the campaign started the media too often fell back into their old habits of overstating the importance of some events and missing the significance of others. They were all the more prone to stumble into these traps because of the vacuous nature of the campaign itself.

The shocks of Vietnam and Watergate had numbed the political system. The war had so confused and divided the Democrats that its end left them in disarray, lacking purpose and direction. As for Watergate, its aftermath—Nixon's resignation and the GOP debacle in the 1974 congressional elections—had stunned the Republicans, throwing them on the defensive.

As it turned out, the candidate best suited to take advantage of this muddle was Jimmy Carter. Lacking imposing credentials or deep convictions, he nevertheless dominated the campaign for the Democratic nomination by the force of his energy and ambition.

Months after my luncheon with Carter in 1974, I checked my old notebooks and found only blank pages where my notes from our conversation should have been. It suddenly occurred to me that here was a man determined to make it to the White House who had said nothing I felt obliged to record. Of course that might have been my fault. The only way to find out what Carter was really about, I concluded, was to talk with him again.

As the 1976 Democratic campaign approached, Carter could not be safely ignored. That year no other Democrat had a clear advantage in the race for the nomination—and Carter was running harder than anyone else. He was campaigning six days a week. By the time I caught up with him in May 1975, eight or nine months before the campaign's official opening, he had already visited forty-five states.

Something else about the peanut farmer from Plains commanded attention. Southern Baptist Carter taught Sunday School and made no bones about being a born-again Christian. With conservative Christians—often called evangelicals or fundamentalists—emerging as a growing force in the political process, Carter might be able to make his faith pay a political bonus.

When I asked Carter about this during an early campaign foray in New Hampshire, he responded with caution. Yes, he said, the evangelical movement numbering some forty million was "deeply committed to establishing government as moralistic and decent." But he obviously was wary of being depicted as a religious zealot. "That doesn't mean I'm anointed," he said. "It means that I have an obligation to discern the best qualities of the American people in government and to put them into effect."

Here was the issue that would remain one of the great enigmas for journalists covering Jimmy Carter. Carter's stress on religion, and the high moral tone he established for his candidacy, particularly his pledge to tell the truth, had special resonance for an electorate shaken by the revelations of the Watergate scandal. But how much of what Carter said about religion and morality did he truly mean, and how much did he say for political effect? Was Carter a man of probity and honor or a self-righteous hypocrite? These questions hung over his campaign for the White House and in the presidency that followed, without ever being satisfactorily resolved.

Carter had many exemplary character traits. In a trenchant critique of his political style, a former aide, James Fallows, later wrote that "If I had to choose one politician to sit at the Pearly Gates and pass judgment on my soul, Jimmy Carter would be the one." But in the political arena, other aspects of his personality overshadowed his virtues. He was often self-absorbed and sanctimonious. Driven from childhood by the need to meet the high expectations of his parents and his own ambition, he was plagued by the fear that he would fail to achieve the goals he set for himself.

To back up his religious faith, Carter had a will of iron. On our trip to New Hampshire, after hearing him make his celebrated and oft-repeated promise that he would never tell a lie, I also followed him to a factory gate where he shook hands with workers. As we were leaving, a truck driver accosted him, bitterly complaining because Gerald Rafshoon, Carter's longtime adviser, had parked his car in the spot reserved for the driver. Carter tried to ignore him, but the man kept shouting, making an unpleasant scene.

Finally Carter glanced at Rafshoon, who had a camera dangling from a strap around his neck because he had been taking photos for a Carter campaign brochure. "He doesn't work for me," Carter told the driver. "He's a photographer."

The confused driver gave up and left. But Carter might just as easily have apologized to him and given him a few dollars for his trouble. Trivial as it was, this incident demonstrated Carter's stubbornness, a trait that would help him reach the presidency, and yet make it harder for him to succeed once he got there. It also illustrated how difficult it would be for the candidate who promised he would never tell a lie to keep his word.

The incident meant little at the time. Carter's name was still obscure, and the race was at a very early stage. But it occurred to me that if Jimmy Carter got anywhere in the race for president, this is what he would be up against—reporters ready to hold him to his promises.

One reason for the press's focus on Carter's vow of truthfulness was that Carter had made his own persona the foundation of his candidacy. "Why Not the Best?" was his campaign slogan as well as the title of his brief autobiography. He treated issues superficially, branding the tax system and the welfare system "a disgrace to the human race," but failing to explain how he would reform them while keeping his promise to balance the budget. Although he repeatedly pledged to reduce the size of the federal bureaucracy, candidate Carter declined to say which agencies he would chop.

Gerald Ford, Carter's opponent in the general election, was no bargain either. Like Carter, Ford was dead set against inflation, which was climbing, and unemployment, which was also on the rise. But he did not say how he would create more jobs and keep *his* promise to balance the budget. And in pledging to curb the rise in the cost of living, neither Ford nor Carter referred to the reality of soaring oil prices imposed by OPEC.

The shallowness of the campaign led naturally to superficial journalism. Candidates did not like to concede that point. Carter for one had claimed that "the national news media have absolutely no interest in issues at all. . . . The traveling press have zero interest in any issues unless it's a matter of making a mistake. What they are looking for is a 47-second argument between me and another candidate or something like that. There's nobody in the back of this plane would ask an issue question unless he thought he could trick me into some crazy statement."

In fact Carter had little interest in answering specific questions about issues. His idea of an issues discussion—and this was all too true of other candidates—was for him to announce some bold promise of reform, such as curing the welfare mess or overhauling the tax code, and then avoid an explanation of how he would carry out this pledge. The truth about the importance of issues to Carter is evident from the memos that Hamilton Jordan and others wrote planning Carter's long-shot bid for the presidency. One can look high and low without finding any sign of issue discussion. From start to finish they are awash with tactics and mechanics, with ideas for exploiting the intricacies of the new system and the new power of the press to Carter's advantage.

Jordan recommended that Carter be the first to declare his candidacy in order to impress the media. "Your being the first to announce will result in your receiving a disproportionate amount of press coverage initially. Your being covered on a continuing basis and being treated as a serious, viable candidate depends to a large extent on your being able to convince the working press that you can—in fact—win the Democratic nomination."

Then Jordan discussed the primary schedule, again with an eye toward influencing the press. He emphasized the importance of the sequence of primaries, pointing out that the results of one primary "can have a profound and irrevocable impact on succeeding primaries and a candidate's abilities to raise funds and recruit workers." Of particular significance, Jordan advised Carter, were the early primaries, because the press took "an exaggerated interest" in these contests. More important than the results, he said, was how the results were interpreted by the press. "Handled properly, a defeat can be interpreted as a holding action and a mediocre showing as a victory."

But none of these machinations were as important to Carter's success as his basic strategy, which contradicted the conventional wisdom shared by most members of the press. The success of George McGovern's anti-war candidacy in 1972, along with Muskie's failure in that campaign, had convinced most reporters that a candidate needed strong ideological appeal to win the nomination in a system dominated by primaries. Consequently few in the media at first paid much attention to Carter, whose successful blueprint was based on an opposite premise.

In a year when ideology held little appeal except to ardent liberals—and even they were badly divided—Carter set out to capture the political center. Failing to understand the route Carter had charted to the nomination, the media first neglected Carter, then, following his early success, overestimated his appeal. As a consequence the nation elected a president whose limitations did not become clear until he held office.

What made Carter's victory possible in 1976 was the disarray among liberal Democrats, who at the time were considered the dominant group in the party. To begin with, most liberals in 1976 had counted on Edward Kennedy running. But he pulled out, chiefly because he wanted to avoid having to answer questions about the 1970 tragedy at Chappaquiddick, where a young woman companion had drowned in his car.

By the time of the New Hampshire primary in February 1976, a flock of liberals had entered the race—the witty and urbane Morris Udall, congressman from Arizona; Fred Harris, a former senator from Oklahoma, who boasted of being a half-blooded Indian and a full-blooded populist; R. Sargent Shriver, the former Peace Corps director and Kennedy in-law who cast himself as a proxy for that charismatic clan; and Indiana senator Birch Bayh, a boyish, folksy liberal who would undermine his candidacy by admitting to being a politician. In addition, a write-in campaign was mounted for Hubert Humphrey, the erstwhile happy warrior of liberalism now scorned by many as an anachronism. But for all their credentials, none of these Democrats had found an argument or an issue to lift himself above the rest.

In the campaign's first major test, New Hampshire's presidential primary, the candidates of the left shared the liberal vote while Carter, the least liberal candidate and most assiduous campaigner, came in first with 28 percent of the vote. Udall was close behind with 24 percent. Carter had already won the Iowa precinct caucuses competing against the same field. All this was enough, as Jordan's memo had foreseen, for the press to stamp the former Georgia governor as the tentative front-runner.

Overlooked in the sudden press enthusiasm over Carter was the peculiar ideological arithmetic in New Hampshire which made his success possible. True, Carter had come in first in the primary, but he had won the backing of only about one in four Democrats. The majority preferred one or another of the liberal candidates. These results presaged difficulties between Carter and his own party which, while they did not scuttle his nomination, later debilitated his presidency. And this weakness the media failed to discern or report.

Carter had another important asset: George Wallace. About all the liberals could agree on in 1976 was the importance of stopping the candidacy of the Alabama governor, who once again, despite his crippling wounds suffered in the 1972 assassination attempt, announced for the presidency. Liberals had underestimated him before, and they were determined not to make that mistake again.

As it turned out, Wallace's impact on the race was greatly overestimated, not only by the liberals but by the media.

In the immediate aftermath of the attempt on his life in 1972, some thought Wallace was finished as a national political leader. He was said to be ravaged by pain and so heavily sedated that he could not function as governor. In the winter of 1973, with a handful of other reporters, I had stood at Wallace's bedside while the governor, wrapped in a blanket which covered his catheter, talked defiantly of running again in 1976. "Maybe I can't campaign as much as I used to," he said hoarsely. "But I can still campaign."

The idea of a Wallace comeback held great natural appeal for reporters, particularly those who wanted to play the talent-scout role. His bullet wounds made him a more sympathetic character than the fire-eating demagogue of yore. And hero or villain, he was far better known than the rest of the cast of active Democratic candidates. By 1975 Wallace had regained some of his strength as a result of a rigorous program of physical therapy. He was still paralyzed from the waist down and confined most of the time to a wheelchair. Yet the press regarded him as a formidable figure because he showed up well in early polls. Although his ratings had more to do with his name recognition than anything else, the press often neglected that point in its buildup of the Wallace bugaboo. One published analysis of the forthcoming campaign predicted that, given the new party rules providing for proportional representation, "Wallace—with an immovable bloc of a quarter to a third of the Democratic electorate—could come to the convention with as many as 40 percent of the delegates."

All through 1975, as Democrats prepared for the campaign, the press was filled with such fervid speculation about the importance of Wallace's candidacy. Few journalists believed that Wallace could actually be nominated. But many speculated that he could disrupt the convention and leave the party once again divided in the general election campaign.

In a state of near panic fanned by the media, liberals sought a candidate who could defeat Wallace in the Florida primary, in 1972 the scene of his greatest triumph. They soon convinced themselves that only a Southerner stood a chance of success, and just as quickly settled on Carter as their choice. If Carter was not exactly a liberal, he seemed at least no worse than a moderate conservative. But for Carter to succeed against Wallace in Florida, the Georgian's backers insisted, the liberal candidates must stay out of the race and leave Carter to fight it out with Wallace on his own.

Morris Udall, the leading liberal candidate, had misgivings about this strategy from the start. "If Jimmy wins down there," Udall told me he had warned the anti-Wallace forces, "he doesn't expect to go back to raising peanuts." But the liberals had only one goal at the moment—beating Wallace. And this was the same objective that drew the attention of political journalists. The major theme of their stories before Florida was not whom the Democrats would choose as a nominee but whether anyone could stop Wallace.

Two weeks after his narrow victory in New Hampshire, Carter defeated Wallace in Florida and became the Democrats' man of the hour. Only then did liberals come to appreciate the extent of Carter's shrewdness and their own ingenuousness. By then it was too late to stop him if they had wanted to.

Not that Carter did not stumble on the road to the Democratic convention in New York. Many of his problems had to do with his calculated fuzziness and his self-righteousness. Carter's theme of love and trust provided his candidacy with the semblance of idealism and served as a substitute for ideology. Although his Atlanta head-quarters staff produced a flood of position papers on foreign and domestic affairs, Carter shifted his ground on these policy matters whenever he thought it convenient and made plain that he viewed such statements as of secondary importance. "I don't care how much you talk about issues or how many numbers of Senate and House bills you can name," he told a group of Washington lobbyists, "if the people don't believe that when you're in the White House you're going to do something about the problem and that they can trust what you tell them."

More even than most of his peers, he resisted committing himself to a consistent point of view. "I never characterize myself as a conservative, liberal, or moderate," Carter said proudly early in his campaign, "and this is what distinguishes me from my opponents."

It was a measure of the Democrats' intellectual exhaustion that they did not require Carter to disclose further his beliefs or intentions. But what of the media? Why did they not expose Carter's haziness and challenge his equivocations?

Most were content to ride the wave of the Carter phenomenon. Those who tried to probe the veneer of moralism that surrounded him were often frustrated by the cunning of his staff and the indifference of the rest of the party.

As Carter gained momentum, *Harper's* published an article by freelance journalist Stephen Brill titled "Jimmy Carter's Pathetic

Lies." The article set out to make Carter pay a price for his rash promise never to tell a lie by citing numerous examples of his over-claiming, corner-cutting, and double-talk. The party's 1972 nominee, George McGovern, thought the article raised "many questions about Carter's real beliefs and his sincerity."

But Carter struck back even before publication. His press secretary, Jody Powell, who would later demonstrate his skill at press manipulation in the White House, got hold of an advance copy of Brill's story and dashed off an eleven-page rebuttal, which he persuaded the *Boston Globe* to print alongside Brill's article, before *Harper's* ever hit the newsstands. Powell also orchestrated a press campaign to attack Brill personally. Brill was depicted as a hatchet man for the liberals, out to smear Carter. The article became "a popgun, not a bombshell," as McGovern put it. "Anyone who had notions that Jimmy Carter and his staff were simpleminded 'Georgia boys,'" McGovern observed, "should have learned from the devastating treatment they administered to their first serious critic."

Carter got into more serious trouble with the press later in the campaign by using the phrase "ethnic purity." Asked by Sam Roberts of the *New York Daily News* about constructing low-income housing in suburbs to counter housing segregation, Carter said he favored giving people the right to live where they wanted. But he added: "I see nothing wrong with ethnic purity being maintained. I would not force racial integration of a neighborhood by government action."

The use of that peculiar expression, with its racist connotations—no less a friend of Carter's than Andrew Young would later describe it as "Hitlerian"—stirred a storm. Wherever he went Carter was hectored by the press. He indignantly denied any racist intent and lectured the press for seizing upon this one phrase to torment him. Finally, after being browbeaten by his staff, Carter admitted he had made an "improper use of words."

Still the controversy raged. What finally pulled Carter out of this jam he had created for himself was the support of civil rights leaders who arranged a rally in downtown Atlanta to demonstrate their continued backing for the Georgian. "I want to find the man so perfect that he has never made a mistake," said "Daddy" King, father of the martyred Martin Luther King, Jr., while blacks in the crowd shouted back their responses.

"I know that I have made mistakes," King cried.

"We all do!" came the refrain from the crowd.

"But if there is a forgiving heart . . ." King began.

"Yes!" the crowd interrupted.

". . . and one who stands to apologize, then this nation, this state, and everyone else has no choice but to accept."

"That's right!" the crowd roared.

And that was that. What this demonstrated was that in many cases the power of the press could be smothered by the power of politicians—in this case the politicians who, having made Carter their champion against George Wallace, had too much invested in his political future to back out. So they enlisted Daddy King in their cause. Thus Carter got by—with a lot of help from his friends.

Meanwhile among Republicans, Gerald Ford, the only appointed president in American history, was having an awful time persuading his party to give him a chance to seek the office in his own right. To me, and to many other reporters, Ford seemed one of the emotionally healthiest human beings to hold high political office in the latter part of the twentieth century. But Ford's link to Nixon, particularly his decision to pardon the disgraced ex-president for his Watergate crimes, had darkened his presidency and damaged his rapport with the press. These relations also suffered from a commonly shared Washington stereotype—the idea that Ford was not the sharpest knife in the drawer. The notion was based in part on Ford's plodding manner of speaking, which may have been an aftereffect of a serious childhood stuttering problem. Another factor was his concentration on the minutiae of Congress, which made him seem unaware of events and ideas outside of Capitol Hill. Finally there were two oft-repeated Lyndon Johnson wisecracks: that Ford "had played football too long without a helmet" and "was so dumb he can't chew gum and walk at the same time."

As such things do in Washington, this perception fed on itself and became a standard component of cocktail-party banter and of conventional journalistic wisdom. It handicapped the new president when he faced a challenge from Ronald Reagan for the GOP nomination. Ford's behavior as president unfortunately reinforced the image. He often mispronounced and misused words—I once heard him praise New Englanders for their "work *ethnic.*" He was generally a dull speaker, and his occasional attempts at cleverness often backfired. Trying to promote the virtues of free enterprise, Ford declared that if the federal government ever decided to produce beer, it would probably wind up charging ten times as much as a local brewery. The *Boston Globe's* account of his remarks began: "President Ford said last night that the government he heads is so inefficient that if it entered the brewery business it could not sell beer for less than $25 a bottle."

Add to these verbal pratfalls Ford's various physical mishaps, such as tripping on the steps of Air Force One and bumping his head in the White House swimming pool. These incidents inspired derision among reporters and compelled Ford's press secretary, Ron Nessen, to remind the press corps that the president had been an all-American football player at the University of Michigan.

Fortunately for Ford, Ronald Reagan had image problems of his own. One perceived flaw was that he was a "mad bomber," along the lines of Barry Goldwater whom he had backed in 1964, ready to blast off into World War III if he ever got his finger near the nuclear trigger. The other notion was that Reagan was still basically just a movie actor who wasn't playing with a full deck when it came to the realities of how the federal government worked.

Ford's managers were shrewd enough to exploit this last notion when they saw an opportunity. A candidate who makes a mistake in an interview or some other impromptu situation can blame it on a slip of the lip. But the Reagan blunder that Ford's campaign concentrated on was imbedded in the text of a prepared speech. It was a proposal for transferring responsibility for a whole slew of federal programs—Medicaid, welfare, food stamps, and the like—to the states. The price tag was a cool $90 billion—the amount Reagan claimed the federal government would save under his plan, which he billed as "creative federalism."

The other way to look at it, of course, was that since Reagan was not talking about cutting the programs but simply shifting the burden, the $90 billion would have to come from somewhere. Where? The Ford campaign had a ready answer: "Out of the pockets of state and local taxpayers."

Having gotten wind of Reagan's speech in advance, Ford's aides prepared an ambush for the challenger. They waited for several months until early 1976, when Reagan's campaign got under way in crucial New Hampshire. Then they struck. On the day Reagan arrived in New Hampshire, Ford's campaign distributed press releases to reporters in Washington and New Hampshire charging that Reagan's plan would cost citizens of New Hampshire, one of the stingiest states in the union, tens of millions of dollars.

With the cooperation of the political press corps, that was all it took to transform Reagan's new slant on federalism into a blunder. From then on, everywhere he went in New Hampshire Reagan was badgered with questions about his $90 billion plan. By the time he had figured out some answers, the initial impetus of his candidacy had been drained.

On the face of it, the furor over Reagan's plan seemed to be just the sort of substantive debate the press was always promising to cover. In fact the debate was a mirage. Reagan's plan was far from an explicit blueprint. Rather, like McGovern's "demogrant" plan, it was little more than a notion vaguely sketched in a few lines from a speech. It was hard to assess the details one way or another in the frantic format of a campaign. But the controversy served the main purpose of Ford's managers, which was not to challenge Reagan's ideology but rather to point up his alleged unreadiness to deal with the real problems of government. It was shrewd thinking by Ford's strategists, but they would not have succeeded without the complicity of the press. In the face of the avalanche of nitpicking that buried Reagan's plan and his hopes for victory in New Hampshire, it would have required a measure of independence and fortitude on the part of journalists to point out that there was less to this furor than met the eye. But few displayed these traits, and Ford's managers made their point well enough to hurt Reagan in New Hampshire, where he lost to Ford by little more than fifteen hundred votes.

By past standards, Ford's margin should have been considered a symbolic defeat for the president, as it had been for LBJ in 1968 and Muskie in 1972. But this time, because Reagan had been ahead in the early polls, expectations ran the other way. "A win is a win is a win," the Ford people claimed. And that was the way the press wrote it. Reagan kept his candidacy alive right down to the convention, but he never regained the opportunity he had lost in New Hampshire. There he had had the chance to deliver a mortal blow to Ford's candidacy, and with the help of the press, he blew it.

After his bruising battle with Reagan, and after the Democrats nominated Carter, polls showed Ford trailing his challenger by thirty points or more. But the president still clung to hope. After studying the opinion surveys, his handlers concluded that Carter's advantage seemed to be based not on any of Ford's substantive actions as president, or Carter's pledges, but rather on contrasting impressions of the two candidates' character.

Perceptions of personality can be altered more readily than concerns about issues, Ford's planners reasoned. And they knew that in a competition based on image, a president usually enjoys an advantage simply because he is president. Accordingly, his managers decided to keep Ford close to the Oval Office and the White House Rose Garden. "He *is* the president; anyone else is a pretender," is the way Dick Cheney, then Ford's chief of staff, put it to me—a conceit that Ford's team labored hard to impress upon journalists.

As Ford's advisers realized, the media could not afford to ignore what Ford did in the White House. The best the press could do was to link the events Ford staged at 1600 Pennsylvania Avenue to the campaign by reminding the public of their political purpose. Television correspondents would sign off their coverage of a Rose Garden event by saying: ". . . with the Ford campaign in the White House." But Ford aide Michael Duval told his colleagues not to worry what the correspondents said as long as the White House was shown on the screen. "People aren't going to remember the voice-over," he contended, "they are going to remember the visual."

The Rose Garden strategy offered another benefit for Ford, beyond underlining his status as president. Just as in 1972, when Richard Nixon had stuck close to home, the political press spent more time and energy on the challenger, in this case Jimmy Carter. That was all to the liking of Ford's strategists, whose main hope for winning the election was in changing the electorate's view of Carter for the worse.

The press had good reason to give Carter the once-over more than once. Being an unknown and an outsider had been "a real plus" for Carter in the contest for the Democratic nomination, as his pollster, Patrick Caddell, acknowledged. He was the man "everyone wanted" but no one knew much about. In the general election, Caddell conceded, that became a drawback. Although voters gave Carter positive ratings in Caddell's surveys, nearly half of those interviewed could not answer most of the specific questions about his qualifications and beliefs. He was perceived as "fuzzy" on issues, and "people were uneasy with him as a person."

This was a problem Carter had difficulty solving. "Because people kept saying that no one knew who Carter was," Jody Powell observed, "there were repeated and painful attempts by us to explain who this man really was, sometimes to the point of absurdity."

Carter's clumsiest and most bizarre effort at self-definition was his notorious interview with *Playboy* magazine, in which he sought to allay apprehensions about his fundamentalist religious beliefs. To prove that he was a regular fellow, Carter volunteered the information that "I've looked on a lot of women with lust. I've committed adultery in my heart many times." And he added: "But I don't think I would ever take on the frame of mind that Nixon or Johnson did, lying, cheating, or distorting the truth." When the media swarmed all over these remarks, Carter's campaign suffered.

As the combination of Ford's Rose Garden strategy and Carter's own foolishness steadily eroded their once-overwhelming lead,

Carter and staff were near desperation. "It was like the Chinese water treatment," Hamilton Jordan, Carter's campaign manager, complained.

Searching for a remedy, Carter and his aides summoned reporters traveling on their campaign plane to an extraordinary off-the-record meeting in a motel room in San Diego. At that session Carter talked to reporters—among whom I was one—as if they were part of his campaign, not observers or adversaries, and he asked for advice on how to straighten out his candidacy. Reporters quickly told him they were not in the business of giving advice to him or any other candidate.

Much as some reporters might yearn for influence over presidential politics, most would prefer to exert that influence through the stories they write or broadcast, rather than via any words of wisdom they might offer a candidate. Journalists have surely been known to offer advice, solicited and otherwise, to politicians, but rarely in the presence of other journalists.*

Since the reporters would not help Carter, Powell had another idea. He suggested that maybe the way to get elected was to shut out the press, as Nixon had done in 1972 and in 1968. "Maybe we'll have to close the campaign," Powell said. I reminded Powell that it was Jimmy Carter's campaign, that he could run it open or closed, and that either way we would try to find a way to cover it.

The meeting demonstrated how efforts to manipulate the media can often backfire. Carter's session with the campaign press corps

---

*During my 1998 conversation with George W. Bush while he was campaigning for reelection as governor of Texas, I was unprofessional enough to suggest that he debate his Democratic opponent, who stood no realistic chance of winning. My argument was that by debating, Bush would seem generous and fair, and gain experience which might later serve him well. Bush flatly rejected the idea. Later he did debate his challenger, Garry Mauro, but only once, and only with extreme reluctance. Bush carried that same aversion to debating into the 2000 presidential campaign, with negative consequences for his candidacy.

86

accomplished nothing except to intensify the focus on Carter's problems as a candidate.

Carter would have been better off, and the press would have done a better job, if both had paid less attention to the inner workings of his campaign and more to the travails of the national economy. After a sharp recession in 1975, conditions were tending upward. But as election day neared, unemployment shot back up. And inflation remained a troublesome threat.

Carter had little to say about these real-life problems, nor for that matter did his opponent. Instead, both Carter and Ford seemed absorbed with finding ways to handle the media, and few reporters had the imagination to remind their viewers and readers of the issues the candidates were neglecting.

Carter's lead continued to dwindle—then Ford put his foot right where the chewing gum used to be. During the second of three televised debates between the two candidates, the president, trying to defend the administration's dealings with the Soviet Union, contended: "There is no Soviet domination of Eastern Europe, and there never will be under a Ford administration."

This was a preposterous statement, as Ford knew as well as anyone. The president probably meant to say he did not *want* the Soviets to dominate Eastern Europe, or that control of their satellite states would not last forever. Whatever he meant, what he said caused him no end of trouble, all the more so because it took Ford five days to admit he had misspoken, just as Carter had delayed too long in dealing with his ethnic-purity gaffe. Meanwhile Ford's blunder remained the focus of press attention and of Carter's rhetorical attacks. "It's time we had a president who understands the facts about Eastern Europe and who will speak up for freedom throughout the world," the challenger declared.

No one believed that Ford's comments on Eastern Europe accurately reflected his view of Soviet power, any more than Carter's ramblings on God and lust were thought to indicate his attitude on religion and morality. Yet the press made much of both gaffes. It was easier for reporters to write about these blunders than to point to the substantive issues that both candidates neglected. In the end, many believed, the furor over Eastern Europe fanned by the media did to Ford what the $90 billion coverage did to Reagan: it slowed his momentum and permitted Carter to capture the White House by a narrow margin.

"After the most extensive press coverage ever accorded a Presidential campaign, Americans might be expected to know more than ever about the candidates," pointed out *Newsweek* as the campaign drew to a close. "Instead," the magazine concluded, "they knew so little of significance about the candidates, they seem to have gathered only the usual abstractions." What this amounted to "is a paradoxical failure of communication. Far from being enlightened by the unprecedented volume of campaign stories—and the most widespread political polling ever undertaken by the media—the public appears, at best, to have been bemused. Record numbers of voters are professing themselves turned off, undecided or only marginally committed to either candidate."

Few people in politics or journalism disagreed with that assessment. It was much harder to find agreement on who was to blame for this failure. Many politicians were quick to fault the media. "Reporters are poisoning the political well by telling Americans no candidate takes any position except to enhance his election prospects," said Frank Mankiewicz, who had been Robert Kennedy's press secretary. "It's automatically assumed that nobody can do anything because they believe in it."

Reporters preferred to pin the apathy on the emptiness of the campaign. "Carter isn't running an issues campaign," said the *Chicago Daily News'* William Eaton as the campaign headed into its final stages. "He's running an anti-Ford campaign at the moment. So that's what's being reported. Here you've got a guy who's shouting 'brainwashed' and 'disgrace' to the nation at Ford, and then complaining that you didn't write about health care that day." And *St. Louis Post-Dispatch* veteran James Deakin agreed that neither candidate had provided any serious discussion of issues. "If it isn't there, you can't cover it," he said.

In truth the campaign furnished enough cause for blame to trouble the consciences of both politicians and journalists. Even more sobering was the prospect that the conduct of the 1976 contest held out for the future. Although the campaign was over, its distortions and confusions would set the tone for press coverage of the governance that followed.

1980: *Hostage to Crisis*

⚑ "THE DOMINANCE OF THE MEDIA over our politics has now led to the creation of a monstrosity that presents a grave danger to what is left of democracy in the United States." This was the judgment rendered by Walter Dean Burnham, then at MIT, now at the University of Texas, when the 1980 campaign was at its height—or, as he might have put it, its depths. "The functions of parties have been taken over largely by media organizations. From a democratic point of view, this leads to an irresponsible politics and a debased currency of political ideas."

This hanging verdict came not from some extremist crank but from one of our most respected political scientists. With its apocalyptic tone, the judgment was somewhat overdrawn, as Burnham later acknowledged. But it reflected the frustration that Burnham shared with a good many other Americans over the growing importance of the media in presidential politics, a feeling that the 1980 campaign would intensify.

Sharing in the frustration—increasingly so as the campaign developed—were members of the media themselves, who began to realize that the transformed political system had cast them as both victims and villains in the campaign melodrama. They had been there before. Four years earlier, at the beginning of the 1976 campaign, journalists had reflected on their coverage and vowed, as *Newsweek* noted, "This year, by God, we'll do it differently." Now, facing the start of a new campaign, they made the same promise.

Criticized in 1976 for not having noticed the significance of the Iowa caucuses where Jimmy Carter began his march to victory, journalists in January 1980 descended upon Iowa like a plague of locusts. They buttonholed every citizen in sight and dispatched camera crews into classrooms, firehouses, and church basements around the state in hopes of capturing the full flavor and meaning of this arcane method of selecting delegates to the national conventions.

Of more fundamental importance, journalistic skepticism, born of Watergate and Vietnam, had hardened, as the feeling spread among political journalists that, like Nixon before him, Jimmy Carter, with his moralistic effusions on the campaign trail, had deluded them and the voters. Indeed, on the eve of the 1980 campaign Carter seemed to have lost control. Humiliated by the Iranian hostage seizure abroad, staggered by runaway inflation at home, most Americans when they took stock of their country worried that it was in sorry shape. As for the president, many felt as one citizen I interviewed put it: "The water is six feet deep, and Carter is only five feet nine."

This attitude was reflected and reinforced by the media. From the start of the Carter presidency, journalists had emphasized the Georgian's unfamiliarity with the ways of Washington. "In his own inexperience, the President could not define a mission for his government, a purpose for the country and the means of getting there," complained Hugh Sidey in *Time*.

Carter's emphasis on nuts and bolts was thought to be misplaced. "The inheritor of a profoundly political office whose most successful occupants have all been experienced and skilled politicians, Mr. Carter seems more nearly to have an engineer's approach—concern with the details of program and policy rather than with the broad appeals and human exchanges of gaining acceptance for them," wrote *New York Times* correspondent Tom Wicker, one of the influential journalists that Hamilton Jordan had suggested Carter seek out early in his candidacy.

Carter's moralizing drew double-barreled attacks. Some journalists charged that his stress on righteousness was impractical. "Upgrading conventional political questions to the status of good and evil is an ingrained habit with Jimmy Carter," lamented columnists Rowland Evans and Robert Novak. Others accused him of hypocrisy, particularly after revelations of the financial finagling of his longtime confidant and budget director Bert Lance, which forced his resignation in Carter's first year in office. "The Lance affair has made Carter seem a bit like Elmer Gantry, not about to live by the rules he preaches," charged George Will.

But perhaps the most significant press complaint pointed to Carter's lack of a coherent system of belief, a view expressed by another *New York Times* columnist and former aide to Richard Nixon, William Safire. "Unless some philosophy is articulated that gives an Administration its character and flavor—unless the trumpet is certain—the diffusion of power loses its purpose," he wrote. "All that is left is squabbling and backbiting and end runs."

Some of this criticism was overstated, but much of it was soundly based. And many of these same points could have been made during the campaign had the press been more willing to look beyond the superficial aspects of Carter's persona and his strategy. Now the press had awakened to his flaws. But it was already too late for him, and for the country.

I learned how vaguely founded were Carter's political convictions when I interviewed him in the Oval Office for a book on his first hundred days in the presidency. When I asked him about his beliefs, he referred me to a just-published volume of his speeches. "There's an amazing consistency in my speeches, in what I emphasize as being important. I'd say basic morality is there—not that I'm better than anyone else," he quickly interjected. "It's hard for me to describe," Carter added, "because it's part of my consciousness."

Say what?

The closest Carter came to defining his beliefs during our hour-long conversation was his reference to "basic morality." For Carter, moralism served as a surrogate for a political point of view. This was a president who viewed the political struggle not as a competition between groups with varying claims on public policy but as a conflict between good and evil in which he rarely, if ever, doubted which side he was on.

But this was not a formula for strong leadership, a point which was reflected by the polls and the media. Carter had faced a drum-fire of criticism in the first two years of his presidency, even when the economy seemed to be earning passing grades. So he was already on shaky ground with the press and the public when times turned bad, as they did in the summer of 1979. With the president in Tokyo for an economic summit conference, a severe gasoline shortage in the midst of soaring inflation aggravated the public's discontent and intensified media criticism. Rushing back to Washington, Carter announced plans for an address on energy, then changed his mind in favor of a broader theme. After conferring for six days at Camp David with about a hundred prominent citizens, Carter delivered his broader message which the press soon dubbed the "malaise" speech. Americans were suffering "a crisis of confidence," Carter declared, and added: "I realize more than ever that as President I need your help." He also declared that "The gap between our citizens and our government has never been so wide." This had been a familiar theme of his campaign, but, as many in the media pointed out, after three years as president, Carter could no longer escape blame for the estrangement.

Whatever benefits Carter might have gained from this theatrical moment were wiped out just after the speech when he demanded the resignation of every high official in his administration and then fired four cabinet members for not being sufficiently loyal. Immediately a chorus of disapproval rose from the press, with the media charging that instead of using the opportunity of the energy crisis to focus attention on the nation's problems, Carter had called attention to his own difficulties and his own weaknesses.

"Carter's manifest intent was to show that, after two and a half years, he has at last taken charge of his unruly and faltering government," *Newsweek* observed. "But his housecleaning instead gutted his domestic policy team of some of its strongest players, signaled survivors that political loyalty has priority over professional competence and sent a seism of anxiety around the world about the stability of his reign."

Carter's behavior made clear that his management techniques had failed, that his much-vaunted personal bond with the voters had withered, and that he was vulnerable to a challenge for the office he held. Just as clear was where the challenge would come from—Edward Moore Kennedy, senior senator from Massachusetts and the heir to his brother's political dynasty. Months before Carter's malaise crisis I had flown to West Virginia with Kennedy to watch him campaign for Democrat Jennings Randolph, the veteran lawmaker who was seeking reelection. Kennedy was running well ahead of Carter in the polls then, and though he insisted he had no plans to seek the presidency in 1980, he acted and sounded very much like a potential candidate. After he finished a rousing speech to several thousand people at an outdoor rally, many in the audience surged around the platform to greet the senator. Kennedy worked the crowd for a while and then turned to me with a grin. "Help me out," he urged. "It's easy. All you have to do is shake their hands and wave at them and they elect you president."

But as Kennedy would learn a year later, when he did decide to run against Carter for the Democratic nomination, the road to the White House was by no means that easy. His challenge to Carter was demolished by a combination of circumstances in which the media played a large part. Mostly, though, Kennedy was the architect of his own demise. Until it was too late, he failed to offer the Democratic electorate a clear set of alternatives to Carter's policies, choosing instead to rely on his personal strengths as a leader. As it turned out, Kennedy had serious liabilities in a contest of personalities. Recollections of the ten-year-old tragedy at Chappaquiddick led to questions from the media which he could not put to rest.

What made all this especially devastating was that he was not prepared for it. Ted Kennedy was accustomed to the kind of press treatment his brothers had received—not quite reverential but certainly respectful. But the mostly youthful reporters assigned to cover his campaign cared nothing for his inheritance and remembered little of his brothers—including the fact that their campaigns had been as chaotic and disorganized as his. "The people who chewed him up," said political columnist Richard Reeves, "were kids in grammar school when John Kennedy ran."

The tip-off on what was to come was Kennedy's interview with Roger Mudd, then a CBS correspondent, which was televised shortly before Kennedy announced his candidacy in November 1979. Ironically, Carter and his staff were filled with apprehension about the interview. They knew that Mudd, a CBS star, was a longtime friend of the Kennedy family who they were convinced would give the senator soft-soap treatment resulting in a boost for Kennedy's candidacy. They soon found out how wrong they were.

Whether it was a sense of professional responsibility or sheer ambition that drove him to it, Mudd showed Kennedy no mercy. "What's the present state of your marriage?" Mudd demanded of the senator, who for some time had been estranged from his wife, Joan. Shaken and stunned, Kennedy stammered out something to the effect that he and Joan had been having "some difficult times" but were making "some very good progress." Then, pressing on in a way that, as one analyst later wrote, destroyed "the myth of Kennedy invincibility," Mudd relentlessly probed Kennedy's personal life, the tragedy at Chappaquiddick, and his political ambitions, raising questions which at times rendered Kennedy almost incoherent. Asked why he might run for president, the best Kennedy could do was to say: "The reasons I would run is because I have a great belief in this country, that it is, has, more natural resources than any country in the world, the greatest technology of any country in the world, the greatest capacity for innovation in the world, and the greatest political system in the world." As Mudd said later, "It was like I want to be president because the sea is so deep and the sky is so blue." In short, Kennedy was about as tongue-tied talking to Roger Mudd as Jimmy Carter had been talking to me. The difference was that the conversation with Mudd took place on network television in prime time.

One single interview, no matter how poorly Kennedy performed, could not change the image he had forged over two decades. But in the long run Kennedy's performance was damaging because of the impression it created among other members of the media. Made aware of Kennedy's vulnerability, they were determined to search for other signs of weakness. That attitude was reflected in the coverage of Kennedy's campaign when it finally got under way in Iowa in 1979, as reporters seized upon his propensity to mangle his stump speeches. Among other bloopers, the scion of the Kennedy family dynasty railed against "the rising price of inflation," vowed to dramatize his differences with President Carter on "the issue of the substance," and introduced the president of Fisk University, whose name was Walter Leonard, as Leonard Fisk. For some reason Kennedy had trouble getting his tongue around the phrase "farm families," a staple for his Iowa stump speech. Instead the words sometimes came out as "fam farmilies." The press leaped upon these fluffs and made much of them, contrasting Kennedy's awkwardness on the stump with the image of his family, built upon the legendary speechmaking exploits of his brothers.

In a way this was unfair and misleading, since some of the reporters making the comparison had never seen either of the elder Kennedy brothers campaign. But the truth was that Ted Kennedy had tapped into their reputations and exploited the Kennedy family legacy to enhance his own political image. When I traveled with him in West Virginia, I heard him recall his brother John's momentous victory there in the 1960 primary, which paved his road to the presidency. "No member of my family has ever felt a stranger in the hills and the hollows, the mines and the cities of West Virginia," Kennedy declared. "My brothers came here, so did my sisters and my mother. It's good to be home again."

Did Kennedy's verbal goofs matter that much? Probably not. But the media's reporting of them would not have mattered much either if Kennedy had had anything of significance to say. Most of the time he did not.

Attempting to distinguish himself from the president he was challenging, Kennedy relied not on differences in specific ends or means but rather on a contrast in "leadership." "He believes in this system and he thinks he can make it work better than President Carter," Stephen Smith, Kennedy's campaign manager and brother-in-law, told me in outlining the premise for Kennedy's candidacy.

Trying to build a candidacy around subjective judgments and hazy perceptions was a perilous course for Kennedy. In effect he was calling on voters to examine and compare his personal traits with Jimmy Carter's, a test for which he was unprepared. Asked about Chappaquiddick, after he had had ten years to reflect on the drowning of Mary Jo Kopechne and his own delay in reporting the accident, the gist of his answers was that he had nothing more to say.

Without mentioning Kennedy's name, Carter's television ads aimed to underline popular misgivings about his challenger. One Carter commercial boasted: "Husband, Father, President—he's doing all three with distinction." Another commercial pointedly asserted: "A man brings two things to a presidential ballot. He brings his record and he brings himself. Who he is is frequently more important than what he's done."

To this point in the 1980 campaign, the media had by and large performed respectably if somewhat negatively. Reporters had pointed to Carter's shortcomings in the course of explaining the disappointments of his presidency, though some of these were weaknesses they had overlooked during his 1976 campaign. And they had been at least as critical in their coverage of the early days of Kennedy's campaign.

But then, as often happens in political journalism, events took over—in this case the seizure of the American embassy in Teheran, Iran, with sixty American hostages. The media, trying to exploit the public's interest in this bizarre episode, and heavily influenced by Carter's response, lost perspective and did the electorate a disservice. The hostage crisis, as it came to be called, provided a dramatic example of the power of a president to shape perceptions and of media susceptibility to that power.

Muslim extremists had stormed the embassy on November 4, 1979, three days before Kennedy was officially to announce his candidacy. At first the incident seemed likely to be another blow to Carter's prestige. After all, it was Carter, yielding to pressure from influential friends of the shah of Iran, who had made the controversial decision to allow Iran's deposed ruler to come to the United States for medical treatment. This stirred the fury of the revolutionary forces in his country and gave anti-American Iranians—of whom there was no scarcity—a motive and a pretext for taking over the embassy. The American compound in Teheran had been captured briefly a few months earlier, but the State Department had failed to enhance security precautions or evacuate embassy employees.

The media, however, generally overlooked these facts, and as the days went by with the hostages still in captivity, the crisis gradually turned into a boon for Carter and a burden for Kennedy, in the midst of his struggles to gain a footing on the campaign trail. Out of concern for the hostages and indignation against their captors—both feelings that were vigorously stimulated by the press and the president—Americans rallied behind their beleaguered commander-in-chief. It was a role that Carter, displaying previously unrevealed theatrical skill, played to the hilt.

Although his range of actions was limited, Carter now dedicated his presidency to dealing with the hostage crisis. The president pulled out of a scheduled debate with Kennedy in Iowa and canceled his other campaign appearances, contending that he could not spare the time for such partisan activity while hapless Americans in the Teheran embassy were captive. That left Kennedy out on the campaign trail alone, cast as an ambitious politician while the incumbent unselfishly attended to duty in the White House.

In creating this perception so beneficial to his candidacy, Carter was aided immeasurably by the coverage of the hostage story by all elements of the press but particularly by television, which made it the most intensely covered news event in years. As the *Washington Post*'s Haynes Johnson wrote: "Americans awoke in the morning to see the menacing figure of the Ayatollah breathing hatred and preaching holy war. They went to bed at night after seeing mobs of Iranian demonstrators marching before the occupied Embassy, waving their fists. News telecasts ended with photos of the American flag and the tolling of the Liberty Bell. The patriotic fervor transcended anything experienced during the Korean or Vietnam wars, approaching the militant levels of World War II."

Competing with one another for maximum coverage of a story that was pulling in huge audiences, the networks abandoned nearly all restraint. Every night ABC news ran an hour long special called "Americans Held Hostage," and in keeping with the media and the Carter-induced mood, church bells were tolled to help remind Americans of the hostages' predicament. "Are they ever going to stop ringing those damn bells?" Kennedy's press secretary, Richard Drayne, asked me. Drayne knew for whom those bells tolled—together with the other hubbub over the hostages, they were drowning out Kennedy's campaign.

Attacks on Carter by the Iranian extremists, prominently reported by the press, inspired the kind of support for the beleaguered president that he had never achieved by himself. And they hamstrung Kennedy's candidacy. The senator was obliged to walk a narrow line, striving to avoid discussing the impasse in Iran on which the nation's attention was centered. As the crisis dragged on, Kennedy's frustration increased. Finally, during a television interview in December, he denounced the shah for having run "one of the most violent regimes in the history of mankind." And he rejected the suggestion, made by Ronald Reagan, then the front-runner for the Republican presidential nomination, that the shah should be allowed to stay in the United States permanently.

Although Kennedy had not criticized the president or his handling of the hostage situation, Carter's allies now assaulted the senator ferociously, and the media gave banner treatment to their attacks. The State Department said Kennedy's comments would make "delicate negotiations more difficult." Robert Strauss, the president's campaign chairman, charged: "It is an error to inject anything in the campaign that could in any way endanger the lives of the people over there." And the media generally parroted the administration line.

Kennedy was badly hurt. As he campaigned in Iowa for support in the January precinct caucuses, a hail of questions from reporters thrust him on the defensive, forcing him continually to reiterate his concern for the hostages and his support for Carter.

Through it all he nevertheless maintained his poise and his sense of humor. When a new poll showed that Kennedy had dropped about twenty points in his race against Carter in Iowa, I nagged his aides into holding a press conference so that he could be forced to account for himself. But the first question at the press conference came from a reporter who wanted to know what Kennedy thought should be done about a new threat facing the United States in the Mediterranean.

"Reinforce the Fifth Fleet," Kennedy said.

"Just what units would you send in?" he was asked.

Kennedy said he would have to think it over.

At last it was my turn. "Senator, the polls show you steadily losing ground to President Carter. At this rate, how long can you afford to keep campaigning?"

Kennedy looked at me and decided to answer the question about the Fifth Fleet.

"Two aircraft carriers, three heavy cruisers, and five destroyers," he said.

This was good for a laugh, but it could not alter the depressing truth about Kennedy's campaign. While his candidacy faded, Carter made headway. Even though he had confined himself to the White House, he managed to make good use of the prestige and power of his incumbency. He spent hours on the phone calling hundreds of influential Democrats in Iowa and other battleground states asking for their support. Some were invited to Washington for "consultations" on inflation and other policy questions. And the president and his cabinet secretaries tried to arrange the award of federal grants when and where they would do Carter's candidacy the most good. But very little of Carter's low-key politicking showed up on the evening TV news shows or in print. Instead the country saw the president as an embattled commander-in-chief fighting for the national interest.

As weeks turned into months, the White House press corps remained immobilized. For each primary contest Carter's aides spun out the same analysis and offered it to the press: the president should not be expected to do well because he had not campaigned. But of course the hostage crisis was the best campaign he could devise. When primaries brought news of Carter's success, as most of them did, the president was made to look that much better because of carefully lowered expectations.

Carter could be seen only in scrupulously controlled situations, usually in the White House for official announcements. When it served his purpose to make news, he did so. On the morning of the Wisconsin primary, the White House released news of a supposedly favorable development in the hostage crisis. The hopes thus raised were soon dashed, but not until after Carter had scored another primary victory in Wisconsin.

In dealing with the press during the early months of the hostage affair, Carter had important advantages—the prestige of his office and a dramatic story to tell. The media certainly could not have disregarded Carter's role as president nor the significance of the story. But reporters should have been far more imaginative and aggressive in their coverage. First, the story should have been put in context by pointing out that the seizure of the embassy in Teheran resulted in large measure from the pro-shah policies pursued by Carter and his immediate predecessors. Then the media should have raised questions about the future direction of U.S. policy in Iran and the Middle East. Beyond gaining the release of the hostages, what did the United States wish to accomplish? Better reporting would have provided Americans a clearer understanding of the problems facing U.S. policymakers in that region as their government followed a path that led from the frustration of the hostage seizure to the embarrassment of the Iran-*contra* scandal to the "triumph without victory" of the Persian Gulf War.

On the domestic side, instead of merely harping on Kennedy's flaws as a campaigner, the media should have put more emphasis on the advantages that Carter gained from the hostage crisis. Reporters should also have provided more coverage of Carter's behind-the-scenes campaigning from the Oval Office. And they should have paid more attention to the troubled economy, which was even then stumbling into the inflationary abyss that would ultimately destroy Carter's presidency.

The media's flawed response to the challenge of covering an incumbent president in a time of international crisis helped Carter to defeat Kennedy and gain the Democratic nomination. But, as Carter soon discovered, running against Ronald Reagan was a different story. As the hostage crisis dragged on and Americans grew more and more resentful of Carter for not doing anything about it, it began to hurt the president, not help him. An abortive helicopter rescue effort sent his political fortunes into a steep decline, hastened by the condition of the economy. Under Carter, Americans were enduring the worst of both possible economic worlds—a recession and inflation.

Ronald Reagan was in many ways ideally suited to exploit this situation. His years in Hollywood had helped make him a master of television—the key to the hearts and minds of voters. "Ronald Reagan was the best electronic media candidate in American history," claimed Richard Wirthlin, his campaign pollster and chief strategist.

More than this, though, Reagan held strong beliefs which he was not ashamed to express. On a February afternoon in 1980, campaigning in the Massachusetts primary, Reagan halted his motorcade to inspect Plymouth Rock, a traditional photo opportunity for any candidate. After this ritual was duly recorded for television, Reagan returned to the campaign bus—which at the moment contained only a handful of reporters, myself included—faced his fellow passengers, and offered a brief epiphany about the Pilgrim Fathers' voyage more than three centuries ago. "If they could come all that way in that little boat," Reagan demanded, "how dare we be afraid of anything?"

The logic of that proposition does not stand close scrutiny, but Reagan's words had a nice ring to them, and he rendered them with fervor. Although the setting was unusual and the audience sparse, it was a typical Reagan performance. His ability to express his reverence for such icons as the Pilgrims, the flag, free enterprise, and church and family, in catchy phrases and with unquestionable conviction, had over the years inspired the admiration and allegiance of legions of conservative Republicans. This same trait also made him an attractive media candidate even when members of the media thought he was offering little more than humbug.

Reagan's ingratiating personality greatly helped to make him the "Great Communicator." His easygoing manner was the spoonful of sugar that helped his polarizing ideological medicine go down. Reagan's mellow demeanor reflected his inherent optimism and self-confidence. One of his favorite stories was of the little boy who, on waking up Christmas morning and discovering a pile of manure under the tree, declared, "There must be a pony here somewhere."

This natural pleasantness helped to frustrate the Carter campaign's efforts to cast Reagan as a dangerous villain. As the Carter team turned desperate, their opinion surveys showed that, as Pat Caddell, Carter's own pollster, later recalled, "The American people simply did not want Jimmy Carter to be their president if they could possibly avoid it. And so we had to find them a reason why they would be forced to keep him."

The best argument they could devise amounted to saying that as bad as Carter might seem, Ronald Reagan in the White House would be horrendous. In effect, Carter's old campaign slogan of "Why not the best?" was transformed into "At least not the worst." The president's advisers resolved, as Jack Nelson reported in the *Los Angeles Times*, to make Ronald Reagan the issue of the campaign and to depict him as "a saber rattling, inexperienced ideologue who lacks the judgment and compassion needed to be President."

Largely because of this negative strategy, the campaign came to be dominated by low blows, cheap shots, and false alarms, leading Professor Burnham and others to denounce the media for having "debased" political debate. But in reality the media served chiefly as a conduit for the charges and countercharges hurled between the two camps. Where journalism failed was in not providing a background for the attack rhetoric so that voters could better understand what the candidates were up to.

Reagan was certainly not without blame for the mindlessness of the 1980 campaign. Striving to deflect charges that he lacked concern for the environment, he remarked that trees themselves contributed to air pollution. This was too much to take even for his press secretary, Jim Brady, who was moved to look down on the redwood forests of California from Reagan's campaign jet and cry out, "Killer trees! Killer trees!"

But Reagan's lapses were muffled by the vehemence of Carter's demagoguery. With minimal justification he accused Reagan of reviving "the stirrings of hate" between the races and claimed that a Reagan victory would divide the nation "black from white, Jew from Christian, North from South." Trying to exploit Reagan's tough talk about nuclear arms negotiations with the Soviets, Carter asserted that the outcome of the election would decide nothing less than "whether we have war or peace"—making clear that he himself favored peace. The reaction to this calumny was so damaging to Carter that he felt obliged to offer an apology of sorts in an interview with TV's Barbara Walters.

Nevertheless Carter's campaign maintained its essentially negative approach, which also shaped the president's strategy toward his other challenger, the independent candidate John Anderson, Republican congressman from Illinois. Anderson's candidacy was to a large degree a consequence of media influence. He had started out as a candidate for the GOP presidential nomination. A vigorous advocate of civil rights and gun control, his distinctive views and his eloquence on the stump gained him respectable support among moderate voters in New England and a disproportionate measure of national attention from the media.

In the spring, *Newsweek* concluded that "Anderson might be out of the race by now if his threadbare campaign hadn't caught journalists' eyes." It was Anderson's contrariness that appealed to reporters weary of politicians mouthing the same platitudes they did not themselves believe. "The worst thing in the past," said Lou Cannon of the *Washington Post*, "was that we didn't give somebody attention who deserved it. Anderson is the classic refutation of that—we've had a role in creating his candidacy. We like odd men out and windmill tilters."

But in their admiration for Anderson's candor and differentness, the media failed to reckon with political and personal realities. The reason Anderson's views seemed novel and fresh for a Republican was that most voters in his party had rejected such ideas. Beyond that, press attention served to encourage Anderson's latent messianic tendencies, a trait that limited his attractiveness, even to independent voters who supported his policies and admired his gumption.

Anderson's beliefs doomed his chances among Republicans but encouraged his backers to take advantage of the prestige he had built in the media to run as a third-party candidate. Appealing to generalized discontent with the nominees of the two major parties, Anderson drew the support of 25 percent of the nation's voters in early polls. His backing was coming from both parties. But Carter strategists concluded that his ever so slightly left-of-center appeal was a greater threat to the Democratic president than to Republican Reagan, and set out to wreck his campaign. In a number of states Democrats made it their business to obstruct Anderson's efforts to get on the ballot. More important was Carter's refusal to take part in a presidential debate if Anderson were included, on the grounds that it would be unfair for him to have to confront two Republicans.

The press reported these tactics by Carter but only in passing. They deserved greater attention because they spoke volumes about the desperation of Carter's candidacy and the failures of his presidency.

Reagan did not escape unscathed by the media, which focused on his shifts away from a hard-line conservative position. As the campaign entered its closing weeks, Reagan's hawkish promises to forge a mighty war machine were scaled down to passing mentions of his pride in the armed forces. Instead of vowing to slash social programs to the bone, he spoke only of pruning waste and fraud. Time and again he pledged allegiance to the Social Security system, which, as the Democrats liked to point out, he once suggested might be made voluntary. And his minions distributed among union workers a revisionist leaflet rejecting the notion that Reagan had once considered subjecting unions to anti-trust laws.

The media's chronicling of this waffling, in print and on television, was one of the brighter spots in an otherwise dark chapter for American politics and journalism. The coverage bumped Carter's troubles briefly off page one and succeeded where the president had failed in forcing Reagan to defend himself. "How could I change my positions?" Reagan asked his media inquisitors, reddening slightly under their constant nagging. "I'm still where I was over these last twenty years."

But the more realistic and significant question, which the media's coverage suggested but failed to emphasize, was how Reagan could have failed to change his positions, given the need to broaden his appeal from the Republican right to a national majority? Instead of merely playing "gotcha" with Reagan's deviations from the conservative rhetoric of his past, the press should have pointed out that the argument between the new Reagan and the old foreshadowed contradictions between ideology and governance. These conflicts could plague his administration and contribute to the towering federal budget deficits that all but crippled Washington's ability to deal with the nation's problems.

Apart from whatever doubts Reagan's revisionism raised about his own fitness for the presidency, his backing and filling reinforced public misgivings about both candidates. The polls showed the low esteem in which the president and his challenger were held by the public, and was reflected in scathing commentary from the press. "There is no way, given the nature of the two prime contenders for the office, that the country is going to elect a President in November who is especially gifted in or suited to the conduct of the office," the *Washington Post* declared. The *New York Times* was even more acerbic: "Someone chases a voter down an alley, points a gun to his head and demands an answer: 'Carter or Reagan?' After thinking for a moment the voter replies, 'Shoot.'" That, the *Times* editorialized, "turns out to be not merely a joke, but the story of the 1980 campaign."

Reagan assured his election in the televised debate with Carter in the closing days of the campaign. Responding to one of Carter's numerous attacks on his record, the challenger remarked, "There you go again," with a shrug and a good-natured smile that devastated Carter's efforts to depict him as some sort of ogre. Then, in his summation, Reagan emphasized the economic debacle that had overtaken Americans by suggesting they look back four years and ask themselves whether they were better off as a result of Carter's presidency. The thundering negative response could be measured from the vote returns that gave Reagan his landslide triumph.

Even though circumstances—the troubled economy at home and the hostage humiliation abroad—were the decisive factors in the campaign, the efforts of the media were evident in the political process. "The media performed an incredible task in exposing the public to everything they could lay their hands on about the campaign and generated torrents of information for the use of the electorate," contended Jonathan Moore, director of Harvard's Kennedy Institute of Politics and editor of an extensive postmortem on the campaign. "Ultimately the voters must be capable of intelligent discrimination and willing to sort their way carefully through a lot of diverse material in making their decision," Moore conceded, "but the information is available."

More than make information "available," the media must at least try to organize the flood of events, place them in perspective, and help in the decision-making. In 1980 this effort, to the extent that it was even attempted, fell woefully short.

Afterward, politicians and journalists once again argued about who was mostly to blame for the sorry level of the campaign. Democrats complained bitterly that the press had given substance short shrift. Even victorious Republicans were dissatisfied. Lyn Nofziger, press secretary to president-elect Ronald Reagan, told a convention of newspaper editors that reporters covering the presidential campaign had failed the public by "looking for what is sensational instead of what is important."

"Utter malarkey," was the response of veteran journalists and campaign chroniclers Jack Germond and Jules Witcover. "If what the candidate says about 'substance' is covered too little, and the tone of his campaign or his personal foibles is covered too much, it's because what he says isn't newsworthy, and what he is doing really is trying to tell the voters more about himself, or often the flaws of his opponents."

The only safe conclusion to be reached about this argument was that it would extend into the next campaign, when the press would have to deal with different circumstances. In 1980 the press could blame some of its failures on hard times and the sour national mood. In 1984, though times improved and the mood brightened, political journalists faced a challenge at least as formidable as any in the past.

S I X

1984: *"You Cover the News, We'll Stage It"*

■ MOST PRESIDENTIAL CAMPAIGNS begin gradually as candidates go through the slow process of canvassing supporters and making up their minds whether to run while the media watches from a distance. But the 1984 contest for the White House started abruptly, one day in December 1982 just before Christmas, nearly two full years before the election. I remember the moment vividly because I was at home, getting ready to take my wife to a holiday party, when I got a phone call from my office.

"Forget the party and get your butt down here," John Brownell the assignment editor for the *Los Angeles Times* Washington bureau, told me. "Ted Kennedy has decided not to run."

Largely because of the media's fixation with the Kennedy mystique, Democratic presidential politics had for a long time revolved around Ted Kennedy as the heir to the family's legacy. Not until he made his decision not to run in 1972 and 1976 did the party's order of battle in those years begin to take shape and the political press begin to pay serious attention to other candidates. In 1980 Kennedy's challenge to Jimmy Carter split the party and distracted the media, which contributed to his undoing. But after Carter's defeat in 1980 and Reagan's rocky start in the White House, Kennedy's steadfastness in his liberal convictions helped him regain some of his past luster, at least in the eyes of political journalists. By December 1982 his decision not to run, which he claimed was made out of respect for the wishes of his children, changed the Democratic political landscape.*

As the story I wrote that December evening pointed out, Kennedy's departure opened the way for Walter F. Mondale, who as Jimmy Carter's former vice president was far better known than any other Democrat and had a stronger claim to support from what was still the party's dominant liberal wing. Mondale moved swiftly to take advantage of Kennedy's departure. Proclaiming himself the front-runner, he easily set the pace in 1983 in collecting money and securing endorsements, notably from the AFL-CIO. He moved so far in front so fast that his nomination was taken for granted by nearly everyone in politics and in the media, ushering in what became the year of inevitability in presidential politics.

The coverage of the 1984 campaign was dominated by the conviction that the outcomes of the only two contested races—one for the Democratic nomination, the other for the White House itself—were inevitable. Walter Mondale would be the Democratic nominee, and later, Ronald Reagan's victory over Mondale would be almost certain. These beliefs were widely held by reporters and by members of the political community. And they turned out to be right.

Nevertheless the 1984 election provided a disturbing lesson for journalists. The contest for the Democratic nomination, which dominated the early months of the year since there was no competition on the GOP side, demonstrated the shortcomings of the media. The struggle between Mondale and Reagan for the White House illustrated the limitations of media influence.

Make no mistake: the forecasts that Mondale and then Reagan would win were based on empirical evidence which turned out to be

*Kennedy never did offer a convincing reason for not running. He did not explain why his children were more opposed to his candidacy in 1984 than they had been in 1980 when they actively supported him. Many politicians and reporters believed his real reason for not running had more to do with his unwillingness to undergo further grilling from the media about Chappaquiddick.

well founded. In Mondale's case, he had almost universal support from party leaders and activists. While these folks no longer wielded the almost absolute power they had exercised before 1968, they had learned from the past few campaigns. In 1988 they were still a force to be reckoned with in the nominating process.

Although the idea of invincibility that surrounded Mondale was shattered early in the campaign by Gary Hart's surprisingly strong showing, Mondale won anyway, thanks to the advantages that had made him seem inevitable in the first place. But once again the media made the mistake of taking something for granted, in this case Mondale's nomination. As a result they helped make the early forecasts of Mondale's nomination a self-fulfilling prophecy. Reporters attempted to recover perspective once Gary Hart burst upon the scene. But if political journalists had been more alert to Hart's potential strength and more sensitive to Mondale's weakness, the nominating contest might have ended differently.

As for Reagan, the main reason for the confidence in his success was simply the state of the economy. Polls indicating that the president personally was held in high esteem were largely a function of the economy. In 1982, when the country was hit by a short but severe recession that drove unemployment to the highest levels since the Great Depression, Reagan's own poll ratings went south with the economy. His party lost twenty-six seats in the off-year election. Even as late as mid-1983 the president trailed Mondale in the polls. But when the economy began to turn around and unemployment dropped, Reagan reaped the political credit.

None of this was clear to the media or anyone else in 1983 when Mondale launched his drive for the Democratic nomination. Mondale's plans reflected his personality and style—they were solidly conceived and executed, but they lacked zeal and imagination. Although his voting record in the Senate stamped him as a full-blooded liberal, Mondale was no firebrand. Moderate in taste, restrained in manner, his climb up the political ladder had been expedited by circumstances. He made it to the U.S. Senate by appointment, to fill the vacancy created by Hubert Humphrey's resignation in 1964. It took his selection as Jimmy Carter's running mate in 1976, after he had given up on a presidential run of his own, to elevate him to the national political stage. As vice president, Mondale was first touted as a champion of progressive causes but turned out to be a disappointment. "Mondale has never been a fighter and never won anything by fighting for it," Leon Shull, who ran Americans for Democratic Action in the capital, told me. "He is by nature a very cautious guy."

Mondale's timorousness smothered his campaign. Signs of weaknesses appeared in 1983 when he lost a straw poll in Wisconsin to California senator Alan Cranston, who mustered supporters of the nuclear freeze proposal—then arousing great enthusiasm on the left—to upset Mondale. Cranston's victory meant little except to demonstrate that even this most unlikely prospect for the White House, whom Howell Raines of the New York Times once likened to a heron, could generate enthusiasm that Mondale could not.

To understand the media's response to the Mondale campaign, it helps to appreciate the environment in which reporters operated. During the long early months of the campaign, political journalists had been so exposed to physical exhaustion or boredom that many had neared the point of numbness. Often starting at dawn, they would spend the day scrambling in and out of buses, school gyms, and union halls in three or four states before hitting the next hotel bed at midnight. Dreary food and dirty laundry were their constant companions. They had to deal with indifferent editors and the constant repetition of the candidate's stump speech.

A typically vapid moment from the campaign trail in early 1984 finds a clutch of reporters killing time in the lobby of the Ramada Inn in Keene, New Hampshire. The campaign has been under way unofficially for nearly a year—though not a single vote has yet been cast—and to the reporters it seems they have been in this lobby all that time. Actually they have been waiting only about three hours while Walter Mondale hobnobs in private with local Democratic chieftains.

Suddenly there is an announcement—the press bus is ready for boarding. The reporters gather their notebooks, tape recorders, portable typewriters (the laptop computer is yet to be invented) and slog through the ankle-deep New England slush to their four-wheeled mother ship.

But wait! No sooner are they on board then the candidate's staff issues an electrifying announcement. Mondale is "going to answer something." No one knows what question Mondale will be asked, or by whom. But on such a barren day no one can afford to pass up any morsel of information. These correspondents, members of an elite corps whose professional status is the object of envy by college journalism students the country over, pick up their belongings and rush back to the cursed lobby.

Mondale leaves the meeting. The great moment looms. But most members of the traveling press can hear neither the question, from a local reporter, or Mondale's answer. Judging from the expressions of those within earshot, however, this exchange will not alter history. Back to the bus and on to the next stop. Then the press can call their editors around the country and report they are on the job, covering the making of the president.

In this campaign wasteland, journalists were susceptible to any event or circumstance that might hold a smidgen of significance or drama. Or, as ABC correspondent Brit Hume gibed at Mondale's press secretary Maxine Isaacs after a blur of indistinguishable events, "We regulars have had our excitement threshold lowered."

As in previous campaigns, the press again tried to correct its past mistakes. To get away from pack journalism, the *Washington Post* switched from "man-to-man" to "zone" coverage. Instead of trailing a particular candidate, reporters were assigned to regions of the country where they covered the different contenders as they traveled through the area. The *Los Angeles Times* had twelve campaign reporters; only two of them traveled full time with individual candidates, and those two often swapped assignments. My boss, national editor Mike Miller, pointed out that reporters who remained in the cocoon of the campaign plane not only ran the risk of going stale but were apt to lose perspective; they could become focused on what he called the "inside baseball" of strategy. Miller used to say, "It does not help a person make a choice of whom to vote for if we go on about how good an organization someone has in Iowa."

Still, reporters heard much the same criticism as in the past. The candidates and their staffs accused the media of neglecting the candidates' positions on the issues, though the truth was that the candidates repeated the same speech many times, usually offering little in the way of specifics. The lesser-known candidates complained that the press concentrated on the rivalry between Walter Mondale and space hero John Glenn, considered to be Mondale's most serious rival, to the detriment of everyone else.

Glenn was my own private choice. I thought the echoes of the accolades he had won as an astronaut would reverberate on the campaign trail, particularly because the movie *The Right Stuff*, dramatizing his role in the race to the moon, was scheduled to premiere just as the campaign was getting under way. It was a bad guess. The movie was a dud, and rather than helping him, Glenn's background seemed to hurt him with voters who considered him to be a space jock, trying to ride his fame into presidential orbit. Glenn is a fine fellow, as I learned, but as a candidate he turned out to be wooden and vague. The ultimate fizzle of his candidacy demonstrated the vagaries of media celebrity. Certainly Glenn got plenty of attention based simply on his renown, but it did him little good.

As Thomas Griffith pointed out in *Time*, "to some extent, newspapers, magazines and television are gatekeepers for those who would be well known, at first to be courted, perhaps later to be disdained." But the role of the media in making or breaking celebrities is easily exaggerated. Journalism can offer an introduction, but whether someone catches on or not is up to the public. The process of celebrity-making may be mysterious but is also measurable, by such devices as network ratings, best-seller lists, record charts, and, in the case of a presidential campaign, opinion polls.

Circumstances can create new political celebrities overnight whom the media are suddenly *forced* to acknowledge, as was the case with Jesse Jackson, one of Mondale's rivals for the Democratic nomination. Early in 1983 Jackson flew to Damascus to help gain the release of navy flier Robert Goodman, who had been shot down over Syria while flying a support mission for U.S. Marines in Lebanon. Before anyone quite knew what had happened, Jackson had established himself as a successful negotiator in international affairs, had been invited to the Rose Garden by President Reagan, and had become a bona fide celebrity. When Jackson appeared at the White House on live TV with Lieutenant Goodman, Reagan eyed him with the wary professional respect an adult actor shows around a precocious child who might steal the scene.

Jackson certainly stole the scene from Mondale. The day Jackson returned from Damascus, the CBS Evening News showed Mondale proclaiming: "Today I begin my 1984 campaign . . ." CBS correspondent Susan Spencer then broke in: "Not so fast! Mondale had to precede his long-scheduled speech," she noted, by first congratulating Jackson. As Mondale was shown doing just that, Spencer added that the former vice president had repeated "his call for withdrawal of the Marines from Lebanon." That was about all CBS felt obliged to tell its audience about what Mondale had intended to be a milestone in his candidacy.

Jackson's dramatic emergence as a hero figure, and the coverage he attracted, probably robbed Mondale of some of the attention he expected at the launching of his campaign. But as is generally the case with front-runners, Mondale's main problem was not how the media treated Jesse Jackson or any other candidate, but how the media covered him. The press rap against Mondale was that he was not exciting. At the end of the year, columnist David Broder of the *Washington Post*, reviewing some of his own errors and misjudgments, concluded, "But no one, I hope, will deny me my one moment of brilliance." As long ago as January 1983, "I wrote, 'Mondale has the capacity to make the Democratic marathon dull.' Boy, did he ever!"

Is it fair that one man in a field of eight should bear the blame if a marathon is dull? Maybe not. But as the front-runner, Mondale set the tone and the pace. The point of the dullness issue was not that

Mondale was not much fun to be around. The real criticism was that his dullness reflected a lack of imagination, a rather useful quality for an occupant of the Oval Office.

In one of the most damning defenses ever uttered, Mondale's own media director, Roy Spence, responding to complaints about his boss's sluggishness, announced that Mondale was a candidate who "dares to be cautious." That trait, Spence told Bernard Weinraub of the *New York Times,* was "a strength" that Americans would learn to value. "I don't think the American people want a quick fix, quick action, without a great deal of thought," he explained.

Another media criticism of Mondale attacked the foundation of his candidacy. In the preceding year he had impressively reconstructed the old Democratic coalition of interests—organized labor, blacks, feminists, and other special-interest groups. This accomplishment gained him prominence and support, but it also made him a target for charges from his rivals and from the press that he was the captive of the groups that had endorsed him. Mondale had a hard time responding to this argument. He felt that to deny the charges of being a toady for the interest groups that had backed him would make it seem as if he were rejecting their needs and concerns.

Mondale's problems, and Gary Hart's potential, became more apparent early in 1984 when a series of nationally televised debates attracted attention to the campaign. At the first such confrontation, on the Dartmouth College campus in New Hampshire, a shouting match between Mondale and Glenn captured most of the headlines. But Gary Hart, who styled himself as the candidate of new ideas, attracted attention with a telling remark aimed at both Mondale and Glenn after one of their spats. "Fritz, John, there you go again," Hart remarked, mimicking Reagan's famous quip in his 1980 debate with Carter. "This party will not regain leadership as long as leaders of the past debate ideas of the past." Hart claimed to offer new leadership and new ideas.

Immediately after the debate, recalled Mark Hogan, a Hart adviser, "It was like a group of media people got together and said, Why not start listening to Gary Hart and writing about his campaign? It was almost as if the curtain lifted on his campaign."

The circumstances were right for Hart. The media were bored and weary of Mondale's inevitability, a myth they themselves had created, and tired of the stale debate between Mondale and Glenn that had defined the Democratic campaign. Hart's aggressiveness at the Dartmouth debate kindled a fire that illuminated Hart's candidacy after a year in the shadows—much like the treatment given twelve years earlier to George McGovern's candidacy, which Hart had managed.

I was as guilty as everyone else. Late in 1983 another reporter on my paper, Sarah Fritz, had traveled to New Hampshire with Hart and watched him campaign. "Gary Hart has really got something going up there," she said. But I was not persuaded. I knew that Hart had very little money, so I could not take him seriously. Even after Fritz's alert, I did not take the time to look for myself at Hart's campaign in New Hampshire.

But in the wake of the Dartmouth debate, Hart realized that his moment had arrived. Mindful that it might not last long, he pounced on Mondale the very next chance he had, which was at another candidate debate in Des Moines. "Name one issue on which you disagree with the AFL-CIO," he demanded of Mondale. The front-runner would not answer directly, muttering something about "they want someone they can trust, not someone they can run." Hart, by directly confronting Mondale, had pushed to the forefront the issue that reporters had been chewing over for months—Mondale's indebtedness to the interest groups that Republicans liked to say actually controlled the Democratic party.

Now reporters followed up Hart's question, hounding Mondale at every stop on the campaign trail. Their pursuit of this issue helped Hart by supporting the point he was trying to make—that Mondale was a tool of the big labor bosses and of the other Democratic constituencies that had supported him. More important, the press response demonstrated that for all their connivance in fostering

Mondale's inevitability, reporters were still eager to poke holes in his candidacy when the chance arose.

Just how eager was demonstrated by the Iowa precinct caucuses, marking the official beginning of the delegate selection process, a few weeks before the New Hampshire primary. Mondale came in first with 49 percent of the vote. Considering that he was up against a slew of other candidates, the returns amounted to a slam-bang victory for him. In second place was Gary Hart with 16 percent of the vote. Remembering Hart's claim that he stood for the political future, Murray Kempton, the legendary columnist, turned to me in the press room and said, "The Democrats of Iowa have seen the future and given it 16 percent of the vote."

That's what I thought too. But, like Kempton, I missed what turned out to be the significance of the Iowa vote. The real winner would turn out to be Gary Hart. One reason was that John Glenn, who had been Mondale's chief rival in the eyes of the press and of most politicians, finished sixth in Iowa. Glenn hung on for a few more weeks, but to all practical intents, Iowa did him in.

Hart now became the beneficiary of the media's preference for a real contest. With the New Hampshire primary a week away, and despite Hart's puny showing in Iowa, the media recast the Democratic race from Mondale versus Glenn, to Mondale versus Hart.

Unfortunately for Mondale, the threat from Hart was not merely an invention of the media. The perception that the media reported, and helped create, was grounded in reality. Hart had not campaigned in every state everywhere, as had Mondale. But, as Sarah Fritz had tried to tell me, Hart had spent an enormous share of his time in New Hampshire, building an efficient organization and mobilizing support. When his second-place finish in Iowa created an opportunity, Hart cashed in. He routed Mondale in New Hampshire by ten points, ended Mondale's front-runner status, and overnight became the media's hero.

"Never before in American political history had the chemistry of a race for the nomination changed so rapidly," *Newsweek* reported. But Hart's ascendancy did not last long. After a few quick primary victories, he ran into a Mondale counterattack in the big Southern primaries on Super Tuesday. One of Hart's managers told me what was wrong. "In New Hampshire people were looking for an alternative to Mondale, and Hart became that alternative," he explained. "The problem was that when people started wondering what Hart was really like, we let Mondale draw the picture of what they saw." Mondale's sketch of Hart was of a cocky, not-dry-behind-the-ears kid with nothing much to back his talk of "new ideas."

"Where's the beef?" Mondale demanded of Hart in their first post–New Hampshire debate. And Hart had no snappy answer. His staff seemed befuddled. Hart had sold himself as the candidate of "new ideas." Nagged by reporters to spell them out, his press secretary, Kathy Bushkin, lamely responded, "Well, actually there are no new ideas."

Having ignored Hart for months early in the campaign, the media now made Hart pay for this oversight. Journalists piled on, trying to find out who this guy Hart was. It soon turned out that he had changed his name, from Hartpence, that he had fibbed about his age to make himself younger, and that many of his Senate colleagues did not much care for him. Rapidly the golden glow that had crowned the Hart campaign was replaced by a darkening cloud of ambiguity.

Another blow inflicted on Hart was the media's interpretation of the voting on Super Tuesday, two weeks after Hart's New Hampshire triumph, in five states. Hart won primaries in Massachusetts, Rhode Island, and Florida while Mondale won in Georgia and Alabama. What did these results portend?

The initial response from network pundits seemed to contradict the widely held view of the media as a quasi-conspiratorial monolith. On Super Tuesday night NBC treated the story as a Mondale comeback, with anchor Tom Brokaw describing the former vice president as "alive and well tonight in this race." For Gary Hart, Brokaw had a sarcastic put-down, likening the Colorado senator to "this season's hit rock-'n'-roll single." CBS's Dan Rather took the opposite view, stressing Hart's success with a labored railroad metaphor. Hart's candidacy "keeps moving like a fast freight," Rather said, while Mondale's "is off the side rails and is moving forward again." But by the next night CBS had given up calling a winner. Instead it showed successive scenes of Hart and Mondale arriving in Illinois, the next primary battleground, introducing both the same way: "The big Super Tuesday winner came to Chicago today."

In the print media, David Broder of the *Washington Post*, as close to a bellwether as there was and is in the trade, seemed to shimmy and shake a bit. His first-edition story reported that Hart "kept his bandwagon rolling as the music continued to fade for his rivals," and a few paragraphs later referred to Mondale's "crippled campaign." But that damning allusion was scrapped in later editions, after more returns came in.

The pundits seemed to agree on several criteria for separating success from nonsuccess in the Super Tuesday primaries, though the public was left to wonder how they arrived at these criteria. Hart, for example, was "expected" to win Massachusetts and Rhode Island, expectations which discounted the significance of his victories in those states. But both those states were heavily unionized and traditionally Democratic. By most standards of logic they should have been safe territory for Mondale, the candidate of the party's past, rather than his rival, the self-styled "Mr. Tomorrow."

Most press analysts seemed to believe that Hart had gained his most important victory in Florida, though his margin there was the narrowest of his three primary triumphs. But not everyone agreed. Roger Mudd scoffed at Hart's success in Florida because it was "not a true Southern state."

Over the next few days, as judgments firmed, Mondale won the benefit of the doubt, for which he could thank some shrewd manipulation by his supporters, among them House Speaker Thomas P. (Tip) O'Neill III of Massachusetts. As soon as the Super Tuesday returns came in, the Mondale team put out the claim that all Mondale had been required to do in the balloting was survive, which he had accomplished by winning Alabama and Georgia. As for Hart, the Mondale backers argued that he needed not just to win but to win "big." And winning three of five states, they said, was not big enough. These claims were put forward by leaders of prestige and influence in the Democratic party, people who supposedly knew what they were talking about when it came to politics. Since Hart's side offered no equivalent interpretative chorus, the media gradually allowed their view of Super Tuesday to be transformed from a Hart victory to a deadlock, and finally to what amounted to a triumph for Walter Mondale.

The media's hesitant response scarcely contributed to its image as a purposeful, dominating force. But it did show that however capriciously, the media can deploy significant power, and that this power can be manipulated by forces competing in the political arena. In 1984 the media went through a cycle reminiscent of 1972, when reporters first built up Muskie, then knocked him down, then built up McGovern and knocked him down. In 1984 history started to repeat itself, with Mondale as the front-runner and Hart in McGovern's insurgent role.

But the 1984 story ended differently. Democratic party leaders had learned a lesson from 1972: they could not prevent Mondale from being knocked down, but they saw to it that he bounced back, with the help of the media. Walter Mondale had traveled a relatively easy road to political prominence, making his way more by conciliation than confrontation. But now in the heat of the campaign, as he sought to recover from the shellacking Gary Hart had given him, Mondale was transformed by his handlers into "Fighting Fritz." And the media, picking up on this sobriquet and repeating it endlessly, helped to propagate the myth.

Like Jimmy Carter's early supporters in 1976, the party leaders and interest groups who had backed Mondale from the start in 1984 had too much invested in him to withdraw in adversity. They continued to support their candidate, and their support carried weight with the media, whose interpretation of the campaign helped to influence a fair number of voters with only shallow allegiance to either Mondale or Hart. They also helped make Mondale the nominee instead of Hart.

While Mondale and Hart carried on their struggle to the finish, another Democratic contender whom almost no one gave a chance to win was getting plenty of attention. This was Jesse Jackson, whose presidential candidacy demonstrated the foibles of the media in dealing with the issue of race. Plunging into the campaign, Jackson challenged business, labor, and his own party to "make room for the locked out" and promised to rally a "rainbow coalition" of all races. But it was to black voters—whose support Mondale assumed he had earned because of his strong record on civil rights—that Jackson appealed most.

As Jackson campaigned around the country, he often complained about a double standard that discriminated against minorities and hindered his candidacy. But Jackson's candidacy benefited from another kind of double standard: kid-glove treatment from other candidates. Fearful of offending black voters, they helped boost Jackson in public opinion polls. So did a flood of almost entirely uncritical attention from the media. It all amounted to what political scientist Austin Ranney, author of *Channels of Power*, called "a new kind of affirmative action."

In the last four months of 1983, even before he gained the release of Lieutenant Goodman, Jackson had more front-page stories in the *New York Times, Washington Post,* and *Los Angeles Times* than any other candidate. This intensive coverage and comparably favorable treatment on TV and in newsmagazines was far out of proportion to his chances of winning the nomination, which were considered nonexistent. It had to do mainly with the symbolism of Jackson's role as the sole black candidate in the race and with his flair for showmanship.

In part this was legitimate. Jackson's candidacy, as a metaphor for the rising political hopes of black Americans, deserved attention in the 1984 campaign. And Jackson's ability to get backing from white liberals demonstrated the appeal of the social and economic issues that he alone among the Democratic candidates raised. But in their coverage of Jackson the media failed to distinguish between Jackson the symbol and Jackson the candidate, competing for delegates against the likes of Mondale and Hart. The press scarcely mentioned the weaknesses of his political organization and the frequent inconsistencies and downright errors in his public statements—just the sort of thing that reporters pounced on when committed by other candidates.

Such a honeymoon was healthy neither for Jackson nor for the media, and could not last. The end was bitter, provoked by an off-the-record session with black reporters, among them the *Washington Post's* Milton Coleman, during which Jackson referred to Jews as "Hymies" and to New York as "Hymietown." When those slurs were attributed to Jackson in a story published by the *Post* but written by another reporter, Jews were understandably angered—but so were many blacks, who felt that Coleman was sabotaging the candidate's push for political power. Speaking on his weekly radio program, Louis Farrakhan, the bellicose Nation of Islam leader, pledged to "make an example" of Coleman. "At this point, no physical harm," he said, "but . . . we're going to keep on going until we make it so that he cannot enter in among any black people."

Despite Farrakhan's outrage, even the *Post's* handling of the "Hymietown" story reflected the media's tendency to treat Jackson as a special case. After all, Coleman had not written about the conversation when it happened. And when the *Post* finally did publish Jackson's offensive comments, it chose to bury them in the thirty-seventh paragraph of a fifty-two-paragraph report about the candidate's relations with Jews. As the *New York Times* pointedly asked, Were they playing down Jackson's comments to avoid appearing racist?

Jackson's candidacy was more in the nature of a civil rights demonstration, which was after all the movement from which he had emerged, than a realistic bid for the nomination. Protest candidacies have a long and honorable tradition in American politics, but they are by definition limited in scope and impact. Too often the media, hoping to placate Jackson's militant supporters, adopted the pretense that Jackson had a plausible chance of gaining the nomination and tried to cover him that way, rather than treating his candidacy for what it was. In so doing they patronized Jackson, did African

Americans a disservice, and provided a distorted picture of the role of race in American politics.

In late spring of 1984, while Mondale was grinding out his victory over Hart and Jackson, I was covering a Mondale rally at a California shopping center when I was accosted by a middle-aged woman, her arms full of packages, who wanted to know what was happening.

"It's Walter Mondale," I said. "He's running for president in the election."

"What do we need an election for?" she asked. "We already have a president."

Answering that woman's question, which might have been voiced by millions of her fellow citizens, was the central challenge facing Mondale as he sought to unseat Ronald Reagan. It was also the fundamental problem confronting the media as they tried to cover the election.

In a year of inevitability, the most inevitable aspect of the election was that it would be about Ronald Reagan. Elections almost always are about incumbents. The most a challenger can do is convince people through the media that they are mistaken if they approve of the incumbent, or reinforce their doubts if they have any. In Mondale's case, his task was especially difficult. Incumbent Reagan was a gifted performer with skilled advisers who devised the television ads that set the tone for his campaign against Mondale.

One, released in September, typified the overall theme. It presented a series of vignettes—a white farmhouse at dawn, a happy wedding party, an elderly man raising an American flag while glowing youthful faces looked on. As the flag filled the screen and misty music played, a voice-over intoned: "It's morning again in America. . . . Today, more men and women will go to work than ever before in our nation's history. . . ." The voice-over went on to talk about the wonders of low inflation and low interest rates, concluding: "Our country is stronger and prouder than ever . . . why would we ever want to return to where we were less than four short years ago?" This mawkishness made even some Republicans gag, but it seemed to suit the mood of the electorate.

What made the commercials work for Reagan—indeed, what made his victory "inevitable"—was the healthy state of the economy. Sure it was far from perfect. Unemployment was still over 7 percent; the rich were getting richer faster than ever while the poor and middle class lagged behind; the deficit was mounting. But the president's critics faced one overwhelming reality: for most middle-class Americans, the conditions of their lives were vastly better than they had been in 1980. And there was a sound basis for their satisfaction. The misery index—the combination of inflation and unemployment which had reached more than 20 percent under Jimmy Carter—had been cut in half under Reagan.

The media had an obligation to remind voters of chinks in Reagan's economic armor, which they tried to do intermittently. But this task was like pushing a large boulder uphill. Any story that focused on the limitations of Reagan's economic policy would have to point out that when it came to the major concerns of voters, such as inflation and unemployment, the indicators were not only greatly improved over 1980 but were continuing to improve. Moreover the press could not hit hard at the flaws in Reagan's economics—the lack of fairness and the looming budget deficit—and maintain its objectivity in the absence of a strong attack by the Democrats on these issues. But the Democrats, shaken by Jimmy Carter's failures, seemed uncertain of themselves and their beliefs, and unable effectively to challenge Reagan.

The Democrats came to believe that the public—the people who read newspapers, watched TV news, and voted—did not seem to want to pay attention. One indication of the public attitude, and the challenge facing the media and the Democrats, came early in the campaign when Mondale's campaign attacked Reagan's foreign policy—his heavy spending on defense, his ill-considered and costly deployment of Marines in Lebanon, and his push for more military aid to the *contras* in Nicaragua. The Democrats had a good case on the merits, and polls suggested that the country was on their side. But one Democratic issues specialist told me at the time: "No foreign policy issue is as strong as 15 percent inflation and 10 percent unem-

ployment." These were the approximate conditions that had prevailed under Jimmy Carter, and the bitter memory of those days still
dominated the public mood. Besides, after four years of relative
peace, few Americans were willing to swallow the old Democratic
warning that a reckless Reagan would lead the country into war.

With contentment reigning in the land, Reagan's handlers were
able to conduct a media strategy of benign neglect. They avoided
clashing with political journalists; instead, for the most part they
simply ignored them. Their attitude was summed up by a sign on the
desk of White House press secretary Larry Speakes which read, "You
don't tell us how to stage the news and we don't tell you how to cover
it."

This approach to the press by Reagan's operatives was based on
their reading of the turbulent recent history of the presidency. They
believed, as Steven Weisman, the New York Times' White House correspondent, wrote, "that reporters' pursuit of information, by its very
nature, disrupts Administration plans and hampers the President's
need to communicate a basic message." The net result, Reagan's
advisers claimed, was the weakening of the institution of the presidency. They looked back at Reagan's most immediate predecessors—
Johnson, Nixon, Ford, and Carter, all of whose White House tenures
had come to unhappy ends—and concluded that their fates had
been largely forged by the media.

Determined to control their own destiny, Reagan and his crew
looked chiefly to television. They believed that the public made its
decisions on public affairs based mainly on what it saw on television,
not on what appeared in print, and they were more confident about
being able to control the ultimate output of television.

On television, their surveys told them, pictures mattered most.
Extended comments by network correspondents counted for little.
"We learned very quickly that when we were presenting a story or
trying to get our viewpoint across, we had to think like a television
producer," Speakes later recalled. "And this is a minute and thirty
seconds of pictures to tell the story, and a good solid sound bite with

some news." When Reagan pushed his education program, the media viewed him sitting at a schoolroom desk, talking to students. If nothing on Reagan's schedule would advance the particular cause he was trying to promote at the time, the White House would say, "No coverage." And, as Speakes observed, "If the press didn't like it, the press didn't like it. There was no need to have the cameras in there and reporters trying to ask questions that would embarrass the president, unless we could get our stories on TV."

Secretary of State George P. Schultz spoke for many people in the administration when he declared, in explaining the decision to bar press coverage of the 1983 invasion of Grenada: "It seems as though the reporters are always against us. And so they're always seeking to report something that's going to screw things up." So the Reagan administration took away the press's opportunity to "screw things up," as Shultz looked at it—or to inform the public, as reporters looked at it. No one complained except the press. A good many Americans seemed to share Shultz's views, as testified to by sundry polls showing the press to be held in ill repute, and also by the lack of public outcry on the Grenada press ban.

While Reagan's efforts to control the news were scarcely brand-new, he and his people seemed more adept at it than any of his predecessors. Not only was he better at executing these tactics—in part because of his background as an actor—but he and his advisers were able to benefit from the experience of those who came before them. Remember, the increased aggressiveness and prominence of the press really began after 1968. So it took a while for presidents to realize what was going on and to develop countermeasures.

After nearly four full years in the White House, the Reagan media manipulation machine was a highly efficient apparatus. Its potency was demonstrated early in the fall of 1984 when Mondale tried something rare for a challenger. He took the initiative in foreign policy, an area usually ceded to incumbents, by arranging a meeting with Soviet foreign minister Andrei Gromyko. Uncharacteristically caught off guard, the Reagan White House at first had no comment for the scores of reporters who called to ask if the Mondale gambit would undercut Reagan's own forthcoming meeting with Gromyko.

Reagan's chief of staff, James Baker, considered scolding Mondale for meddling in the affairs of state. But Baker then decided this would make Reagan seem petty. Instead Baker and Reagan's other press strategists agreed on a company "line": the president had "no problem" with Mondale's tête-à-tête. That response would show the president to be above partisanship, while at the same time, by the use of the word "problem," subtly suggest that Mondale's gesture might not be altogether kosher. So when reporters again asked Speakes for comment on the Mondale-Gromyko meeting, the press secretary replied nonchalantly: "We don't have any problems with it." Afterward, when the president himself was asked about the meeting, he replied, just as casually, "I have no problem with that at all." These ho-hum responses, which sounded totally spontaneous, even as they used much the same language, did what they were designed to do: deprive Mondale's meeting with Gromyko of much of its potential for drama and significance.

Even as poll results underlined the seeming inevitability of Reagan's triumph, hundreds of reporters dutifully trooped around the country trying to cover the news. Many of them thought the most efficient way to do this was to board one of the candidate's jets. There the physical and psychological compression provided surroundings which were, as *Time* observed, akin to the atmosphere generally inflicted only upon recruits in basic training or inmates in an asylum. In past campaigns the standard rationale for putting up with such conditions was that the campaign plane offered the only assured access to the candidates and their staff. But given the campaign ground rules restricting coverage, the journalistic fellow travelers of Mondale and Reagan had little to show for their schlepping beyond the credit-card receipts for the air fare.

On Air Force One the eleven-member press pool was seated in the rear, well behind Reagan, and relied on briefings from press secretary Speakes. These supposedly fortunate few then shared the information with the rest of the press traveling on a separate "zoo plane." By unwritten agreement, Reagan was not to be photographed without due notice; when United Press International transmitted a photo of him wearing sweatpants, the White House raised hell.

It might be expected that the regimen on a challenger's plane would be more relaxed. But not challenger Mondale. Daring once again to be cautious, he had early in the campaign issued a ukase that put everything that happened on board off the record. Nagged by the press, Mondale eased the rule, but then he and his aides made themselves scarce to the reporters on board.

The campaign gave the media only one chance to challenge the prevailing doctrine of inevitability. That came as a result of Reagan's stumbling performance in his first debate with Mondale. Watching the seventy-three-year-old president grope for words and numbers, and struggle to organize his syntax and his thoughts, his aides feared the reemergence of the "age issue," which had been dormant since the 1980 campaign. They were right to worry.

In the wake of the debate, network sound bites featured Reagan's lapses, not the snappy one-liners the voters were used to hearing. Then the *Wall Street Journal* published a page-one story speculating on whether the septuagenarian president's mental faculties had become seriously eroded.

The very next day reporters descended upon the president's own doctor, the normally reserved and retiring Daniel Ruge, and pried from him the admission that Reagan had "tired" during the debate.

Had he lost stamina over his four years in office?

"I don't know; you'll have to ask him," Ruge answered before a campaign staffer succeeded in hustling him into a waiting car.

Fortunately for the Republicans, the campaign schedule offered its own solution for the problem created by the debate—another debate, and a chance for Reagan to lay the age issue to rest once and for all. The old pro did not blow the opportunity. When one of the reporters on the debate panel asked him about his age, Reagan must have subconsciously licked his chops. He answered with a line he had made up in the back of his limousine months earlier. Of course he felt up to the job, he said, "and I want you to know that also I will not make age an issue in this campaign. I am not going to exploit for political purposes my opponent's youth and inexperience."

Everyone laughed, even the hapless Mondale. The networks had their sound bite, and scarcely any journalist, on television or in print, attempted to challenge the notion that merely by a well-prepared quip Reagan had disposed of questions whether his advanced years undermined his fitness to serve. Instead the media almost universally accepted the Republican claim that Reagan had buried the age issue. The president had won not only the debate but the election. Mondale was fortunate to carry a single state, his own Minnesota.

The media, which in the past had been accused of dominating the political process, now faced charges by liberals of neglect of duty, of having failed to expose the deficiencies of the Reagan presidency. In seeming response to such criticism, James Reston, perhaps the most respected columnist in all of newspaperdom, wrote after the election: "Not since the days of H. L. Mencken have so many reporters written so much or so well about the shortcomings of the President and influenced so few voters." In the wake of the number of articles that targeted the president's "windy theorizing" and "zigzag contortions," Reston contended: "Mr. Reagan beat the newspapers by ignoring them." He pointed out that Reagan did not hold a single national news conference in the weeks following his renomination and generally "dismissed the White House press corps with a wave and a smile."

But in saying that Reagan "beat" the press, Reston missed the point. Reagan was not competing against the nation's newspapers and television journalists. He was running against Walter Mondale, who did not put up much of a show. Most of the reasons for that had to do with the favorable state of the union as perceived by its citizens. Even so, Mondale did a poor job of challenging the Reagan presidency. Most notably he failed to take advantage of the moment of maximum exposure for any challenger, the convention that nominated him. With tens of millions watching, Mondale picked as a running mate New York congresswoman Geraldine Ferraro, whose slim qualifications for the position persuaded voters that Mondale was even more desperate than they had thought. Then, in his acceptance speech, he lent credence to the Republican depiction of Democrats as the party of taxation by promising to raise taxes, without spelling out how Americans would benefit from this additional bounty granted to their government.

In short, Mondale did next to nothing to alter the attitude of the woman at the shopping center who told me, "We already have a president." His failure made it difficult for the media to go beyond the role of not-entirely-innocent bystander in the campaign, which did little more than ratify Reagan's presidency. Members of the press now had four more years to contend against Reagan and his team of manipulators. The next election would test whether they could profit from the lessons learned under the spell of the Great Communicator.

SEVEN

1988: *Character Study*

❧ THE TROUBLE for Gary Hart started in April 1987, on his very first presidential campaign trip. Hart had officially launched his candidacy that morning with a press conference in Denver at which he tried to argue that voters really cared about issues, not personalities. "I don't get all excited about personalities," he told the assembled reporters. "I think people care about arms control, about toxic waste in their backyards, about whether the President can negotiate with Mr. Gorbachev. I think they care about defense. The real question facing the voters," Hart said, "is the future of the country, and who is best prepared to govern."

Yet whether Hart liked it or not, the politics of personality—or the character issue, as it came to be called—dominated and shaped the 1988 campaign for the Democratic presidential nomination. In the process the reach of the media extended into hitherto untouched areas, creating a host of new conundrums about the role of the press in campaigns and generating a legacy of controversy and confusion that clouded the competition for the presidency for years to come.

As for Hart, who helped trigger it all, it was easy to understand why he wanted no part of the character issue. He had emerged from the 1984 campaign, in which he nearly edged out Walter Mondale, as a quirky kind of guy. And quirkiness is not one of those traits considered presidential. To be sure, Hart had plenty of political assets: his strong run in 1984, his rugged good looks, his quick mind, his success in depicting himself as someone who could lead the Democratic

132

party away from the supposedly stale traditions of its liberal past into a yuppified high-tech future. These attributes helped make him the front-runner in the contest for the 1988 nomination, after Ted Kennedy had once again taken himself out of the race.

Still, there were those oddball tendencies. Questions from reporters about changing his name and his birthdate had slowed Hart's early momentum in 1984. And he had ruined whatever chance he had for the nomination in late spring, when just before the primary in New Jersey he could not resist a wisecrack linking the Garden State with toxic waste dumps. The Republican governor of New Jersey immediately demanded that Hart apologize. Mondale supporters claimed the faux pas reflected Hart's insensitivity to New Jersey's real problems. The media seized upon the incident as another example of Hart's consummate fecklessness.

But Hart's character problem extended beyond such occasional episodes of sophomoric behavior. Political insiders knew that his interest in feminine companionship was not restrained by his marriage vows. And it did not take long before such inside gossip reached the outside world via the media. In the week before Hart announced his candidacy, both *Newsweek* and the *Washington Post* carried stories alluding to Hart's supposed reputation as a "womanizer" and "lady's man." *Newsweek* quoted a 1984 campaign aide as saying, "He's always in jeopardy of having the sex issue raised if he can't keep his pants on."

This made it inevitable that no sooner had Hart's campaign plane taken off on its maiden voyage, the candidate would be asked whether he was concerned about a flood of stories about his sex life. His response: "Sooner or later someone is going to write the story about how this gossip is coming out of other campaigns."

That was a strange reply by Hart. While his own purity might be hard to establish, the charge that other campaigns were trying to wreck his front-running candidacy was obviously more compelling. When I asked Hart if he had any evidence to support his accusation, he tried to back off. But it was too late. Stories about his allegations against the other candidates dominated the media coverage of the start of his trip. And it helped assure that character would play a prominent part in the contest for the Democratic nomination, though no one yet knew how prominent and destructive that role would be.

Character had been a major factor before in presidential politics, particularly in 1976 when, in the wake of Watergate, Jimmy Carter had campaigned as the apostle of truth and the press had responded by probing his personality. But in pursuing reports of Hart's alleged philandering the media was venturing into an area that had previously been off limits, a departure that reflected the national cultural upheaval triggered two decades earlier.

A. H. Raskin of the *New York Times* used to tell of overhearing presidential candidate Estes Kefauver instructing a hotel clerk in the 1950s, "Send up whiskey and women in that order"—but never printing a word about Kefauver's well-known proclivity for wine and women. Another Timesman, R. W. Apple, recalls staking out the lobby of Manhattan's Carlyle Hotel, where President Kennedy was spending the night, to observe the comings and goings of politicians. Kennedy's only visitor was a stunning woman, whom Apple later realized was actress Angie Dickinson. "No story there," Apple's editor told him.

Kennedy was probably the last president to enjoy this journalistic double standard of personal behavior. He was able to put his personal assets and virtues on public display to his political advantage while remaining confident that his personal shortcomings would be cloaked in privacy. That state of affairs began to change soon after JFK's tenure in the White House ended, as profound changes in sexual attitudes and behavior swept through American society and engulfed the media. Many of the children of the middle class began living in what used to be called sin. Premarital "tryouts" and extramarital relationships became commonplace. Homosexuals asserted their identities. And journalists too abandoned previous restraints and began to publish more of what they saw and knew of the private life of political leaders.

In a way it seemed paradoxical that with the relaxation of American sexual mores, the new freedom of the press led to politicians being held to a stricter standard of conduct. Some journalists may have been influenced by the "Personal Is Political" credo of the burgeoning feminist movement—the notion that individual problems are rooted in larger political issues, thus tending to politicize private life.

But the main reason for the change was that the media began to see more importance in the personal behavior of presidents, including their sexual behavior, and for this presidents had themselves largely to blame. Following the pattern established by JFK, presidents have been eager to collaborate with the media to advertise their personal virtues, and in this way they have opened the way to scrutiny of their weaknesses.

This examination was heightened by two great national traumas, Vietnam and Watergate, which seemed to make apparent the connection between character defects and disastrous policies in the nation's highest office. Lyndon Johnson and Richard Nixon, two very different men, each from a different party, were seen as mendacious and deceitful, driven to self-destructive actions by internal forces they could not control.

In the aftermath of these national tragedies, some presidents benefited by their skill in manipulating the character issue. Among the Democrats, Jimmy Carter's promise never to tell a lie helped vault him from obscurity to the White House. From Republican ranks, Ronald Reagan used the media to present himself as an icon of rugged individualism. Blue-collar Democratic voters who had a hard time buying into Reagan's supply-side economic theories nevertheless gave the Gipper their votes, polling data showed, because they viewed him as a man with "high morals," "a John Wayne straight shooter" who had "the guts to stick to his guns."

But then the country was shaken by another White House–generated trauma, which, like Vietnam and Watergate, could be linked to presidential character. This was the Iran-*contra* fiasco, which blighted the last two years of Reagan's presidency. As sundry official investigations and the probings of the press made clear, the convolutions of Iran-*contra* represented the dark side of Reagan's fabulously appealing political personality. One reason Reagan was so good-natured and congenial, it became apparent, was that he did not burden himself with the sort of things that make most people cranky. He made decisions, as one aide put it, "like an ancient king or a Turkish pasha, selecting only those morsels of public policy that were especially tasty."

The hubbub about Iran-*contra,* which colored the public's view of the presidency just as the 1988 campaign was getting under way, provided another reason for the press to look hard at the personalities of the competing candidates. And this mandate assumed by the media also included sexual conduct if it seemed to shed light on a candidate's character.

Mindful of all this, and keenly aware that Gary Hart, because of his erratic behavior in 1984, was an obvious target, Hart's campaign launched a preemptive offensive. "The campaign is planning to make character a major issue," Hart's campaign manager Bill Dixon told reporters a few weeks before the official announcement of Hart's candidacy. "We are trying to tell the story of who Gary Hart is."

Overcoming Hart's own resistance to the idea, his staff arranged a visit to his boyhood home in Ottawa, Kansas, where Hart renewed friendships with former schoolmates, strolled along Main Street, and visited his parents' grave. The sentimental journey was climaxed when Hart, talking about his parents before a crowd of about seven hundred old friends and well-wishers, lost control and nearly wept. His staff was overjoyed. "Anything that humanizes him, helps him," said one aide. But Hart himself still seemed to hold back. When asked later why he had choked up, he would say only, "It was an emotional day"—without even looking up from the autograph he was signing.

"I am not a traditional politician," Hart told his home state paper, the *Rocky Mountain News.* "I mean, most politicians are pushing themselves and their families forward ad nauseam. They cast everything in personal terms, and I've never been particularly attracted to that. And so, because I don't talk about myself much, then suddenly I become mysterious."

Typically, the cerebral Hart had formulated an intellectual rationale for defending his privacy. When I talked to him about values, the rhetorical handmaiden of the character issue, he sought to draw a distinction between "public" and "private" values. "Each of us has his own set of personal values," he said. "But there also are an identifiable set of public values. The reason I belong to the party I belong to is that my party comes closest to the set of public values that I think this nation stands for—equality, regardless of economic background, legal and social justice, and equal opportunity."

But did not personal values also have political significance? "Only because society has a right to regulate personal behavior that affects society as a whole," Hart said. "Otherwise people should be free to behave as they please."

Still, as a matter of practical politics, I asked, did not licentious behavior offend some groups and hurt at the ballot box?

Such puritanical attitudes, Hart replied, were held only by religious minorities. "This nation from Jefferson on has always said no minority could impose its religious values on the community," he argued. He pointed out that he himself had once been a member of a religious minority with strong conservative beliefs, the Church of the Nazarene. "The church didn't believe we should go to movies. So we didn't go to movies. But we didn't picket to try to close down the theater," he said. "It's one thing to tell your adherents to observe your values. It's another thing to impose those values on the community."

Hart would soon discover that whatever might have worked in Jefferson's day no longer held true for Gary Hart in late-twentieth-century America.

As part of their effort to defuse the character issue, Hart's staff persuaded him to submit to lengthy interviews about his background—an idea that inevitably backfired. Hart resented the probing and prying into his personal life, not only because he had things to hide but because he considered himself to be above such petty concerns. His arrogance had as much to do with his downfall as his libido.

"I'm going to answer about three more of these, and then I'm not going to answer any more," he snapped at one interviewer, asking about some episode in his past. "I was thirteen at the time. It's nonsense. Who cares what Ronald Reagan was thinking when he was thirteen?" On another and, as it turned out, more significant occasion, when E. J. Dionne of the *New York Times* asked about his womanizing, Hart's exasperation got the better of him. "Follow me around. I don't care," he said. "I'm serious. If anybody wants to put a tail on me, go ahead. They'd be very bored."

Unfortunately for Hart, the *Miami Herald* took him at his word. The *Herald* was drawn into the picture because it had run a story about the character issue that was sympathetic to Hart, by its top political writer, Tom Fiedler. The story pointed out the difficulties of campaigning "in a media-intensive age, where the scrutiny seems less intended to test a candidate's intelligence quotient than to expose his or her private life."

One Miami woman who read the story found it especially relevant. She called Fiedler and told him: "Gary Hart is having an affair with a friend of mine. We don't need another president who lies like that."

The *Herald* then dispatched reporters to stake out Hart's Washington town house, where they discovered that while his wife of twenty-eight years was away, the candidate was billeted with a twenty-nine-year-old model named Donna Rice. Hart at first claimed he was considering Rice for a job on his campaign staff. But then it became known that Hart and Rice had cruised to Bimini together on a yacht all too appropriately named *Monkey Business*. Hart's denials of misconduct were drowned out by inconsistencies in his own story and a barrage of questions from an unrelenting press corps. His darkest moment came when he was asked during a press conference whether he had ever committed adultery.

"I do not think that's a fair question," he said. Fair or not, Hart soon had to confront the *Washington Post*, which demanded that he comment on information, bolstered by photographic evidence, that he had conducted a longtime affair with a Washington woman, a lobbyist who was a former Capitol Hill staffer.

That did it for Hart. He pulled out of the race eight days after the *Herald* had disclosed his liaison with Donna Rice, but not without giving the press corps and the rest of the political world a piece of his mind. "I refuse to submit my family and friends and innocent people and myself to further rumors and gossip," Hart said. "I believe I would have been a successful candidate and I know I could have been a good President . . . but apparently now we'll never know." Hart called for changes in the nation's political system—which he charged had destroyed his candidacy by slighting more significant issues and exaggerating the importance of his personal behavior and character. "For most people in this country," he said, "that's not what concerns them."

A fair number of other politicians echoed his words. Another Democratic presidential contender, the Reverend Jesse Jackson, who had always resisted answering questions about his own freewheeling personal life, charged that Hart "was sabotaged." The episode, claimed Jackson, "raises some profound questions about journalistic ethics and limits." And Charles T. Manatt, co-chairman of Hart's campaign, told a reporter: "It's more the media than the public that's interested in such details of personal behavior, and when a newspaper does a stakeout to get the details, that's beyond the pale, it's gone too far."

But such arguments flew in the face of political reality. Hart's own campaign had recognized the importance of character when it sought to promote the more wholesome aspects of Hart's background before disaster overtook him. "Character is singularly important, more important in the presidency than in any other office," said Michael Robinson, a specialist on the press and the presidency at Georgetown University. "I worked hard to get Lyndon Johnson elected as the peace candidate, and then he almost shipped me off to Vietnam. That was a function of Johnson's character." And Duke University's James David Barber, the reigning academic expert on presidential character, claimed: "Hart's fantasizing about how campaigns develop. In the real world, the press is going to be looking at him. For him to say, 'I'm going to lead my personal life the way I want to and you guys just report on my position papers'—that's just not the way it works."

But is that the way it should work? Journalists themselves disagreed then and now. The story provoked internal debate in the newsrooms of many newspapers. "My God, people asked, are there no limits?" wrote *Washington Post* deputy managing editor Richard Harwood. "Will surveillance teams now be put on the trail of every politician?"

Harwood wondered aloud if the media should adopt rules or standards to govern what should be printed and what should not. But then he rejected the idea, pointing out that the media were too amorphous and variegated to regulate effectively, that no professional societies existed to undertake such a task, and that any such effort by a government agency would immediately be condemned—and properly so—as violating the First Amendment.

What this breast-beating overlooked was that Hart had done himself in. The *Herald* would have been derelict not to pursue the tip about his rendezvous with Donna Rice, and the other papers had no choice but to follow up the story. The verdict on Hart was handed down not by the media but by the political community that withdrew its support—not merely because of his liaison with a model but because of the recklessness and insolence that conduct betrayed. When later that year Hart made an abortive attempt at a comeback, he found that his fellow Democrats still regarded his behavior as politically unacceptable.

Yet if most of the criticism of the media's coverage of Hart's philandering was misdirected, the media nonetheless fell short of their obligations to the public. They had performed responsibly, but once again their sin was one of omission. What political journalists should have done, more thoroughly than they did, was first to point out that Hart's philandering was part of a general pattern of unsteady behavior which caused unease among his associates, then remind the public of the link between the personal weaknesses of Nixon and Johnson and the disasters that had overwhelmed their presidencies. While these connections may have been obvious at the time of Watergate and Vietnam, decades later many citizens had forgotten the crucial details and others had been too young to be aware of them. By failing to provide this information, and thus to explain their own role in Hart's downfall, journalists left a residue of confusion over the political significance of character that would plague both candidates and the press in campaigns to come.

What was clear in the wake of Hart's withdrawal was that, for better or worse, the character issue would be a prominent part of the 1988 presidential campaign. "It seems to me that the press and the public are going to feel after Hart's case that we have to hold all the candidates to the same standard of scrutiny," predicted David Keene, senior political consultant to Republican presidential contender Bob Dole, the senator from Kansas. "It's going to create a different scenario for campaigns," warned Democratic National Committeeman John Roehrich of Iowa, where his party's delegate selection process was to begin. "The American people are going to expect their candidates to be as pure as Caesar's wife. And that's going to be the norm."

Sure enough, it was not long before character scrutiny claimed its next victim—Senator Joseph Biden of Delaware. Just as adultery had driven Hart from the race, in Biden's case it was plagiarism. But underlying these episodes were deeper misgivings about both men which revelations of their conduct seemed to confirm. With regard to Hart, it was a perception of his general unsteadiness of judgment and disregard for the possible consequences of his private actions. With Biden, it was a suspicion that his career in politics was veined with superficiality—that he offered more sizzle than steak. In what was certainly the fundamental irony of Biden's presidential candidacy, those misgivings were grounded directly in what everyone agreed was his greatest political strength—his oratorical skill. Biden was able to rouse Democratic audiences to enthusiasm in a way none of his rivals—except civil rights leader Jesse Jackson—could match. His boyish good looks and Irish charm endowed him with what one admiring observer called "earthy magnetism"—the promise of an electricity that the Democratic party had not been able to offer the nation since the Kennedy brothers.

Yet for all his dazzle, skeptics noted that Biden, though he had been in the Senate for nearly sixteen years, was, as the *Almanac of American Politics* pointed out, "without any major legislation to his name." This modest record invited the suspicion that not much lurked beneath the flashy surface. Biden's problem was comparable, as New York governor Mario Cuomo once warned him in a private conversation, to that of a beautiful woman whom no one will credit with intelligence. "If you want to be the dumb blonde of the party," Cuomo needled Biden, "the guy who can give you a speech but can't count, I'll be glad to go around the country billing you that way."

Biden's undoing followed the discovery that he had borrowed— without attributing it—a dramatic passage of personal reminiscence from a videotaped speech by British Labour party leader Neil Kinnock to use in his own campaign speeches. Biden's delivery left the impression that his remarks had sprung from his own head and heart. Finding out about this deception led the press to seek other cases of such "borrowings." And they found them. In little more than two weeks Biden quit the race, blaming an "exaggerated shadow" of mistakes that he complained had begun "to obscure the essence of my candidacy." But his mistakes would not have mattered that much if they had not lent credence to doubts that already existed about his character and his candidacy.

Biden's forced departure from the race cleared the way for the nomination of Massachusetts governor Michael Dukakis, who appeared to have no noticeable human frailty beyond excessive smugness. It remained for George Bush's board of strategy, in what was certainly its most creative act, to find—or rather create—a weakness in Dukakis and with it to smother his hopes for the presidency.

Gaining the initiative in the campaign just after the Republican convention, Vice President Bush's managers won not so much because of the media but despite them. The guiding principle of the

Bush campaign was the same as it had been in 1968 when Richard Nixon gained the nomination by all but eliminating uncontrolled public exposure. But the expanded reach of television and advances in technology permitted Bush's manipulators to achieve an even higher level of control.

"The camera is neutral, but the camera is everywhere," pointed out Reuven Frank, a former president of NBC News, in a post-election critique. "No candidate is ever unaware of the camera. Every day print reporters were fobbed off with position papers while handlers wrote speeches for candidates as full of 'sound bites' as chocolate chips in a David's cookie."

The sound bite, as Frank defined it, was "a picture of the candidate talking, short enough to fit into the time limits and pithy enough to satisfy the producer's criteria of pith." The refinement of technique both by the media and the candidates had reached a point, Frank lamented, that had robbed campaigning of any spontaneity or suspense. "Everybody is so sure of everything, it is remarkable that there is a loser."

Of course there was a loser, a big loser—the citizenry.

In exploiting these techniques, Bush's handlers started off with a tremendous advantage because of the economy. It was even more robust than during Reagan's 1984 "Morning in America" campaign.

Nevertheless, by late spring Michael Dukakis led George Bush by about 10 percent in the polls. How did this come about? One reason was that at this early point in the campaign, voters were not thinking seriously about the decisions they would make in November. Another was that most Americans knew little about Dukakis except that he had successfully defeated Jesse Jackson, his only remaining rival in the closing weeks of the Democratic campaign. They knew a bit more about George Bush, and what they knew did not especially endear him. In his years in the vice presidency, Bush had created an impression of effeteness—"wimp" became the all too familiar shorthand term—and many considered him to be little more than a Reagan stooge. These qualifying factors behind the Dukakis lead should have been pointed out by the press when it reported the polling figures. But this is one of the media's habitual failings—to report polls without explaining the limits on their significance. The margin of sampling error is always mentioned. But the more meaningful margin of error, rarely mentioned, is a result of the shallow and tenuous nature of voter attitudes.

In any event, Bush's handlers were confident they could change the poll numbers. They swiftly concluded that the key to victory was to turn the focus of the election from George Bush to Michael Dukakis. This meant shielding Bush from attack and then hammering Dukakis. "We know we can't elect George Bush," Eddie Mahe, a member of the Bush planning team, told me at the outset of the campaign. "But we can defeat Michael Dukakis."

The result was the most negative presidential campaign in modern times. Before Bush's operatives could mount their attack, however, they found themselves on the defensive, dealing with a crisis within their own camp stemming from Bush's choice of Dan Quayle for vice president. The decision to select this little-known and little-distinguished senator from Indiana led reporters, probing his background, to unearth tales of how Quayle's wealthy and powerful family had used its influence to gain enrollment for young Quayle in the National Guard, which allowed him to avoid service in Vietnam.

A tremendous furor ensued, which Quayle was ill-prepared to handle. Some Republicans thought he would have to be jettisoned from the ticket, à la Eagleton. Despite the media storm, this did not happen in part because Bush and his advisers, fully mindful of what had befallen George McGovern in 1972, and more confident of their own ability to shape opinion, decided to face the criticism and not back down. They were quick to point out that the parallels with Eagleton were limited. They denied that Quayle had received special treatment and pointed out that his accusers had little solid evidence to support their charges. And whatever had happened, it had happened two decades earlier when Quayle was a young man, not yet in public life. Bush's aides set out to turn around the press's attacks on Quayle by exposing the press to the public.

They did this by having Quayle and Bush, after leaving the nominating convention in New Orleans, make their first stop in Quayle's hometown of Huntington, Indiana. There townspeople greeted their now most celebrated citizen like a conquering hero. A forest of signs in the crowd testified to the prevailing sentiments about Quayle and the media: "Quayle Country: media poachers beware. No hunting or trapping." "We're proud of our National Guard. Sam Donaldson go home." In an adroit piece of stage managership, Bush's handlers decided to hold a press conference immediately after the rally. Local citizens were on hand to cheer their hometown hero and boo the touring villains of the press corps.

Quayle stayed on the ticket. He probably did Bush no good in the campaign or later as vice president, except perhaps to bolster support from conservatives who were never wild about Bush to begin with. But Quayle did not prevent Bush from winning the election. And his continued presence on the ticket and in office served as a living refutation of the theory of media domination of the political system. The supposed power of the media to make or break politicians depends on context and circumstances. The exposure of Eagleton's psychological problems and Hart's philandering brought them down because the charges against both seemed disqualifying, and neither man could satisfactorily explain his problem. Quayle's conduct was not necessarily damning on its face, and he and his allies did a better job defending him than any of his foes did attacking him. But Quayle's triumph over the media was overshadowed by the crippling of the media in the last two months of the campaign, as Bush trained his guns on Dukakis.

Bush's campaign was built on character and values—the character and values of Michael Dukakis. In mounting their assault on Dukakis, Bush's managers adopted a strategy that in a way paralleled the views Gary Hart had expressed to me. Drawing a distinction between public and private values, Hart had suggested that private values were strictly personal while public values were a fit subject for political debate. The Bush campaign, adopting that reasoning, saw public values as an opening to make their case against Dukakis.

Using paid commercials and the so-called free media—the obligatory press coverage of their campaign events—Bush and his operatives launched a massive attack on Dukakis's public values as a way of indirectly attacking his character. By focusing on several controversial aspects of Dukakis's gubernatorial record—such as his veto of the law requiring teachers to lead their classes in the pledge of allegiance, his opposition to capital punishment, and the weekend furlough he had granted to a convicted killer, Willie Horton—Bush sought to define his opponent as outside of what Bush called "the mainstream" of American beliefs and values—in other words, as unfit to be president. The Republican campaign did not just stumble on this line of attack. Earlier that year, hidden behind a two-way mirror, Bush campaign manager Lee Atwater, famed for his aggressiveness, and other top aides had watched as one of their researchers dispassionately told a focus group of thirty New Jersey Democrats about Dukakis's low crimes and misdemeanors. By the time the presentation was over, only fifteen of the thirty still backed Dukakis, and Atwater was licking his chops. As he later recalled: "I realized right there that we had the wherewithal to win, and that the sky was the limit on Dukakis's negatives."

Bush himself led the attack, bringing up the Willie Horton issue repeatedly in his stump speeches. "Clint Eastwood's answer to violent crime is: 'Go ahead, make my day,'" he told campaign rallies. "My opponent's answer is slightly different. His motto is: 'Go ahead, have a nice weekend.'"

From the nature of the charges lodged against Dukakis, it was clear that Bush's attacks had little to do with substance or public policy. Asked after the election why he had dwelled on such matters as the flag pledge and the prison furlough, particularly when he had peace and prosperity on his side, Bush claimed that these parts of Dukakis's record were "symbolic of an approach to government that does not track with common sense." But as Bush's strategists would tacitly acknowledge, they were used because they packed a powerful emotional punch.

In their chronicle of the campaign, *Whose Broad Stripes and Bright Stars*, political reporters Jack Germond and Jules Witcover concluded that Bush's assault on Dukakis's record added up to "a degree of negativism" unprecedented in presidential politics. They also contended that the media "were too often timid in telling their readers, with the bark off, what was happening in the campaign."

Certainly the press should have been more vigorous than it was in exposing the negativism and vacuousness of Bush's tactics. But the media were limited in how far they could go in this direction without undermining their own objectivity and credibility. In the final analysis, if Bush's attacks were to be answered effectively, it was up to his opponent, Michael Dukakis, to carry the burden. It was Dukakis's responsibility to show why such issues as the economy and homelessness mattered more than saluting the flag, and what proposals he had for dealing with these substantive problems.

But the Democratic standard-bearer was not up to the challenge. Even as his poll standings dropped under the weight of Bush's barrage, Dukakis denounced the attacks as "shameless," "disgraceful," and "irrelevant." But Dukakis's bloodless style on the stump inhibited him from spelling out his own values in ways that stirred voters' feelings. He seemed incapable of engaging issues emotionally. And his own attempts at symbolic communication generally fell flat, or backfired.

The most memorable example was Dukakis's decision to take a ride in an M1 tank to demonstrate that despite Bush's charges, he was at heart a patriot who recognized the need for a strong national defense. Unfortunately, with only his head and shoulders visible, and wearing a tie, an ill-fitting helmet, and a foolish grin, Dukakis appeared like a caricature of himself, in danger of being swallowed up by this mechanized monster. The Bush campaign turned the news clips of Dukakis's ill-fated ride into a devastating Bush campaign commercial which lambasted Dukakis both as a hopeless dove and a hypocrite. "I was trying to define Michael Dukakis in terms of foreign policy and he defined himself," gloated Roger Ailes, Bush's top media adviser.

Where were the powerful media in interpreting these events? They might as well have been out to lunch. The Bush campaign, and to a lesser degree the Dukakis campaign, had in effect rendered the press irrelevant, or at least peripheral to the process. Satisfied with the results their candidate was getting from the press coverage of their carefully packaged events and speeches, Bush's handlers called an end to press conferences. They had no interest in dealing with impromptu questions that might dilute the impact of their orchestrated sound bites. The result of this edict was illustrated at Newark Airport when Bush arrived there on a mid-September afternoon. When the candidate landed, dozens of reporters, television crews, and photographers were waiting behind metal police barricades his aides had stationed about fifty yards away. "Come over here," journalists bellowed at the vice president, trying to get him close enough so they could shout questions at him. Bush cupped an ear, in a manner made familiar by his mentor, President Reagan, who genuinely had a hearing problem, and disappeared instead into his limousine.

On the other side of the political fence, Michael Dukakis had been steadily losing ground to Bush since the Democratic convention. Yet in September Dukakis sharply cut back on his own press conferences, persuaded that his contacts with the press were hurting his efforts to compete with Bush. "This is one campaign that is very strong on issues and challenges," Dukakis explained. "So you've got to make sure that's the message, not the response to what somebody said at ten in the morning."

Given the state of Dukakis's campaign and his failure to produce a coherent message, it is hard to see what harm he feared from the press. In his convention speech, Dukakis had presented himself as ideologically neutral, a sort of "Governor Goodwrench" who could fix whatever was wrong in the country. This led to the perception among the voters and the media, as the ABC anchorman Peter Jennings put it during one of the televised campaign debates, that the Democratic candidate was little more than a "technocrat—the smartest clerk in the world." The best response that Dukakis could muster was to say, "I care deeply about people."

Perhaps so, but Dukakis had a hard time expressing his cares and convictions in terms that the media could communicate and that voters could grasp. When Bush harried him about his pledge-of-allegiance veto, Dukakis responded with a legalism, contending that he was bound by an advisory opinion that the law was unconstitutional. Had he been a better legal scholar and a more articulate politician, he could have made a more compelling case for the right to dissent by citing a historic Supreme Court decision that struck down just such a flag law as the one he vetoed. "Freedom to differ is not limited to things that do not matter much," former Justice Robert Jackson wrote in his eloquent 1943 opinion. "That would be a mere shadow of freedom. The test of its substance is the right to differ as to things that touch the heart of the existing order."

Instead of striving to get the electorate to understand his beliefs and actions, Dukakis seemed obsessed with what had become the mantra of the campaign trial, the battle cry of the manipulators in both parties: "We don't want to step on our message." The trouble was, in Dukakis's case there was no message worth stepping on.

In response to the restrictions imposed by the candidates, and the inability of the Democratic standard-bearer to defend himself, reporters complained and grumbled to themselves, and some carried their grievances to their readers and viewers. NBC correspondent Lisa Myers, in a report on the manipulation of the media, emphasized the contrast between Bush's packaged media events and his rare meetings with the traveling press corps. She included a film clip from one of the few Bush news conferences in which the vice president, trying to deny he harbored a trace of bigotry, said: "I hope I stand for anti-bigotry, anti-Semitism, anti-racism. This is what drives me. . . ." Pointing out that Bush was "prone to misspeak," Myers said Bush's aides liked it better when they were "limiting access and managing the news."

But these reprisals were little more than pinpricks on the armor of the Bush presidential juggernaut. "Apparently there is no cost for ducking the press conference and no reward for doing it," observed Michael McCurry, press secretary for Dukakis's vice presidential running mate, Lloyd Bentsen. McCurry said his candidate faced the press regularly and still managed to get his message across.

"We are aware that there are few complaints to which people listen with less sympathy than those that emanate from a press that considers itself wronged," the *Washington Post* editorialized.

But there is much more than journalistic resentment at issue here.

In an age of public financing of presidential elections, you would think that at least one hour a week out of those 168 might be given over to the candidate's taking questions from the journalists who are trying to understand and report on his campaign; you would think a man confident enough to imagine himself as president would be confident enough to face Q-and-A sessions with the press.

But to date, on both points you would be wrong.

What should the press do? "The premise we have to challenge as journalists is that the candidates have the exclusive rights to control the dialogue," contended David Broder of the *Washington Post*. Because taxpayers financed much of the cost of the general election campaigns, Broder argued, the candidates should devote at least one hour a week to answer questions.

Maybe so. But in the absence of such a statutory requirement, some journalists argued that the media ought to take matters into their own hands. Broder's *Washington Post* colleague Richard Harwood contended that the press needed to be more assertive. "This may not mean, as someone has said, that the press will be successful in telling the electorate how to think," said Harwood, "but it may succeed in telling them what to think about."

But if it was to fill such a role, the press, as Harwood put it, would need "to clean up its act." That would mean reporters for both print and television would have to practice a more thoughtful type of journalism. They would need to bring to their reporting and to their readers enough background to put events in context and clarify their importance. At times they would have to be willing to sacrifice the chance for one day's front-page headline or prominent slot on the network news in the interest of pursuing a potentially more enduring or significant story, even knowing the effort might come to naught.

It was a formidable challenge, and not many journalists thought they and their colleagues were up to the task, given their inherent limitations as onlookers. Instead, some pinned their hopes for improvement on the practitioners of the process they sought to cover—"some smart politician," as *Time* put it, who would come along and tap the resentment of the sorry state of campaigning. "Fortunately, every established campaign style is eventually challenged by someone who figures out that he can win by rebelling against the system. Keep an eye out for the next guy who tries."

Sure enough, in the very next election someone came along to challenge the patterns that the media had established since 1968. But his method and the results were scarcely what *Time* had had in mind.

EIGHT

1992: *Beat the Press*

▶ EARLY IN THE 1992 presidential campaign, when I had the chance to talk to Governor Bill Clinton one-on-one, I asked him whether he thought a candidate's personal behavior was a relevant guide to his performance as president.

Clinton seemed to be riding high then. We had just flown into Manchester, New Hampshire, where the polls showed him far ahead in that state's vaunted primary. Clinton had that same week been anointed as the likely winner of the Democratic nomination by cover stories in *Time* and *Newsweek*. And with the country suffering through a severe recession, whoever won the Democratic nomination figured to have a better than even chance of capturing the presidency. Still, persistent rumors about his past conduct lingered over Clinton's candidacy, and my query obviously touched a nerve.

"That is a question that every American has to answer for himself," he said as we motored into downtown Manchester. He paused to survey the snow-covered New Hampshire landscape. "But the question I would ask back," he continued, "is to what extent is that the real reason the press pursues these matters with such relentlessness?"

That was a characteristically shrewd response, intended to put the onus for the so-called character issue on the press rather than on the candidate. Clinton's gibe at the motives of the press prefigured a series of thrusts at political journalists that would be launched not only by Clinton but by the campaigns of Republican George Bush and independent Ross Perot. These attacks were an attempt by politicians to deal with the media's growing influence in presidential campaigns, and amounted to a new strategy for trying to manipulate the media. Beating up on the press was a way to win support from various elements of the public that had their own reasons for resenting the press. It was also a way to keep the press back on its heels—and off the backs of the candidates.

In Clinton's case, the aggressive approach to the press, like the overall shape of Clinton's candidacy, had its roots in the disastrous Democratic presidential campaign of 1988. In the wake of Dukakis's defeat, Stanley Greenberg, a pollster favored by Clinton and other self-described centrist Democrats, pointed out in a landmark article in *American Prospect* that Dukakis's inarticulateness in the face of Bush's assault had left Lee Atwater's "savage caricature" as the dominant image of the Democratic party.

It was a political party, Greenberg wrote in his essay—which would have a profound impact on the Clinton campaign—that had lost the support of middle-class Americans. They had come to view the Democrats as short on patriotism, weak on national defense, soft on criminals and minorities, and indifferent to values of work and family. Middle-class voters now saw themselves as squeezed "between the rich and the poor, neither of whom play by the rules but seek their rewards through shortcuts and special claims—tax breaks, windfalls, and welfare." If they were to win them back, Greenberg wrote, Democrats needed to show that they stood up for people "who play by the rules."

To make Greenberg's approach work, Clinton and his aides realized they needed to take the initiative away from the opposition—and this included the press. Clinton's advisers were convinced that one reason Bush's attacks on Dukakis had scored so heavily was that Dukakis did not fight back; he simply took it on the chin. Clinton himself echoed that view in a speech in the summer of 1991 at a Chautauqua lecture series. Calling Bush's unanswered attacks on Dukakis on such issues as the pledge of allegiance and the Willie Horton furlough "devastating," Clinton said that Dukakis "didn't understand, as I tried to tell him, that where I come from people won't vote for you for President if they think you don't like to pledge allegiance to the flag."

For 1992, the Clintonites decided, the best defense was a strong offense. Anyone who struck at Clinton would get answered back in kind and then some. This came to mean that Clinton and his staff would use the press to attack rival candidates. And when this did not work, the campaign would attack the press itself, or at least find ways to put it on the defensive.

This macho posture was personified in the leadership of the campaign by the combative consultant James Carville, the "ragin' Cajun" who created the "war room" as the center for planning Clinton campaign strategy. Just as Clausewitz saw war as an extension of diplomacy, Carville and his cohorts regarded presidential politics as another form of warfare, an attitude reflected in the bellicose metaphors that rolled off their tongues. "I think we're going to have to go to war," Carville admonished his colleagues during one of the campaign's many crises with the press. "This is full-scale nuclear war," press secretary Dee Dee Myers echoed.

Their best-defense-is-a-good-offense blueprint was particularly crucial to Clinton's advisers because of their candidate's vulnerabilities, of which they were uncomfortably aware. Nearly everyone in politics or journalism in or out of Arkansas whose business it was to know about prominent politicians had heard rumors of Clinton's womanizing. Reporters did not have to ask politicians about Clinton's extramarital activities—politicians asked *them*. The problem had been enough to keep Clinton from running for president before, particularly in 1988 when Gary Hart's forced withdrawal turned the Democratic competition into a wide-open race. But 1992 was different, mainly because of the Gulf War which created a misconception, fostered by the media, that greatly altered Democratic politics.

When the Gulf War ended in a military triumph, however incomplete, it was widely hailed by the press as making Bush invincible in the 1992 election. The press buildup started as early as the U.S. military buildup in the Gulf—"Desert Shield," as it was called. "Success

Would Virtually Assure His Re-Election," the *Los Angeles Times* trumpeted about Bush, months before the first shots were fired by U.S. troops. That analysis seemed confirmed after the war ended early in 1991, as Bush's poll ratings soared to record-setting levels.

In the face of the media landslide for Bush, one by one the leading Democratic presidential prospects allowed their supposedly astute judgments to be overwhelmed and found excuses not to run. What none of them anticipated, however, was that the economy would turn sour in 1991. As it did, so did Bush's reelection prospects. Now Clinton had the advantage of knowing that the climate was right for a Democratic victory, and that his competition for the nomination was made up of politicians who had neither a strong following nor overpowering credentials.

Mindful that the real threat to Clinton's candidacy came not from his rivals but from himself, his strategists set out to inoculate the candidate against the danger of the press unearthing his past. In September 1991 Clinton arranged to be the guest at a press breakfast in Washington, surprising his hosts by bringing with him his wife, Hillary. He was clearly braced for questions about his personal life. When the first one was asked, he jumped on it like a cleanup hitter going after a fat pitch and dismissed the subject as unworthy of public discussion in a great republic. "This is the sort of thing they were interested in in Rome when they were in decline, too," Clinton told his inquisitors.

Then, with Hillary Rodham Clinton at his side, the governor sought to cut the ground out from under any future inquiries into his past. "What you need to know," he told the assembled elite of Washington journalism, "is that we have been together for almost twenty years and have been married almost sixteen, and we are committed to our marriage and its obligations, to our child and to each other. We love each other very much. And we intend to be together thirty or forty years from now, regardless whether I run for president or not. And I think that ought to be enough."

So there it was, cards face up. Clinton had gone up against the cream of the capital's political press corps and refused to answer their questions before they even had the chance to ask them. What's more, he told them they had no business asking him about what he did not wish to discuss. *"What you need to know,"* Clinton made plain, was only what he was willing to tell. For reporters to ask more than that was not just an intrusion on his privacy but a sign of moral decadence befitting the last days of the Roman Empire. That was where matters stood when I interviewed Clinton on the way to Manchester and he implied that press questions about his behavior were really a manifestation of hypocrisy.

As it turned out, our brief exchange was far more timely than I could have imagined. Later that very day Clinton was confronted with the allegation, published in the tabloid newspaper the *Star*, that he had carried on an affair with a Little Rock nightclub singer named Gennifer Flowers, whom he had helped place on his state's payroll. The gist of Flowers's story, for which the *Star* had paid an undisclosed sum, was that she and Clinton had had a sexual relationship over a period of a dozen years, concluding in 1989. What really stung was that Flowers had tapes to back up the story. Indeed, the *Star's* story included quotations from Flowers's conversations with Clinton, who at one point advised her that "as long as everyone hangs tough" there would no problems for either of them. "If they ever hit you with it, just say 'no' and go on," he added.

The story threw the Clinton campaign into turmoil, but it also caused consternation among the media. Some journalists, considering themselves members of a professional elite, resented having to deal with such tawdry matters when they should be free to concentrate on loftier concerns. Then too, many reporters who were of Clinton's baby-boomer generation may have felt themselves susceptible to the same urges to which Clinton had submitted.

The day the story broke, and before I had even heard of Gennifer Flowers, I saw an ABC News reporter questioning Clinton in the lobby of the Manchester Holiday Inn. After hesitating, I walked over and listened while the reporter brandished a copy of the story. Clinton, actively shrugging his shoulders and rolling his eyes, offered an unconvincing denial of Flowers's account, a denial he would soon repeat on national television.

Afterward I told the reporter that I had not meant to intrude but that I would not have expected him to be conducting an interview in the hotel lobby about an exclusive story.

"I wouldn't have done that if it was a story I had any respect for," the ABC reporter said.

I was stunned by his response. Here was the leading candidate for the Democratic nomination facing a serious accusation that could wreck his campaign. Yet this reporter was only one of a number of journalists who believed the Gennifer Flowers story was beneath them.

A "shabby accusation" that "distorted and contaminated not only the political system but the judgment of some in the news media," said Albert Hunt of the *Wall Street Journal. Newsweek* columnist Jonathan Alter sought to distinguish between the Gennifer Flowers allegations and the Donna Rice affair which had driven Gary Hart from the race four years earlier. "When Gary Hart was caught during the 1988 campaign spending the night with Donna Rice, he got what he deserved," Alter wrote. "He had betrayed his supporters and staff by thinking with an organ other than his brain. The recklessness spoke to his judgment and maturity and was thus a legitimate campaign issue." The difference between Clinton and Hart, Alter argued, was that Clinton, unlike Hart, had not lied about his past,[*] nor did he dare reporters to follow him. "Informal rules are obviously imperfect, but perhaps the line on adultery should be drawn at current conduct," Alter argued.

This argument ignored the very plausible notion that how Clinton had conducted himself in the past would suggest what he would do in the future, a supposition that was eventually borne out by the

---

[*]In fact Clinton did lie about his relationship with Gennifer Flowers. Six years after he denied her story in New Hampshire, during grand jury testimony he admitted having a sexual relationship with Flowers.

events of his presidency, with grave consequences for Clinton's tenure in the White House and for the country.

Clinton and his aides, mindful that Alter's attitude was by no means universally shared by his colleagues, were not prepared to rest the fate of his candidacy on the lenience of the press. Instead, in keeping with their understanding of the lessons of the 1988 campaign, they counterattacked with a ferocity that caught the media off guard. Their main theme was the press's tendency to dwell on sensational aspects of their candidate's personal life rather than the substantive issues that confronted the country.

On the night the Flowers story broke, Clinton dispatched his sharp-tongued media director, Mandy Grunwald (whom one friend described as "Lee Atwater in a Chanel suit"), to make that case on Ted Koppel's *Nightline* show. Koppel, one of the most formidable interviewers in television journalism, never had a chance against the sense of outrage Grunwald managed to generate.

Was it possible to put a story like this in "perspective"? Koppel began, gently enough.

"Well, programs like this are not a help," Grunwald shot back. "This is the first program that *Nightline* has done on any topic relating to the Democratic presidential candidates. You haven't been talking about the middle class. You haven't talked about why Bill Clinton has captured people's imagination."

"Oh now, wait a second," Koppel protested. "We've done a number of programs on the middle class, the issues, unemployment."

But the relentless Grunwald brushed that aside and hammered away at the celebrated interrogator who now found himself on the wrong end of the gun barrel. "People are about to go out there and vote," she said. "And you're choosing with your editorial comment, by making this program about some unsubstantiated charges that started with a trashy supermarket tabloid, you're telling people that's something you think is important. You're setting the agenda, and you're letting the *Star* set it for you."

Grunwald's attention-getting assault, followed by similar outbursts by other Clinton staffers, appeared to have a chilling effect on many in the media. Most mainstream outlets gave the controversy over Flowers's charges and Clinton's denials scant coverage or none at all. Yet the story would not go away. Word of mouth, talk shows, and the persistence of some mainstream journalists kept it alive.

A week after the Flowers charges became public, Clinton's own pollster, Stanley Greenberg, conceded that the candidate's position remained "precarious," pointing out that opinion surveys suggested that a significant number of voters would not support a presidential candidate whom they believed had engaged in extramarital sex. On Capitol Hill talk was rife among Democrats of trying to persuade one or more of the party leaders who had earlier dropped out of the race for the presidency to change their minds.

The Gennifer Flowers story confronted the so-called respectable media with a dilemma: how could they print "trash," hot off the supermarket press, which arguably smeared not only Clinton but the whole political process, including the media? But how, on the other hand, could they ignore it and thus seem to be suppressing the news, particularly when this news, however sleazy, might have great impact on Clinton's candidacy?

The respectable media—most newspapers, the networks, and local television stations—resolved the dilemma by covering the story more or less indirectly. They reported the impact the story was having on Clinton's candidacy, but in doing so they also recounted Flowers's charges. For instance, the CBS Evening News pointed out that Democrats were worried that as vulnerable as George Bush seemed to be because of the nation's economic pain, their front-running Bill Clinton might have a hard time defeating him because of Clinton's personal troubles. And in explaining these troubles, CBS recounted Gennifer Flowers's story and displayed her photo.

But press coverage of the political impact of Clinton's personal problems too often suffered from superficiality. Reporters focused on polling responses by voters to the question of whether the allegations about Clinton's womanizing would change their minds about whom to support. The vast majority of voters invariably said no, and so the reporters concluded that the revelations did not matter.

To find out the real impact, reporters needed to dig deeper. When pressed—as a *Los Angeles Times* focus group made clear—voters did acknowledge that the charges had influenced their overall reaction to Clinton, and not for the better. Repeatedly the eight voters in the focus group who were gathered by the *Times* to watch a televised debate among the Democratic candidates insisted that Gennifer Flowers's charges should have no role in the campaign. Nevertheless their comments, as staff writer David Lauter reported, showed that the charges had colored their overall view of Clinton and his candidacy.

"I'm not sure he's willing to level" with voters about the costs of his economic program, said Dan Harkinson, a thirty-nine-year-old lawyer. "I felt he was holding something back," twenty-nine-year-old Jackie Lawson, an accountant, said when asked about Clinton's position on health care. "I don't quite trust him," said Bob Ciderberry, a fifty-two-year-old construction contractor.

"At first glance the polls on the adultery charges give Clinton the benefit of the doubt," said Harrison Hickman, pollster for Nebraska senator Bob Kerrey, another Democratic presidential contender. "Does it matter in itself? For most people, the answer is 'no.'" But what his own surveys also demonstrated, Hickman said, was that the character issue, raised by the adultery charge, "opened the door" to questions about Clinton's basic credibility.

That door stayed ajar for the rest of the campaign and for Clinton's two terms in the White House. But the *Times* focus group was the exception to the coverage of the so-called character issue. The indirect but critical impact that it showed seemed too subtle a point for most journalists to follow up.

The significance of the character issue was heightened two weeks after the airing of the Gennifer Flowers charges when a new and in some ways even more serious controversy about Clinton's past erupted. This time it was the disclosure that in 1969, while Clinton was a Rhodes Scholar at Oxford, he had schemed to get himself a future admission to the ROTC program at the University of Arkansas in order to avoid being drafted during the Vietnam War. But then

Clinton had passed up the chance to join the ROTC and reentered the draft at a time when circumstances suggested he probably would not be inducted.

In this case too, Clinton had the sympathy of some reporters of his generation who had themselves avoided service in Vietnam through college deferments. Their reluctance to pursue the draft controversy was particularly irksome to aides to Bob Kerrey, who had won the Congressional Medal of Honor and lost a leg in Vietnam. On Valentine's Day, just before the February 18th primary in New Hampshire, Kerrey's campaign manager, Billy Shore, was inspired to compose a couplet that served as a bitter comment on the press's attitude toward Clinton's draft problems.

Roses are red,
Violets are blue,
Clinton dodged the draft
And so did most of you.

Despite this attitude, the weight of the Flowers and draft-dodging allegations demolished Clinton's front-runner status and left him trailing Paul Tsongas, the former Massachusetts senator whose candidacy had been endorsed by the *Boston Herald*. Praising Tsongas's "decency and strength of character," the *Herald* declared—in an unmistakable allusion to the unfortunate Clinton— "At a time when voters are weary of candidates with feet of clay, Paul Tsongas is a man whose integrity is unquestioned."

With his support melting away, Clinton struck back at the *Herald* and other critics. "The real character issue and the real patriotism issue in this election is, who has a vision for the country, a plan for the future, and the ability to get it done," he contended. Blaming his troubles with the draft and Gennifer Flowers on the scheming of his political enemies, Clinton retorted: "The people whose character and patriotism is really an issue in this election are those who would divert the attention of the people, who destroy the reputations of their opponents and divide the country we love." Clinton did not say exactly which "people" were doing the diverting and destroying, but clearly the press was among them.

At the same time Clinton's aides took after Tsongas, questioning his reputation for probity and rectitude. "Who does this guy think he is?" Paul Begala, one of Clinton's most aggressive propagandists, asked me. "There are some things about 'St. Paul' of Massachusetts that you guys ought to look into," and Begala pointed to supposed links between Tsongas's voting record in the Senate and the interests of big contributors to his campaign.

In a curious way, the furor over Clinton's past helped him by hampering his rivals. Coverage of Clinton drowned out the efforts of the other candidates to make themselves heard and helped set the stage for Clinton's first great spin triumph on election night in New Hampshire.

I could see it coming in the closing days of the New Hampshire campaign as Clinton managed to regain some of the ground he had lost in the polls. His aides reminded reporters how far their candidate had come back: after trailing Tsongas by nearly twenty points, he was now fewer than ten points behind. They did not mention that he had once led Tsongas by more than twenty points.

"It looks like Clinton's taking it on the chin here," Bernard Shaw of CNN told me over lunch in the coffee shop of the Holiday Inn on primary day.

"That's not the way Clinton's people will look at it," I told him. "They are going to claim a moral victory."

Shaw snorted. "They can't get away with that," he said.

But that night Clinton transformed reality. The returns showed him in second place, losing to Tsongas by eight points. While the winner waited for the final votes to be counted, Clinton rushed to CNN's cameras and, using a phrase crafted by his staff, announced to Bernard Shaw and the world: "New Hampshire has made me the comeback kid." Shaw, who had been so disdainful of Clinton's performance in New Hampshire over lunch, did not contradict the ebullient candidate.

With that masterly stroke of spinmanship, Clinton robbed

Tsongas of the psychological boost that he should have expected from his victory in New Hampshire. Instead it was Clinton who had somehow conned the media into crediting his candidacy with momentum as the campaign moved on.

More serious than their acceptance of Clinton's spin was the failure of the media to point out the relevance of Clinton's behavior. Put simply, his personal conduct—the revelations of philandery and draft avoidance, and the later disclosures of chiseling and connivery in the Whitewater land deal—contravened the whole set of middle-class values that was the cornerstone of his drive for the White House. For it was Clinton's presidential candidacy that brought to fruition the character issue as a double-edged sword. No candidate in modern times was the target for so much criticism and controversy because of his personal behavior. And no candidate before him was so calculating and determined to use his personal life and values as a weapon on his own behalf.

Early in his candidacy Clinton talked to reporters of the difficulties he faced growing up, including dealing with a stepfather who often physically abused his mother. On one occasion, as Clinton told the story, when he had reached the age of fourteen and stood a head taller than his stepfather, he confronted the older man and told him there would be no more violence. "I couldn't wait to get big enough to know there would be peace in my home," Clinton recalled.

By his own account, as well as the recollections of friends and close associates, the bringing of peace to his mother's home was a defining event for Bill Clinton, one that set a course for his life and his life's work. And the telling and retelling of the story helped to shape his image in the press. The searing experiences of his childhood had strengthened his own character, or so Clinton and his supporters sought to suggest. Moreover, the young man supposedly became imbued with an impulse toward reconciliation well suited for the stewardship of a fractious nation. Efforts to dramatize these youthful experiences demonstrated the extent to which Clinton and his inner circle were willing, even eager, to use the press to exploit his personal life in order to advance the public man.

This emphasis on Clinton's personal side, on the version of his character and values presented by himself and his allies, became one of the keys to his candidacy's success—even as the candidate complained bitterly about the excessive attention paid to his personality. "My life is a testament to the fact that the American dream works," he cried on his way to the White House. "I got to live by the rules that work in America, and I wound up here today running for President of the United States of America."

No one in the media thought to question which rules it was that Clinton had lived by. Nor did any of his rivals, with the notable exception of Medal of Honor–winner Kerrey. He had held his tongue during the Gennifer Flowers furor, but when Clinton sought to blame the disclosures of his draft avoidance on unnamed political enemies, that was too much for Kerrey. "Let me tell you where I go over the edge on this thing," the former Navy Seal told reporters. "It should not surprise you to discover that it was the men and women who went to Vietnam who suffered. All of a sudden in this campaign the sympathy is going to someone who didn't go." Yet Kerrey's words received scant attention from a press corps still looking at poll numbers to judge the "impact" of Clinton's character.

In the wake of the draft controversy came revelations of the free-wheeling financial dealings of Bill and Hillary Clinton in Arkansas, particularly in their joint investment in the Whitewater real estate venture. But the charges were complicated and hard for the press to explain or the public to grasp. And Clinton, now emboldened by the ability to face down his accusers, fought back vehemently. During a campaign debate two days before the Illinois primary vote, when former California governor Jerry Brown attacked the Clintons for their alleged conflicts of interest in Arkansas, Clinton, without answering the charges, called Brown a liar who was "not worthy of being on the same platform" with Hillary Rodham Clinton.

"Let me tell you something, Jerry," said Clinton, shaking his finger in anger at Brown. "I don't care what you say about me. But you ought to be ashamed of yourself for jumping on my wife." That's what made the sound bite for television and the lead for newspapers as they covered the debate. Thus Whitewater was buried during Clinton's candidacy, only to reemerge during his presidency when it served as the springboard for his impeachment.

Blessed with remarkably weak opposition, bolstered by the reluctance of the press to challenge his carefully spun strategy, Clinton stumbled through to the nomination. But he was "damaged goods," as his pollster Stanley Greenberg later admitted, and to repair that damage, his advisers set out by every available means to change the public's view of their candidate in the general election. "We had decided that biography was critical," Greenberg said.

Clinton himself, of course, was cast in the lead role in this makeover. But the most important supporting role was played by the so-called new media—chiefly television and radio talk shows—on which Clinton could ramble on about himself without fear of the pointed questions he might be asked on more conventional interview programs. He was willing to take any route around the traditional media, even if he had to pay for it. This practice had begun in New Hampshire when, tired of being grilled by reporters about his troubles, he bought a half-hour of local television time, corralled a group of friendly voters, and let *them* ask the questions. In a way, it was a throwback to the programmed Nixon campaign of 1968.

After that, at every critical moment in the campaign, Clinton looked for ways to communicate with the voters over the heads of the traditional media. In the New York primary campaign, when he was hard pressed by Jerry Brown, Clinton made himself at home on the show of bawdy talk-show host Don Imus. After the California primary, when the polls showed him trailing both George Bush and the wild card in the race, Texas billionaire Ross Perot, Clinton found a friendly forum on the Arsenio Hall show, toting his own saxophone. The relevance of what he said and did was often far from clear. Asked whether his appearance on the Arsenio Hall show wearing wraparound sunglasses and playing the saxophone might make him seem unpresidential, Clinton replied: "I've been playing the sax since I was nine. It's a part of who I am." His strategist Carville added: "This was the real Bill Clinton. That's not to say he wears sunglasses indoors. But it is to say that he likes to have fun."

Pretty flimsy, perhaps. But it was one way to accomplish what Clinton desperately needed—persuade voters to forget his past behavior.

The final symbolic strokes came at the Democratic convention. First came the presentation of an hour-long film biography turned out with the slickness to be expected from its producers, Harry Thomason and Linda Bloodworth-Thomason, creators of the TV sitcoms "Designing Women" and "Evening Shade." The Clinton film focused on every obstacle the candidate had overcome, every hardship he had confronted, in the long climb from his starting place in the little town of Hope, Arkansas. "I still believe in America," Clinton declared at the conclusion. "And I still believe in a place called Hope." Then he accepted the nomination "in the name of all those who do the work, pay the taxes, raise the kids and play by the rules," and once again recounted the tribulations he had overcome since childhood.

Clinton stayed with that biographical theme for the campaign against Bush, pointing to his early life as a refutation of the suspicions about his character. "I believe the best way for me to demonstrate my character is to make sure people know the whole story of my life and my work and my family and what I'm fighting for in this election," he told the editors of *Time* magazine at convention time.

In his struggles to revive his candidacy, Clinton had been forced to contend against an unexpected and unpredictable rival whose own drive for the White House was born of the same discontent with the troubled economy that Clinton had been striving to tap. This was Ross Perot, the most bizarre phenomenon of a bizarre election. Nothing so dramatized the volatility of the media, their fascination with aberrations, and their rapid swings from veneration to scorn as the roller-coaster course of Perot's political fortunes. It was only natural that Perot, the world's only billionaire populist, would rely on the so-called populist media, the talk shows of radio and television, to introduce himself to the political world. The hosts on these shows coddled him, treating him more like a flustered philanthropist than an ambitious politician.

What did Perot know about the global environmental conference scheduled in Rio de Janeiro, Larry King wanted to know?

"Not a thing in the world," Perot blithely responded.

At which point King shrugged, smiled, and went on to the next question.

When he ran out of friendly talk-show hosts, Perot reached into his wallet and bought time himself, just as Clinton had done in New Hampshire, but on a much larger scale.

It was Larry King, though, who had launched Perot's presidential career. "I was his New Hampshire," said King, a man never hindered by modesty.

The timing of Perot's emergence as a prospect for the White House, in late February 1992, was auspicious. Paul Tsongas's victory in New Hampshire had just left the Democratic party in confusion and anxiety. On the Republican side, the recession had ground down President Bush's once stratospheric approval ratings. Three weeks earlier, the monthly economic indicators showed a sharp drop in the growth rate to nearly zero while unemployment climbed.

When the folksy billionaire told Larry King he might indeed run for president, the impact was seismic. Over the next three months Perot transformed the presidential campaign, taking over the leadership in the polls, with the incumbent president trailing him and Bill Clinton, the presumptive Democratic nominee, in third place.

At first the traditional media, finding Perot's brand of politics a refreshing change from the tarnished Democratic campaign, gave impetus to the boom that had been born on the new media. The mainstream newspapers and networks seemed to accept the image that, as the *Los Angeles Times* pointed out, Perot had carefully cultivated over the years: "Perot the man who took on General Motors. Perot the philanthropist. Perot the daring rescuer. Perot the champion of education. Perot the bigger-than-life Texan who still puts his pants on one leg at a time, like everyone else."

This attitude began to change as Perot came under increasing scrutiny, raising questions about the kind of man he was and the kind of president he would be. The *Wall Street Journal* reported that Perot lobbied for federal aid to build a Fort Worth airport that would benefit his family's nearby real estate development. The *Washington Post* published the complaints against Perot's management tactics in lawsuits filed by his former colleagues at Electronic Data Systems, the firm he founded. And the *New York Times* told how Perot seemed to have lost interest in the Texas schools after the reforms he pushed through were watered down. But such information did not seem to slow Perot's surge in the polls, not at first anyway. He was doing more than running against the political establishment; he was also challenging the media establishment. Plenty of other politicians had done this, but the maverick Perot used a different tactic. Most politicians attacked the media for not caring about substance. Perot and his team charged that the media put too much emphasis on substance.

The reason for Perot's stance was that the press had become increasingly weary of Perot's hazy answers, and Perot had grown impatient with being prodded for specifics. Grilled by "Meet the Press" host Timothy Russert on his promise to eliminate government waste and fraud, Perot snapped: "Give me a little time to get all this nailed down."

Perot and his aides decided to borrow a leaf from Clinton's campaign book and hit back at the press. "The media is mainly interested in litmus test, chart issues," said James Squires, spokesman for the Perot petition committee. " 'Are you for the Brady bill or against the Brady bill?' That's what's wrong with the system. That's why Mr. Perot is running for president. He's defining himself for the American people, not for Sam Donaldson or Tim Russert."

"I am sick and tired of having everybody want to know what my positions are," Perot said. "So it's not for the people. This is for the media, who apparently can't breathe without it." The news media, Perot charged, put candidates through a "hazing process," with one exception: "An incumbent president doesn't have to put up with anything because he's so shielded."

But the incumbent president in 1992 did not seem to be shielded from anything. Bush was being pounded every day in the media as he became the punching bag for the nation's hard times. In better days the media had had difficulty finding anything bad to say about the man in the Oval Office. In hard times it was having trouble finding anything but bad things to report. The main reason was the economy: the country was deep in recession. A grim new term, "downsizing," had crept into the public vocabulary, and familiar phrases, such as bankruptcy, had taken on a more urgent meaning. That old standby of incumbent presidents, the Rose Garden strategy, could not work for Bush because roses were blooming nowhere else in the land. It was Bush's additional misfortune that the recession had hit especially hard in New Hampshire, site of the first presidential primary, where he faced a challenge from the conservative columnist and former Nixon aide Patrick Buchanan.

Buchanan took off after Bush in the Granite State, spreading empathy for the downtrodden wherever he went. In Buchanan's arsenal was a simple but devastating commercial which repeated Bush's now notorious 1988 "read-my-lips" pledge not to levy new taxes, a promise he had broken only months before. The drama of the feisty Buchanan taking on an incumbent president who not so many months earlier had been considered invulnerable was a natural for the press. And nearly every story shot another hole in Bush's image.

Bush won the New Hampshire primary, but not by enough to impress the media. Charles Black, a senior adviser to Bush's campaign, was in the midst of pointing with pride to his candidate's success on election night on CNN when anchor Bernard Shaw abruptly cut him off. "Charlie Black," said Shaw—the same Shaw who later that night would be hamstrung by Bill Clinton, the "comeback kid," but now

sounded like an exasperated teacher lecturing a wayward student—
"Patrick Buchanan taking 44 percent out of George Bush's hide has
got to be an embarrassment."

Although Bush won, he was repeatedly depicted as the loser. "A
wounded president," CNN's Ken Bode called him. Buchanan "has
certainly staggered the sitting president of the United States," NBC's
Tom Brokaw observed. As it turned out, by the time all the votes
were counted Buchanan did not win 44 percent of the vote—only 37
percent, with another 10 percent going to ex-Klansman David Duke.
But the damage to Bush had been done.

The collapse of Buchanan's campaign soon after New Hampshire
did little to help Bush as his nomination neared. His fortunes continued to plummet as Clinton's soared, just after the Democratic
convention. Frustrated by his prolonged battles with the press, Ross
Perot abruptly pulled out of the race—temporarily, it turned out—
with a backhanded salute to Clinton, which helped to boost Clinton
far ahead of Bush in polls.

The tendency of the media to ride a trend wave was never more
apparent than during and immediately after the Democratic Convention. Clinton and his managers, with the help of Clinton's filmed
biography, created a story line—poor Arkansas boy from broken
home makes good in national politics—that in the absence of anything else dominated the media's attention. Then came Clinton's six-
day cross-country bus trip with his new vice presidential candidate,
Al Gore—referred to by *Time* as "Bill and Al's Excellent Adventure."
Such a tongue-in-cheek view was the exception to the generally
gushing coverage, which typically displayed Clinton and Gore and
their wives, Hillary and Tipper, linking arms, singing "God Bless
America," and sitting on carefully arranged hay bales at a Midwest-
ern farm.

This exuberant confidence offered the media an irresistible contrast with the travails of the nation's beleaguered chief executive.
ABC news showed President Bush in the cabinet room, dismissing
"crazy rumors" that he was about to drop Vice President Quayle from
the ticket. Democratic nominee Clinton was then shown addressing

a huge crowd in St. Louis, drawing cheers when he contrasted his choice of Gore as running mate with Bush's selection of Quayle. On CBS, Dan Rather reported that Bush "had to put down talk that his reelection campaign is in retreat and in disarray"—which of course added to Bush's difficulties—while Richard Threlkeld announced that "Bill Clinton's campaign is now off to the best start of any Democrat in the last sixteen years." On NBC, Tom Brokaw reported that Bush is "a distant second and fading" while Andrea Mitchell asserted that Clinton's crowds have "exceeded anyone's expectations."

Embittered by this coverage and having little else in the way of a strategy, Republicans now decided that they too would attack the media, using their convention as a springboard for the assault. First, Vice President Quayle charged journalists with foisting "sleaze" on the American people by questioning Bush about an alleged extramarital affair. Motivating the questions, claimed Quayle—still smarting from the pain inflicted on him by the media in 1988—was "a desire to hurt the president and help Bill Clinton." The party's national chairman, Richard N. Bond, echoed Quayle's charge of bias. "We know who the media want to win this election," Bond said, "and I don't think it's George Bush and the American people." Later, at a meeting with *Washington Post* editors, Bond conceded that the GOP attacks were intended in part to soften up the media, much as Little League coaches yell at umpires in the hope, as Bond put it, that "maybe the ref will cut you a little slack on the next one."

Such feeble stratagems suggested the now desperate plight of the party that had been accustomed to dominating the media in the course of winning three presidential elections. Instead of a unified message that had been the hallmark of GOP success, the convention was marked by discord—conservative leaders such as Pat Buchanan delivered harsh, ideologically strident messages from the podium, and moderate leaders such as Jack Kemp fired back, scolding the conservatives.

In the absence of a coherent theme for his campaign, Bush himself attacked the press, a tactic which at least boosted the enthusiasm of the Republican party faithful. "Annoy the media," Mr. Bush cried with evident delight at a Montgomery, Alabama, rally, repeating a slogan from a banner being held aloft in the enthusiastic crowd. "They wouldn't know good news if it hit them in the face." Later that day, at another rally in a high school gym, Bush did not hesitate when a young journalism student asked him for advice. "Be objective," he shot back. Both remarks drew roars of approval, but these jabs at the media were more than applause lines. They were part of a broader White House effort to argue that the media were costing the GOP the election by refusing to report improvement in the economy.

Bush added a paragraph to his stump speech to make that point. "Have you heard this on television at night?" he asked his audiences. "That unemployment claims have gone down to the lowest in two years? Have you heard that inflation is down, that interest rates are down, that total employment is 93 percent, inflation 2.5 to 3 percent, home mortgages are 8 percent?"

Truth to tell, Bush had a point. The economy *was* improving, and the media's reporting of these hopeful indicators lacked the emphasis Bush would have liked. But it would take a long time for this slight betterment to be generally experienced among a bitter and hard-hit public. Given Bush's earlier passivity in the face of hard times, the voters had no confidence in the president's ability to keep the indicators headed up. The media could do little to alter that attitude.

Bush had company in his press bashing. Ross Perot, who redeclared his candidacy early in October, now spent a good part of his time on the stump lambasting the media for unfairness. At first, reporters gave Perot's renewed candidacy generally positive coverage, with stories that focused on his climb in the polls. But that changed when Perot told "60 Minutes" that the Bush campaign had plotted to disrupt his daughter's wedding. Headlines and commentators described Perot's behavior as "crazy," "loony," "zany," "bizarre," "peculiar," and "Perot-noia." NBC's Lisa Myers reported that at the computer firm Perot founded, lying was known as "Rossing."

Perot replied in kind, calling reporters "jerks" and "teenage boys" and declaring at a news conference, "I am sick and tired of you all questioning my integrity." Seeking to rebut press coverage that suggested he had no chance of winning the election, Perot aired a commercial telling his supporters: "You got to stop letting these folks in the press tell you you're throwing your vote away."

Some of his backers, however, intended to do just that. When I asked a New Jersey woman who said she was going to vote for Perot what sort of president she thought he would make, she gasped: "Oh my God, you don't think he can get elected, do you?"

The only real contest at this point was between Bush and Clinton. And the only hope that the Republicans had to offset the bleak economic conditions rested on the public's suspicions of Clinton. Trying to drive that point home in his convention acceptance speech, Bush pointed out that both he and his Democratic challenger promised change, but he advised Americans to ask themselves, "Who do you trust to make change work for you?"

"The biggest thing that's going to happen in the next seven weeks is that people are going to know a lot more about Clinton than they do now," Bush campaign pollster Fred Steeper told me in September after both conventions ended. But the Republicans were unable to tell voters much more about Clinton than they already knew. Some would never vote for him for these reasons; others had made their peace with Clinton because of what they already knew about Bush. In the abstract, the argument about trust seemed potent. But coming from the man who had instructed the country to "read my lips" the last time he ran for president, it became painfully hollow.

Distress over the economy overcame the public's anxieties about Clinton, allowing him to prevail over the media and over Bush. But the concerns and tensions that Clinton's candidacy had provoked did not disappear with the election. The campaign left a legacy of mutual suspicion between the new president and the media which shadowed his first term in office and the reelection campaign that followed.

1996: *Not the Russian Revolution*

✍ IN THE SPRING of 1995, as the media began to lay plans for the next presidential election, the landscape they surveyed was far stranger than any in recent memory. In the wake of the historic Republican midterm victory of 1994, the Democratic president seemed to have vanished from the national political scene while the Republicans made hay and headlines with their conservative revolution. When Clinton called a news conference in April 1995, only one of the three broadcast networks, CBS, chose to put it on the air—and he spent most of the time fielding questions about the Republican congressional agenda. Almost inevitably, he was asked point-blank about his own shrunken role in the national debate.

Not since Richard Nixon, in the midst of Watergate, insisted that he was not a crook had a president sounded so defensive at a press conference. "The president is relevant, especially an activist president," Clinton replied. "The Constitution gives me relevance; the power of our ideas gives me relevance; the record we have built up over the last two years and the things we're trying to do give me relevance."

But such talk seemed like whistling against the wind, with the Republicans, led by new House speaker Newt Gingrich very conspicuously in command on Capitol Hill. "You've done some things very well since we took over the Congress," the speaker told the president, when he and Clinton met at a Washington dinner that spring. "But now you have to face how hard this campaign is going to be. Right now, if I had to guess," Gingrich added, "I'd say your chances of winning are about one in three."

The president did not take umbrage at this gratuitous observation, or so Gingrich claimed when he later told me about their chat. Indeed, at that moment in political time, not many in Washington, certainly few journalists, would have had much ground for disagreeing with the speaker's assessment.

What no one—in the White House, in the rampant Republican majorities on Capitol Hill, or in the media—could guess was how dramatically the political scene would be transformed within the next year. Yet the seeds for this turnabout were already being sown as a result of miscalculations by the Republicans and blunders by the media.

The media's biggest mistake was inflating the importance of the Republican 1994 midterm victory. Yes, the takeover of Congress, particularly the House of Representatives, for the first time in forty years was dramatic. But the press transformed this political happening into an ideological watershed—portending a sea change among voters in their attitudes toward government and the two parties.

As far off base as the media were in this appraisal, their performance contravened two staples of criticism of the press. The extensive coverage of the implications of the 1994 elections undercut the claim that the press cared only about the horse-race aspects of politics. In the aftermath of the 1994 midterm vote, the press explored what was presumed to be substance—though they made too much of it. The media's behavior also contradicted the standard conservative criticism that the media are biased in favor of liberals. Most reporters, as some surveys suggest, may tend to vote Democratic and think liberal. But they cannot afford to let that inclination get in the way of their work. In early 1995, political journalists, casting their own biases aside, reacted as if the whole fabric of American politics had been rent asunder and then reassembled in a totally different pattern.

My own paper, the *Los Angeles Times*, was quick to read profound significance into the returns from barely 40 percent of the electorate when my editors inserted into a story under my byline the claim that the GOP victory signaled "a sharp turn away from the message of activist government on which president Clinton campaigned in 1992." How the editors knew this the story did not say, for the exit polls offered scant information to support such a sweeping judgment. Opinion surveys provided more evidence to suggest that what did the Democrats in was Clinton's failure to keep his promise to use government to improve living standards for middle-class and working-class families. These voters, either by staying home or defecting to the GOP, accounted for much of the Republican success in the midterm vote.

Nevertheless such nuances were ignored by most of the press, which insisted on elevating the conservative revolution, an oxymoronic fancy, to mythic proportions. For weeks after election day, headlines announced the GOP's confident assaults on the government establishment while timorous Democrats retreated in disarray: "Republicans Seek Sweeping Changes in House Rules," "Gingrich Comes Out Slugging with His Team," "GOP Blitzkrieg Shakes Capitol: Democrats Aghast as Pillars of U.S. Health Care Crack," "Hill's GOP Freshmen Poised for Historic Impact," "Democrats in Congress Seem Stuck in Denial Stage of Grief." Even into the fall, when the GOP uprising already showed signs of faltering, the press kept up its portentous drumbeat. As late as September the *Washington Post's* justly esteemed David Broder could write that the 104th Congress "will go down in history as one of the most significant in the last half-century," having inflicted upon the Democrats "a rout of historic proportions."

In leaping to their conclusions about the significance of the GOP takeover, the media were in large measure taken in by the rhetoric of Republican leaders. "They thought it was the Russian Revolution," said David Keene, a longtime Republican operative and chairman of the American Conservative Union. "And so they set expectations for the public and their own troops that were unrealistically high and led to disappointment and frustration."

Leading the charge was Gingrich, who made clear at the start that he intended to yield no ground. "I want to draw a distinction between two words," he said. "I am very prepared to cooperate with the Clinton administration. But I am not prepared to compromise."

As would become clear before long, such bombast was based on half-baked assumptions and sloppy reasoning, which the media conspicuously failed to challenge. Gingrich and his cohorts had sold themselves on the Contract with America. Republicans had unveiled this ten-point conservative manifesto as a sort of party platform during the campaign but had never got around to selling it to the public. Exit polls on election day showed that only about one in four voters even knew about the contract, and only half that number supported it—a piece of information that was rarely mentioned by the press.

But probably the basic fallacy, which the press accepted as underlying the 1994 vote, was the belief that voter discontent with Clinton's stewardship, as exhibited at the polls, could be channeled into support for drastic cutbacks in the federal government. As Republicans and the media would learn from the success of Pat Buchanan's candidacy when the presidential campaign began in 1996, voters' anger was not directed mainly at big government but more generally at other forces that seemed to dominate their lives, including big business.

To see the pitfalls in Gingrich's course, the Republicans and the media did not need to be clairvoyant. All they required was a sense of history, and fairly recent history at that. They could have recalled the Reagan era when GOP cost-cutters, in their determination to trim the school lunch program (perhaps the most popular single program in the entire federal budget), were inspired to label ketchup and pickle relish as substitutes for vegetables. The ploy would have allowed the government to avoid the expense of serving green beans or carrots to 26 million children in nearly 100,000 schools around the country. However much money that shift might have squeezed from the budget, once the Democrats and the media got hold of it, it touched off a national wave of indignation and ridicule which cost the GOP dearly.

As if that episode had never occurred, Gingrich and his co-revolutionaries in the House went after the school lunch program again twelve years later, and also tried to cut back Medicare, education, and environmental protection, all of which rubbed raw the nerves of middle-class voters. Although still caught up in the revolutionary spirit, newspapers and television networks reported enough about these instances of excessive conservative zeal that the first wave of public discontent with the new Republican order began to ripple. Asked in late March which danger they feared most—that Republicans would go too far in helping the rich and cutting needed services, or that the Democrats would go too far in preserving costly and wasteful government programs—by a margin of nearly two to one voters named Republican skimping as the biggest threat.

For the time being, though, the Republicans did not need to worry much about the media deflating the GOP's revolutionary balloon. Political journalists, demonstrating their deep-rooted fixation with celebrity and personality, had become absorbed with recently retired General Colin Powell, creating a presidential boom that had little connection with political reality. Although a complete novice in politics, having never so much as run for alderman, Powell earned rave reviews from journalists. ABC's normally tough-minded Sam Donaldson declared that the first black chairman of the Joint Chiefs of Staff "would make a good president and it would be good for the country. I think this man is extraordinary." *U.S. News & World Report,* in its second cover story on Powell in two years, declared: "He may have an extraordinary opportunity to try to forge a new centrist American coalition." After putting Powell on its cover twice in a few months, *Time* announced: "No other candidate can hope to match Powell's inspiring tale." The latter of two *Newsweek* cover stories seemed to sum up what was on the minds of all the media: "Can Colin Powell Save America?"

None of this was quite as spontaneous as it seemed. In his time on the national stage Powell had shown himself to be a master at the art of polishing his own image by cultivating the media, referring to the *Washington Post*'s famed Bob Woodward as "a friend," dropping in at a New Year's Eve party at the home of former *Washington Post* editor Benjamin Bradlee and his wife, Sally Quinn, giving a speech to a scholarship fund-raising dinner sponsored by the columnist Carl Rowan, and phoning Sam Donaldson to wish him well soon after he had undergone cancer surgery. Powell had deftly fueled speculation about his White House ambitions—tantalizing the media and the political community by disclaiming interest in a political career on one hand, and on the other refusing to close the door on the possibility. He disdained interviews, claiming he needed to spend the time working on his memoirs, but this was no handicap; the general benefited from the contrast between his own restraint and the clamorous striving of most of the acknowledged aspirants for the presidency. When his book, *My American Journey,* was published in September 1995 it was greeted with a crescendo of multimedia attention, assuring Powell's opus best-sellerdom and giving his presidential prospects another boost in the polls.

For all of that, anyone who listened to what Powell had to say about American politics soon realized it would be hard for him to fit in anywhere. He rejected the Democrats out of hand, saying they had run out of "intellectual energy." Some of his admirers urged him to run as an independent, but Powell did not wish to pursue a course that would involve "enormous difficulties." That left the GOP, or so it seemed. But the more Powell talked, the more that prospect too seemed to fade. His views on some subjects, notably his support for affirmative action, had little in common with the party's conservative core; conservative leaders in fact banded together to protest publicly the very idea of Powell seeking the GOP's presidential nomination.

Powell took a few weeks that fall to bask in the continued media spotlight, boost the sales of his book, and brood about his political future. By November he announced he would not run. The media's Powell binge was over.

Meanwhile another and more strident voice was making itself heard with increasing force on the hustings. This belonged to Malcolm S. Forbes, Jr., multimillionaire publishing magnate and ardent advocate of supply-side economic theory, known to his friends—of whom he seemed to be acquiring more every day—as Steve. In short order Forbes was able to demonstrate that a candidate with enough money can make the media seem irrelevant, at least for a time.

Forbes's candidacy got under way in the fall of 1995, in what at first seemed to be the traditional manner. The publisher stumped around the land trumpeting his theme of "hope, growth, and opportunity." And the media paid little attention to him. His announcement of candidacy rated no more than a wire story in the *New York Times.* The *Washington Post* reported that the reaction of the Washington political establishment to Forbes's entry into the race was "lighthearted amusement."

That was before Forbes launched a massive television blitz which for a time changed the shape of the contest for the GOP nomination, giving it a sharply negative cast. Of course some of Forbes's commercials simply plugged his proposal for a flat tax. "I say scrap the tax code," Forbes intoned in one ad. "Put in a low flat tax. It's simple, it's honest—and that's a big change for Washington." Or: "I'm Steve Forbes. If you take away the tax code, you take away the power of the Washington politicians."

A large segment of the Forbes video barrage, though, was made up of attacks on his rivals, particularly the front-runner in the race, Kansas senator Bob Dole. One sample: "Bob Dole—Washington Values, Steve Forbes—Conservative Values." The standard Forbes campaign technique was to take a grain of truth and expand it into a mountain of calumny. One commercial denounced Dole for putting off a Senate vote on the term-limit amendment; the Republican leader had done so only because term-limit backers had asked for the delay.

Heightening the impact of the commercials was their sheer volume. Forbes far outspent his rivals, particularly in the key states of Iowa and New Hampshire. In the last three months of 1995 Forbes spent more than $15 million on television, nearly as much as Dole had spent during the entire year on all the expenses of his campaign.

The media may not have been paying attention to Forbes, but the folks who watch television were. They could not help themselves. "Forbes is on the tube more than Dionne Warwick and the Psychic Network," complained Tom Rath, an adviser to another Republican contender, former Tennessee governor Lamar Alexander. The result of all this exposure could be seen in polls at the start of the election year that showed Forbes's stock rising fast.

The media now had no choice but to pay Forbes the attention his money had earned. Suddenly the publisher had replaced Colin Powell as the GOP phenom of the month. In January 1996 both *Time* and *Newsweek* put him on their covers. And he was getting almost as much free television time on interview shows as he was buying for his commercials. Unlike the homage paid to war hero Powell, however, the coverage of Forbes, who fit too readily for his own good into the stereotype of the ruthless tycoon, had a hard edge to it. "Are you trying to buy this nomination?" Cokie Roberts asked Forbes on ABC's "This Week with David Brinkley." In its cover story, *Time* predicted that Forbes's refusal to disclose his tax returns "was bound to fuel charges that he has something to hide."

Forbes's commercials, at least for the time being, were overwhelming the media's reservations. By late January this political tyro had stormed past Dole's other rivals and was threatening the frontrunner himself. For his part, Dole admitted that Forbes's attacks had stung. "Millions of dollars of negative advertising—it's terrible. I might not even vote for myself," he joked.

Actually Dole's predicament offered little to joke about. His advisers were worried, and not just about Forbes. The publisher's rise had been so swift and unexpected that they could not be sure what if anything could be done to stop him. At the same time, and of more fundamental concern, the national political climate once so favorable to the Republican cause had deteriorated as a result of Democratic success in the image war with the Republican congressional leadership over the budget battle.

This was a story at first largely neglected by the media, or at least by the national media. In Washington the pundits of the press were preoccupied with Clinton's strategy of "triangulation," crafted by his quasi-Republican adviser Dick Morris as part of an effort to maintain and establish his image as a New Democrat who had broken with the traditional shibboleths of his party. The success of triangulation depended upon Clinton, who represented the apex of the triangle, playing off the other two sides, the Republicans and the congressional Democrats, against each other to his own advantage.

While the national media tracked such distractions, congressional Democrats, feeling themselves betrayed by their party's president, pursued their own strategy, dubbed E^2M^2. This was to depict the Republicans as enemies of the environment, education, Medicare, and Medicaid. It was implemented by dramatizing Republican budget-slashing efforts in their congressional districts, through local newspapers and television. The Democrats' approach worked so well that even Clinton joined in, vetoing the GOP tax and spending cuts that would have decimated a number of federal programs cherished by the middle class, notably Medicare. Nevertheless the Republicans pressed their case. When the deadline passed without agreement on a new budget, the federal government in effect shut down for the longest period in its history. Republicans reasoned that Clinton would get blamed, but they were wrong. As newspapers and television carried word that Yosemite and Grand Canyon national parks had been forced to close, and that federally backed home loans were drying up, polls showed that a wide margin of resentful middle-class voters found the Republicans at fault. After all, as the leaders of the GOP revolution had proudly told everyone, they had taken charge in Washington.

Soon thereafter Gingrich's forces backed down on the budget, and the government went back to work. But the episode proved to be another headache for front-runner Dole. Having already been battered by Steve Forbes's commercials, Dole, who as the chief Senate Republican shared with Gingrich the leadership of GOP forces in Congress, had to contend with fallout from the budget fiasco.

When Dole's lack of a coherent message, and voter backlash against Forbes's attack commercials, created an opportunity for an underdog, conservative columnist Pat Buchanan promptly exploited it. Buchanan received an important though certainly unintended boost from Texas senator Phil Gramm, his chief rival for conservative support. Gramm set himself up as the big loser in the expectations game by predicting that he would easily win the Louisiana caucuses, which in 1996 took on extra importance because they had moved ahead of Iowa on the election calendar. Such characteristic braggadocio made Gramm the least favorite candidate of most reporters, who took their revenge by faithfully recording his overbearing demeanor, a style particularly ill-suited to the retail politics of the early contests.

In January, on a visit to Robie's general store, a campaign landmark in the New Hampshire town of Hookset, Gramm agreed to a game of checkers with the seventy-seven-year-old proprietress. TV cameras rolled and onlookers crowded around for a better look at this charming vignette in front of the store's potbellied stove. It did not last long. On the second move Gramm double-jumped his opponent. Ten minutes later the senator walked off triumphant, as pleased as if he had just vanquished one of his presidential rivals.

"Senator, you *beat* her," Gramm's shocked New Hampshire coordinator, James Courtovich, pointed out as the campaign bus pulled away.

"If someone wants to play checkers with me, I'm going to play checkers," Gramm replied.

This Vince Lombardi approach to presidential campaigning did not help Gramm in Louisiana, where he lost badly to Buchanan in a stunning upset. The press was thus able to declare him "bruised and battered," as New Hampshire's WMUR-TV put it, since Gramm himself had promised victory. The Texan promptly went out on a limb again, saying he would quit the race unless he finished among the top three in Iowa. When it became clear that such an outcome was unlikely, Gramm started hedging. But it was too late; he finished fifth, and that finished him.

Nothing so became his candidacy as the announcement of his departure, in which he provided a hint of self-deprecating humor that had hitherto been foreign to him. "When the voters speak, I listen," Gramm said, "particularly when the voters are saying someone else's name."

Buchanan, who had shrewdly allowed Gramm to shape expectations, got a huge boost from Louisiana and emerged as the real victor in Iowa, only a point behind Dole who limped in first. Still the media were slow to grasp the significance of the Buchanan candidacy, just as they were tardy in catching on to the issue that provided its underlying force—middle-class discontent with the economy.

This continuing and profoundly important story was almost totally ignored by the major media, with one notable exception. Early in 1995 the *New York Times* had published a memorable seven-part series, "The Downsizing of America," on the economic anguish that persisted long after the end of George Bush's recession. Later that year, more than three years after the recession had ended, the *Times* published a national "economic insecurity" survey which showed that a considerable majority of Americans thought the country was headed down the wrong track, that twice as many thought conditions were getting worse as believed they were improving, and that more than half thought it unlikely their children would be able to enjoy a better life than they did.

But few other newspapers and networks made much of an effort to examine the sharp-edged anxieties that had become part of American life at the close of the twentieth century. Certainly few journalists, even those on the *Times,* sought to connect the economic distress with the political campaign.

When it was "issue time" at a press conference or an interview, the questions asked had to do with all the old standbys—abortion, welfare reform, street crime—none of which had as much direct impact on the lives of the voters as the economy that was not working for millions of middle-class Americans. For the better off it was working fine, and there were numbers to demonstrate their satisfaction, numbers which convinced the media that the whole country was thriving. Corporate profits soared. The Dow Jones average went through the roof. And millions of new jobs were being created, as the Clinton White House never tired of boasting. What the media seemed to overlook was that the pay for these new jobs was far below that of the jobs that had somehow disappeared in the new economy of the past ten or fifteen years. "Our people say, 'I know there are eight million new jobs—I got three of them,'" Andy Stern, president of the Service Employees Union, told me.

So the American Dream was in extremis, but few in the media or among the presidential contenders seemed to notice.

Patrick J. Buchanan did take note, though hardly anyone in the press paid attention to him at the start of the 1996 campaign. Despite his strong early challenge to Bush in 1992, most reporters dismissed him as a hard-line right-winger obsessed with such "social issues" as abortion and pornography. Some also suspected that his main reason for running was to promote his television career and boost his speaking fees.

It was true that Buchanan yielded to no one in his defense of what he chose to view as traditional values. But he had another cause too, which he had discovered in 1992 in the course of challenging George Bush in the midst of the recession, and this was the economic grievances of the middle class. Buchanan was one of the few to realize that while the recession had officially ended, some of its causes and symptoms lingered on. And this understanding gave unexpected vitality to his candidacy.

While most in the press corps concentrated on Dole, Forbes, and Gramm, Buchanan found a fertile field for his rhetoric of discontent in Louisiana, where cheap foreign competition was crippling efforts at economic recovery in the state's textile industry. "We conservatives believe in free enterprise, we believe in the values of family and community," Buchanan told his campaign rallies. "But when go-go global capitalism is uprooting entire communities and families, I ask conservatives to figure out what it is we're trying to conserve."

This appeal gave Buchanan his stunning victory over Phil Gramm, bolstered his campaign in Iowa, and helped build his mo-

mentum in New Hampshire. By that time even his opponents realized that feisty Pat was on to something by hammering away at economic insecurity. "We did not get a single question about flag
burning or school prayer," Lamar Alexander's man, Tom Rath, told
me after his candidate had staged an issues forum in Concord. "We
got asked about tax policy and employment policy. Every question
was about the economy."

Dole reeled before the Buchanan onslaught. When the senator
did try to address the economic anxieties of the middle class, he lent
himself to ridicule. "I didn't realize that jobs and trade and what
makes America work would become a big issue," Dole declared as he
toured a factory on the eve of the Granite State vote. The candor of
his statement was all too painfully obvious.

Meanwhile Buchanan was making hay and having fun by derid-
ing the leaders of the party. "We've got them all on the run," he joy-
fully told his followers in the closing hours of the New Hampshire
campaign. "All the knights and barons will be riding into the castle,
pulling up the drawbridge. And all the peasants are coming with
pitchforks after them."

The peasants turned out in force on primary day, enough to give
Buchanan a narrow victory over Dole that stunned the political
world. "We're going to give voice to the voiceless," Buchanan told his
supporters, who were so numerous that fire marshals had to turn
hundreds away from his victory celebration in Londonderry.

But Buchanan's success gave Dole's campaign something it had
previously lacked—a purpose, which was to save the party from Buchanan. Dole instructed Republican primary voters that they must
decide "if we are the party of fear or of hope, if we are angry about
the present or optimistic about the future."

Over the years as a talk-show host, columnist, and then a vehe-
ment advocate on the campaign trail, Buchanan had given various
groups many reasons for indignation. He embarrassed even some of
his conservative allies when he dubbed AIDS nature's "awful retribu-
tion" against homosexuals; questioned whether the bombing of abortion clinics was any worse an offense than the act of abortion itself;

and verged on anti-Semitism with his criticism of supporters of Israel.

But what particularly outraged and threatened the GOP hierarchy were Buchanan's nationalist and populist themes, such as his calls for retaliatory tariffs and his denunciations of corporate America. These blows struck directly at the economic interests that formed the backbone of the GOP. Now these leaders mobilized all their resources to crush Buchanan's insurgency.

"We didn't understand the level of fear that the Buchanan candidacy created in mainstream Republican leaders," said Tom Rath, whose candidate, Alexander, struggled to survive in the race after his own third-place finish in New Hampshire. "They felt that his success would be damaging to their position as ranking Republicans. And they also thought it would mean electoral disaster."

This response was only to be expected. More striking was the reaction to Buchanan of most of the media, whose thinly disguised disapproval of this obstreperous candidate to a remarkable degree mimicked the views of the GOP establishment. Just as striking was the contrast between the post–New Hampshire Buchanan coverage and the treatment given other insurgents who had achieved unexpected success. George McGovern and Gary Hart among the Democrats, and George Bush among Republicans, in his first presidential run in 1980, had all enjoyed at least a brief moment of glory while the media celebrated the virtues that had brought them into prominence. Not so for Pat Buchanan. He finally got the media's attention, but the media seemed determined not to praise him but to bury him.

From the cover of *Newsweek* a grim-faced Buchanan stared out at voters under the headline: "Preaching Fear. Why America Is Listening." *U.S. News & World Report* did portray him as smiling, but the headline was ominous: "The Loose Buchanan. The GOP's Panic Attack." *Time* refused to award its cover to Buchanan, but a banner line called attention to the story inside: "The Case Against Buchanan," which reported that the New Hampshire victor "is under growing fire."

A good many of the journalists involved in these stories knew Buchanan personally from his long years in Washington dating back to the Nixon presidency, but the relationship did nothing to soften their treatment. Some, in fact, reacted in a way that suspiciously suggested envy. "He's insufferable," Fred Barnes, a columnist for the conservative *Weekly Standard,* said as the first New Hampshire votes showed Buchanan in the lead. "Come about ten o'clock tonight he's going to be even more insufferable. I like Pat personally, but he's suddenly gotten carried away with his own rhetoric."

Others objected to Buchanan on ideological grounds. "There are an awful lot of journalists who find what Buchanan says utterly abhorrent, but they have been giggling along with him," said Joe Klein, political correspondent for *Newsweek,* who had been unmasked as the anonymous author of *True Colors,* the novel that romanticized Clinton's 1992 presidential candidacy. "Part of every one of us is a theater critic, and he is appealing to that part. But the policy wonk in me is appalled."

The ardently pro-Israel *New York Times* columnist William Safire, who once worked side by side with Buchanan on behalf of Richard Nixon, calculated on "Meet the Press" that Buchanan was an "extremist" whose anti-Semitism would rank at a level four or five on a scale that put Adolf Hitler as a ten and Nation of Islam Muslim leader Louis Farrakhan as a seven.

A few reporters dissented in print from the anti-Buchanan barrage, among them Tom Oliphant of the *Boston Globe.* Fed up with stories tarring Buchanan as racist because a campaign aide had appeared at forums that also featured white supremacists, Oliphant accused his colleagues of invoking a time-dishonored tactic to smear Buchanan—guilt by association. "It has been open season" on Buchanan, Oliphant charged, "with an ethically challenged press now fanning the flames."

But if Oliphant hit back at Buchanan's critics, Buchanan lacked anyone who could defend him against his own worst enemy, himself. After New Hampshire "Pat got sort of bombastic," acknowledged Buchanan's Louisiana media consultant, Roy Fletcher. To say the least. Following his victory in New Hampshire, Buchanan's spokesman, Greg Mueller, told me that he thought his candidate should have stressed his kinder, gentler themes, which Buchanan had labeled "the conservatism of the heart." Instead his rhetoric sent chills through the Republican establishment and their middle-class constituents. "We are taking back our party as a prelude to taking back our country," Buchanan thundered on the night of his New Hampshire triumph. "We do not apologize for the fact that we're going to take control of our national destiny."

Even more disturbing was Buchanan's bellicose behavior. In Arizona, which held its primary a week after New Hampshire, Buchanan at times behaved something like a reincarnation of Emiliano Zapata, an unlikely paradigm for a Republican politician. He stalked around in a black hat, at one point waving a shotgun over his head and warning, "These aren't just for shooting ducks." The *Sturm und Drang* he generated made him seem more like a rabble-rouser than a tribune of the hard-pressed middle class, drained his momentum, and assured the nomination of Dole who, aided by his bounteous campaign treasury and the active support of GOP leaders around the country, ground the remaining opposition into the dust.

The media was not chiefly to blame for the Buchanan flop after New Hampshire. His presidential bid expired from self-inflicted wounds. But press coverage left Buchanan vulnerable to attacks from his foes, tended to exaggerate his missteps, and overall damaged his ability to compete against Dole. More thoughtful reportage might have helped Buchanan survive longer and would certainly have changed the political debate if not the outcome of the contest. More important, the press fell down in its obligation to the public it is supposed to serve by missing the import of Buchanan's candidacy and what it revealed about the country's anxiety over the economy, which was widely assumed to be thriving.

Following Buchanan's New Hampshire victory, leaders of both parties swung into action on Capitol Hill, seeking to push measures that responded to the economic anxiety of voters he had won over with his populist rhetoric. Arizona senator John McCain spoke for

Democrats and Republicans when he declared that Buchanan had "identified a serious problem" in American society. "I violently disagree with his solutions," McCain said. "But what he has done is a significant contribution. It was not being addressed by either party or the president."

But when Buchanan's candidacy collapsed, the economic anxiety issue seemed to disappear from the political and journalistic radar screen. With no candidate on the hustings applying pressure, the leaders of both parties went back to catering to those interests that normally have first call on their energies. As for the media, they went back to covering what the leaders did.

Just as the story of media coverage of the 1996 Republican race hinges on might-have-beens, so does the media's role in the general election. Buchanan's success had demonstrated the political potential of voter concern about economic inequities and uncertainties. Had the media paid attention to these pockmarks in the rosy landscape the Clinton administration painted, the Republicans might have gained a purchase on the issue. But Dole, unlike Buchanan, was incapable of taking advantage of economic anxieties.

Dole did have another weapon in his issues arsenal—welfare reform, but this was muzzled by divisions within his own party, another story largely neglected by the media. Intraparty divisions shaped the Democratic response to the welfare issue too, giving political journalists an opportunity not only to help the public understand how politics really works but to show how political decisions are shaped by the two-century-old structure of checks and balances devised by James Madison. Madison's purpose was to guard against the tyranny of either the executive or legislature by assuring that these two branches of government would almost always be at each other's throats. As a consequence he established an institutional rivalry that makes it hard for political parties to function in harmony.

The way the welfare issue played out in the 1996 campaign demonstrated the Madisonian system operating at full efficiency. The stakes were high because Clinton in his 1992 campaign had promised "to end welfare as we know it." But he had already vetoed two welfare reforms pushed by the Republican Congress on grounds that they were too harsh. Now the latest Republican proposal also seemed severe, so much so that it would injure key Democratic constituencies among minorities and in the cities. This meant Clinton faced a choice between breaking his pledge to reform welfare or causing himself trouble within his own party.

That was good news for Bob Dole. "We always felt that the most important part of our issue cluster on values was going to be on welfare," Scott Reed, Dole's campaign manager, told me after the election. "Clinton had made statements that he would end welfare as we know it. He was very vulnerable on that issue. Our point to the House and the Senate was, 'Why let him off the hook?' We wanted them to stick it to Clinton and put the failure of welfare reform on his ticket."

But a good many House Republicans, having looked at the polls, had already given up on Dole's chances of winning the White House and were more concerned with protecting their own seats. Nearly one hundred Republican House members, determined to pass a measure that stood some chance of becoming law, signed a letter calling on GOP leaders to offer Clinton a compromise bill that he could sign and that they could brag about to their constituents. "The House and Senate were in a survival stage," Reed acknowledged. "They both feared a Democratic sweep. So they put their selfish interests ahead of the nominee."

"Bob Dole's running his race," was the way Republican Representative Jim Bunn, a freshman from Oregon, put it. "I'm running mine." Somewhere James Madison must have smiled.

Largely because of the welfare compromise, Clinton turned the week following the Republican convention into a triumph for his campaign—and a disaster for Dole. The president signed welfare reform and two other new laws on which Republican lawmakers, desperate to save their jobs, had no alternative but to share credit with him in order to impress their own constituents.

But the enactment of welfare reform, even its compromised version, sharply divided Clinton's own party. Half the Democrats in the

House and Senate, including the party leaders in both bodies, voted against the welfare bill that the president signed. Andrew Stern, president of the Service Employees Union, whose members help to form the backbone of what remains of the traditional Democratic party, warned that the new law would "devastate the lives of welfare recipients and hard-working people," adding, "This is a sad day for workers across the country."

Press coverage of welfare reform enactment focused on the merits of the legislation, which were certainly significant. The drastic changes encompassed by the new law raised questions that would take years to resolve. While some publications dealt with the political cross-pressures that led to the compromise on the Hill and to White House approval of the measure, they generally failed to spell out the broader implications of this maneuvering.

Enactment of welfare reform was bad news for Democratic challengers who hoped to unseat Republican incumbents by branding the 104th Congress as extremist. The credibility of that argument was badly damaged by the Democratic president literally giving his stamp of approval to Congress's arguably most extreme accomplishment.

But frustration among Democrats was of little benefit to Dole. The compromise on welfare left the Republican standard-bearer with just one more card to play—the character issue. Here again, he might have done better with an assist from the media. Clinton's tendency to self-indulgence and his resistance to accepting responsibility when things went wrong had become evident in his 1992 campaign for the presidency and soon manifested themselves when he entered the White House. First came Travelgate, the high-handed dismissal of veteran White House travel office workers; then, as a sequel to the furor over Gennifer Flowers, came the Paula Jones sexual harassment lawsuit. Meanwhile Whitewater, the rubric for the various connivings by the president and the First Lady stemming from an Arkansas real estate venture, raised more questions about the Clintons' past conduct than the First Couple seemed willing to answer. These controversies—and, just as important, Clinton's unwillingness to deal with them directly—demonstrated what veteran journalist Elizabeth Drew described as the president's "seemingly unshakable tendency to walk away from responsibility for things that had gone wrong. . . . And worse to put these things in self-pitying terms; that people didn't understand him . . . or that others did bad things to him."

This judgment, which many of Drew's colleagues undoubtedly would have endorsed, certainly seemed relevant to Clinton's performance as a political and moral leader. Yet the media, though they dutifully covered Clinton's various embarrassments, were rarely able to explain to the American people why they should care. "There is a lot of drip-drip-drip that there's something wrong with Clinton," said Dole adviser Don Sipple about the press coverage. "But it's hard to get a handle on it. Voters have to see a consequence for them before it becomes a relevant, salient issue."

With the media unable to make that point clear to the voters, it was up to Dole to get the voters to understand. He did not have an easy task. Character is a complex matter, covering far more than moral behavior. To most people it includes empathy as well as integrity. And when it came to empathy, as Democrats liked to point out, Bill Clinton overwhelmed Bob Dole. Asked in a national poll which presidential candidate they would choose to care for their children, voters favored Clinton over Dole by nearly two to one.

Dole's best chance for raising the character issue and perhaps derailing the Clinton bandwagon came—and swiftly passed—during the first televised debate of the campaign. Did Dole believe, the moderator Jim Lehrer asked midway through that confrontation, that there were relevant differences between him and Clinton "in the more personal areas?" For a moment anxious Democrats everywhere held their breaths while Republican pulses raced with joy. The "character issue," the jugular of Clinton's campaign, had been exposed, and Dole had been handed a dagger. He only needed to drive it home.

But Democrats need not have fretted. Dole had no such intention. "I don't like to get into personal matters," he said. "As far as I'm concerned, this is a campaign about issues."

Scolded by his aides, Dole tried to revive the character issue in the second debate ten days later. But his scattershot sniping at the president failed to demonstrate Clinton's unsuitability for the Oval Office.

As it became known during the campaign, Dole had his own area of vulnerability about character, which probably helped to explain his awkwardness in dealing with the issue. That summer his staff had learned that at least two publications, *Time* and the *Washington Post*, had uncovered a sixty-three-year-old woman named Meredith Roberts, an editor for a Washington trade association, who had told them that she and Dole had carried on an affair from 1968 through 1970. At the time Dole was still married to his first wife, whom he later divorced before he wed Elizabeth Hanford Dole, better known as Liddy, who herself briefly ran for president in 2000.

Desperate to prevent publication, Dole's handlers met with the top editors at *Time* and the *Post*, arguing that since the affair had been over for nearly thirty years it was irrelevant to Dole's fitness for the presidency. But Dole's own rhetoric could be used to refute their arguments. After Gary Hart had dropped out of the 1988 presidential race, Dole observed: "Once you declare you're a candidate, all bets are off. Everything up to that point is fair game." More recently, in 1994, Dole had asserted that the personal lives of politicians—including marital infidelity—were "fair game." Besides, had not the Dole campaign been claiming that Dole's character was superior to Clinton's?

At the *Post* an intense debate raged over the story. Bob Woodward, who had helped bring down Richard Nixon, and many other reporters argued that Dole had made trust and character an issue. Thus adultery, even from the distant past, was relevant. But the *Post*'s editors shied away from this controversy. "The *Post* and its owners, the Graham family, did not want to get into the business of investigating the dalliances of presidential candidates," *Newsweek* (which is also owned by the *Post*) reported—though this was a different stance from that taken by the *Post* in 1984 when the paper aggressively poked into Gary Hart's extramarital entanglements.

Time ultimately reached the same decision. Managing editor Walter Isaacson said he "wasn't comfortable" with the story, particularly that late in the campaign. "The bar is a little higher a couple of weeks before the election because everything is more explosive," he said.

The *National Enquirer* also learned about the story. After offering to pay Meredith Roberts and being turned down, the *Enquirer* decided to publish it anyway. But before the weekly came off the press, the *New York Daily News*, the nation's largest-circulation newspaper, beat the *Enquirer* to the punch with its own account. At this point the *Washington Post*, the paper that had triggered Watergate but had waited almost a month to publish its first story about Paula Jones's sexual harassment complaint against Clinton, and which had decided against publishing the story of Roberts's relationship with Dole, fell back on one of the oldest ploys in journalism. Instead of reporting the story directly, the *Post* managed to get it into print indirectly. It noted that Dole had been questioned about the *Daily News* story by a reporter as he left his hotel on his way to his campaign motorcade. As the *Post* reported it, Dole, in a sour mood anyway because of the final collapse of his presidential hopes, glared at his interrogator, waved his arms dismissively, and snapped, "You're worse than they are."

It seemed not by coincidence that on that same day Dole launched his fiercest attack on the news media. He accused the press of giving a free daily "transfusion" to the president by refusing to investigate scandals involving foreign campaign donations, though the media had unearthed that story in the first place and continued to pursue it. In fact many Democrats blamed the flood of stories about fund-raising abuses with destroying their once-favorable prospects for regaining control of the House of Representatives.

In any event, Dole's tirade served as more than simply a venting of frustration by a losing candidate. By blasting the press for bias, even though his attacks were seemingly unrelated to the disclosure about his own personal life, he served notice on nervous editors of what they could expect if they were to follow the lead of the *Inquirer* and the *Daily News*. Whether because of Dole's tactics or not, the story received relatively minor attention.

Andrew Rosenthal, Washington editor of the *New York Times*, summed up the rationale for most in the media who ignored the story. "This was a story about an alleged affair that happened thirty years ago. Big deal."

But as Howard Kurtz, media analyst for the *Washington Post* pointed out, other behavior from the past had been considered relevant in campaign stories—such as Bill Clinton's use of marijuana in 1969, and his efforts to avoid the draft. And during the 1992 campaign President Bush had tried to make an issue of Clinton's 1969 student visit to Moscow, suggesting that it was a sign of disloyalty to his country.

The handling of the Dole story by the media reflected the same murkiness about the relevance of personal behavior to political performance that had appeared during Clinton's 1992 campaign for the White House. That irresolution again surfaced as a new sex scandal tarnished Clinton in his second term and as political journalists and candidates wrestled with the character issue in the first contest for the White House in the new millennium.

TEN

2000: *Seduction on the Straight-talk Express*

⚑ IN MIDWINTER OF 1999, while the media were gearing up for the start of the 2000 presidential campaign in the two early battle-ground states of Iowa and New Hampshire, the first votes of the struggle for the White House were cast in an unlikely venue, the floor of the U.S. Senate. In that hallowed chamber on February 12, 1999, a verdict of acquittal brought the impeachment trial of Bill Clinton to an end. Few political journalists comprehended the full significance of the day's proceedings.

The stories written and aired that day concentrated naturally enough on the fact that Clinton had been acquitted by a healthy margin. The president's opponents could do no better than fifty votes for conviction, when they needed a two-thirds majority of sixty-seven. And many stories predicted that the Republicans would suffer dire consequences for having sailed against the wind of public sentiment on the impeachment.

The *Washington Post* sounded the alarm even before the vote. "The impeachment of President Clinton has inflamed long-standing ideological divisions within the Republican Party, weakened the party's image among independent and swing voters and now threatens to inflict long-term political damage," warned two of the *Post*'s top political writers, Thomas B. Edsall and Dan Balz. The *Boston*

Globe's political correspondent Michael Kranish, a couple of days after the vote, depicted Senate Republicans who had been "listening to the impeachment trial as they watched their public approval ratings plummet," and now were struggling for a way "to rebuild the tattered party."

To be sure, many Americans did resent the unyielding partisanship of House Republican leaders and the heavy-handedness of special counsel Kenneth Starr. And most were opposed to forcing Clinton out of the White House, particularly given the booming economy and the generally satisfied public mood. But the fact that Americans did not wish to risk upsetting the apple cart of national well-being by ditching their duly elected president did not mean they had been untouched by the disclosures of his private conduct and by the ugly public controversy that resulted. Indeed, the exposure of Clinton's behavior had a far broader impact on the public than most of the press first realized, setting off a reaction that would reverberate through the long campaign to choose his successor.

The public's concern was a point understood by both Republicans and Democrats in the Senate, as demonstrated by their conduct on the day of the acquittal roll call. In addition to the fifty senators who voted for Clinton's conviction on the charge of obstruction of justice, another thirty-two signed on to a censure resolution—blocked by a filibuster threat from reaching the floor—which stated that by his conduct the president had "brought shame and dishonor" to himself and to his office, and had "violated the trust of the American people." And afterward many rose on the Senate floor to make individual statements of condemnation. All told, eighty-two Senators, more than four-fifths of the membership, went on record in one form or another to denounce the president's conduct.

The media's failure to grasp the import of the Senate action was part of a pattern of cumulative miscalculation that led to confusing and misleading coverage of the 2000 contest. This erratic behavior may not have altered the outcome of the campaign, so far as who won and who did not. But the press performance contributed to the befuddlement of the electorate, making it harder for voters to evaluate the rival contenders and the arguments they made to support their candidacy. The flaws in press coverage had little or nothing to do with the usual suspect—ideological bias. Instead they reflected the standard syndrome of political journalism—competitive pressures, superficial thinking, and the zest for dramatization, much of it tinged with a misunderstanding of the character issue.

The media's difficulty with the character issue had to do largely with their dependence on and confusion over the polls. Journalists tended to accept too readily survey data that seemed to suggest that voters cared little about presidential character, a finding that required close and skeptical analysis. Contradicting the notion that the public totally discounted the Lewinsky scandal, a massive *Washington Post* survey, in collaboration with Harvard University and the Henry J. Kaiser Family Foundation, indicated that about half the country believed that beyond his job performance, the president had a "greater responsibility" to set "an example with his personal life."

Not many months after the Senate voted on impeachment, the character issue began to appear on the presidential campaign trail in ways the media could not ignore. It was the candidates themselves, namely the two front-runners in each party, Republican George W. Bush and Democrat Al Gore, who pushed character to the front because they could not help themselves. Regardless of what the press wrote or what the polls said, they sensed that character would be a major force in the making of the president in 2000.

Even before the official start of his candidacy, when Bush and I had talked during his successful campaign for reelection as governor of Texas, he made plain that he intended to give his campaign for the White House a strong moral tone and thus take advantage of public disillusionment with President Clinton. Once Bush made his official announcement, he promised to usher in "a new responsibility era" during which "each American must understand that we are responsible for the decisions that each of us makes in life." In his very first campaign foray into New Hampshire, Bush declared: "I think it's important for any of us who assume high office to understand that when we put our hand on the Bible, that we're swearing not only to

uphold the laws of the land, but that we are swearing to uphold the
dignity of the office to which we've been elected." As the cameras
clicked he added, "It is a pledge I made to the voters of Texas and a
pledge that I have upheld, so help me God."

In making such lofty declarations, Bush sought to distract attention from his past, when by his own account he drank more than was
good for him and reportedly strayed from the straight and narrow in
other ways, possibly by snorting cocaine. But given his emphasis on
morality and character, reporters naturally pressed Bush about vague
but persistent allegations that he had used drugs in his younger
days—as they had once struggled to confront Clinton about his sexual behavior, ultimately without much more success.

Initially Bush brushed off such questions, calling them irrelevant. "You know what happens, somebody floats a rumor and it
causes you to ask a question," Bush responded to one such query in
the summer of 1999, a year in advance of the nominating conventions. "And that's the game in American politics, and I refuse to play
it," he added, his voice rising with irritation. "That is a game, and I
refuse to play."

Did he think such rumors were "being planted"?

"Do I think they are being planted? I know they are being
planted," he shot back. "And they are ridiculous and they're absurd
and the people of America are sick and tired of this kind of politics
and I am not participating."

That was the way he had been dealing with such questions since
he first ran for governor in 1994, refusing to say if he had ever used
illegal drugs, often trying to laugh the matter off by replying, "When
I was young and irresponsible, I was young and irresponsible." But
as time wore on, the humor in that riposte came to seem increasingly lame, and the press grew more persistent.

The *Dallas Morning News'* resourceful chief political correspondent, Sam Attlesey, brought the situation to a head when he found a
new way of asking about drug use. The question, as Attlesey framed
it, was whether Bush would insist that appointees to a Bush administration be required to answer standard FBI background questions

about drug use. And further, could Bush himself meet that standard, which required that applicants had not used drugs within the past seven years?

This was one question Bush realized he could not duck, because it applied specifically and concretely to what he might do if he were president. "That is a relevant question to ask," he said. "It is a very good question." Yes indeed, Bush was glad to say, he could meet that standard.

But Bush's aides quickly pointed out to him that he could not let the matter rest there. His response had left open the possibility that he might have used drugs as recently as seven years ago, or well into his forties, which would contradict one of the basic premises of his campaign—that he had sown all his wild oats as a young man. So the very next day Bush expanded his original denial, now claiming that not only could he pass the background check and the standards applied to the Clinton White House, but he could have passed the more stringent standard, demanding no drug use within fifteen years, that had been in force when his father was inaugurated president in 1989. That answer effectively ruled out drug use since 1974, when Bush was twenty-eight.

Nevertheless Bush had not really made full disclosure. He refused to answer other questions about his use of illegal drugs before age twenty-eight, questions that senior government employees seeking security clearances are required to answer. "I am going to tell people I made mistakes and that I have learned from my mistakes," he said. "And if they like it, I hope they give me a chance. And if they don't like it, they can go find somebody else to vote for."

All in all, the Bush people were pleased with themselves after this fracas. "We're actually better off now than we were forty-eight hours ago, because we've now pushed the story back a quarter of a century and demonstrated that Governor Bush will not ask anyone who serves in his administration to meet a standard that he is not able to meet himself," claimed Ralph Reed, a GOP strategist and Bush adviser. Moreover Reed contended that Bush had gained points with the public by in effect learning from the example of President Clinton not to allow himself to be thrown off course by the storm of scandal. "You can keep your head down and plow through it," he said, "and after you have, you're a stronger candidate because people see you're not going to be knocked out by it."

Bolstering Bush's determination not to respond to further questions was a poll for CNN and *Time* which showed that more than four of five of those interviewed believed that even if Bush had used cocaine in his twenties, it should not disqualify him for the presidency. All this served to provide ammunition to media supporters of Clinton such as *New York Times* columnist Frank Rich. "The best place a candidate can be in 2000," Rich told his readers,"is in opposition to the fulminating moralists in public life, whether those of the press or of Mr. Bush's own party. Bill Clinton's bipartisan legacy is this: Given the choice between scolds and scamps, the country opts for scamps."

The trouble with this argument, apart from its frivolousness, is that not even Bush believed it. Had he accepted the notion of "scamp" appeal, he would not have tried to stake out the moral high ground for himself. It was not the job of the press to prove that Bush had used drugs illegally. And even if he had done so, that conduct by itself would not necessarily disqualify him for the presidency. But it was the press's responsibility to remind voters that Bush seemed to want to have things both ways. On the one hand he was determined to travel the high road of morality, urging Americans to accept responsibility for their own behavior. On the other hand he refused to conform to that standard by owning up to his own past conduct. After all, cocaine use is a felony in every state. And Bush supported Texas legislation to jail persons for possession of a single gram of cocaine or less.

Bush's unwillingness to accept accountability seemed to be obscured by another torrent of polling results with dubious significance, reminiscent of the data on the political consequences of the Lewinsky scandal. For example, a majority interviewed in one poll believed that reporters should not be asking Bush about cocaine use. But reporters who frequently, and justly, criticize politicians for blindly following polling data should surely set a better example. While it is not the business of journalism to gain the approval of public opinion, it is important for journalists to have credibility and a measure of respect if their work is not to be drained of much of its meaning. But establishing credibility does not mean obeying the whim of the public as hinted at by the polls. Rather, in this case the road to credibility was to do a better job of explaining to the public why questions asked of Bush about his drug use were, to use one of the candidate's favorite words, "relevant."

Gore, like Bush, had to face character problems from his past. Heavily involved in the fund-raising excesses of Clinton's 1996 re-election campaign, he had to defend himself for attending a political gathering at a Buddhist temple in Los Angeles where money was raised, then for making dozens of fund-raising phone calls from his White House office—barely skirting a federal law that banned that sort of activity. Gore said he did not realize that the meeting in the temple was a fund-raiser. As for the phone calls, he famously contended—in a disastrous press conference—that there was "no controlling legal authority" prohibiting the phone calls, repeating that legalistic phrase so often that he made himself a laughingstock. The vice president got a huge break when the Justice Department decided that the charges against him did not merit investigation by an independent counsel, a probe that well might have wrecked his presidential ambitions. Afterward Gore avoided defending or explaining his conduct, apparently concluding that his best course was to hope memories of his behavior would fade away. And he counted on his advocacy of campaign finance reform to help erase the stain on his integrity.

But it was not only his own past that posed a character problem for Gore, it was also that of the president whom he had loyally served for more than six years. Realizing that recollections of the White House sex scandal were still too fresh to ignore, Gore set about separating himself from the sleazy side of the Clinton presidency as soon as he announced his candidacy. He lamented the time the nation had wasted because of the Lewinsky affair and labeled

Clinton's behavior "inexcusable" so often that the White House later made known its displeasure. Turning to the future, Gore promised to "take my own values of faith and family to the Presidency" and to use the "moral leadership" of his office "to fight for America's family."

No sooner had Gore sounded these lofty notes than Republicans hammered him for his tardiness in seeing the light. "Al Gore was totally silent while the controversy about the White House sex scandals was at its height," contended the most recent Republican vice president, Dan Quayle. And Elizabeth Dole asked pointedly: "Where was Al Gore when his partner, Bill Clinton, robbed the Oval Office of its moral authority?" That was a question the press should have raised directly with Gore but rarely did. If Gore was so offended by Clinton's conduct, why did he not resign? The world will probably have to wait until he publishes his memoirs to learn the answer.

As the campaign heated up, the press became increasingly intrigued with the character issue and its impact on the contest to choose Clinton's successor. But reporters covered character in a misguided fashion. Instead of focusing on relevant questions—such as whether the actions of Bush and Gore were consistent with their high-minded rhetoric—they tended to go off on superficial and trivial tangents. Journalists covering Gore focused on what was widely described as his "woodenness," his frozen demeanor and stilted mannerisms, and pointed to this as one of the fundamental weaknesses in his candidacy. The *Washington Post* summed up this argument in March 1999 by breathlessly reporting poll results suggesting that "most voters want the country to continue on the path laid out by President Clinton but are not convinced Albert Gore is the person to do it." Public opinion polls indicated, the *Post* reported, that "doubts about Gore's leadership capacity and coolness to his personality could tip the election to the Republicans."

What should Gore do about this? One answer came from Judy Sandler, a retired fashion consultant in Marco Island, Florida, interviewed by the *Post*. "I think he could use some public speaking teaching," Sandler said. "I think he's boring. I wish he had more charisma."

Gore seemed to feel the same way, as suggested by efforts to make himself seem more interesting, most of which boomeranged. Thus when he announced that as a legislator he "took the initiative in creating the Internet," he opened himself to derision from reporters who pointed out that when the Internet was launched in 1969, Gore was just graduating from Harvard. Few stories took into account that Gore, as even Newt Gingrich had acknowledged, had actually played an important role in popularizing the Internet while he was in Congress. Such facts were drowned out by stories reminding everyone how Gore had earlier claimed that he and his wife Tipper had been the models for the ill-starred couple in the celebrated tear-jerker novel *Love Story*. He was in part, according to author Erich Segal; Tipper was not.

All this helped contribute to a rising volume of stories about Al Gore's presidential campaign facing serious trouble, stories that were preposterous on their face. The accounts of Gore's candidacy in crisis were being written more than a year before the November election that would decide his fate, long before most citizens who did not happen to be political operatives or political journalists were giving serious thought to that election. Worse yet, the stories about Gore's troubles, to the extent that they were read, stirred further concerns about his alleged shortcomings among politicians who should have known better, leading to more such stories—and so on and so forth. This foolish circle contributed to public confusion and even alarmed President Clinton, leading to a *New York Times* story headlined: "Clinton Admits to Concerns as Gore Campaign Stumbles." So distressed was the president, reported Richard L. Berke, that "he had personally coached Mr. Gore on how to loosen up and appear less remote and rigid on the campaign trail." With friends like Clinton to help him, Gore needed no enemies.

The truth was that Gore did have problems. He was not an easy person to like because it was hard for him to behave naturally. And

Gore compounded this problem by overcompensating, which only made him seem more synthetic. Back in his Senate days I had once tracked him from Washington to Tennessee, where he was attending a Democratic party get-together, seeking a promised interview for a story I was doing on the political impact of the global economy. For two days, until he finally consented to talk to me, I waited in a hotel corridor outside a room where Democratic state leaders were enjoying a modest bacchanal.

"What was it you wanted to ask me about?" Gore asked.

I reminded him, and he nodded, cleared his throat, and said, "Let me see if I can compose a statement."

I thanked him but told him what I had in mind was not a formal statement but some give-and-take on the subject—a conversation, so to speak.

That seemed to throw him off stride, and he stared at me for a moment, nonplussed.

"Look," he said, "let me tell you a joke I just heard. It's a bit off color, so I want to make it off the record."

I could see no way of stopping him, so I listened. His anecdote, inspired by the recent embarrassment of a Republican congressman who had seduced an underage female intern, was more than a bit off color; it was flat-out vulgar. Worse, it wasn't even funny. I will respect his confidence by not repeating it.

When he was finished, I managed to pry out of him a few words of wisdom about the global economy, which went into my story along with quotes from Bill Clinton and Richard Gephardt, neither of whom had thought to tell me a bad dirty joke.

After I got over my annoyance, it occurred to me that being stiff might not be such a bad handicap for Gore if only he could learn to live with it himself rather than trying to prove he is a regular guy.

Most of Gore's problems, though, reflected the nature of the vice presidency. Vice presidents make a sort of Faustian bargain. In return for the media attention that goes with the territory, they surrender the right to speak their minds in public on anything that much matters. This makes them boring, the most common criticism leveled against Gore, and the same charge once made against George Bush, and Walter Mondale before him. Frustration with this image led Gore to overstate his role in developing cyberspace, and to speak grandiloquently about the mundane business of streamlining the federal bureaucracy, which Clinton had grandly dubbed "reinventing government." Gore also hired the feminist author Naomi Wolf at $15,000 a month to help make over his personality, touching off another wave of hoots and jeers from the media.

In the face of sustained media criticism and a party challenge from former New Jersey senator Bill Bradley, Gore decided to move his campaign "lock, stock, and barrel" to Nashville in his home state of Tennessee. The move was part of a campaign overhaul that was mainly intended to establish his identity apart from Clinton's. It also included an updated wardrobe and a livelier stump speech.

Yet none of this seemed to impress the media favorably. "Will the new look really help fix wobbly poll numbers and a bickering staff?" *Newsweek* asked skeptically. "New Gore, Old Problems: Candidate Relaxes But His Rhetorical Wanderings Sometimes Bring Stumbles" headlined the *Washington Post*.

Skeptical about Gore's supposed transformation, reporters began to look with increasing interest and favor on the vice president's sole rival for the Democratic nomination, Bill Bradley. Here was a man of impeccable character, whose integrity had never been questioned even by his rivals, a former Rhodes scholar and star professional basketball player who exuded idealism, a man who ever since he had entered public life many Democrats had regarded as their dream candidate for president.

Along with his other virtues, Bradley also had a keen sense of humor, albeit a very dry one, as I had discovered during the course of covering him over the years while his admirers waited to see if he would fulfill their dreams and at last run for the White House. Once, when I had a date to interview him in his Senate office about his future and his party's, he left me cooling my heels for more than two hours in the reception room while a stream of other visitors entered and left his inner sanctum. Meanwhile things I needed to do before deadline went undone.

Finally Bradley admitted me to his presence and without much of an apology said, "Let's get started right away." While I took out my notebook and tape recorder, Bradley lay down on his back on the floor of his office and commenced to do sit-ups with considerable vigor. "Please don't let this distract you," he said. "Just go ahead and ask your questions." All the while Bradley kept a straight face, though I could not keep myself from breaking up. But droll as Bradley can be, his sort of humor is an acquired taste, which few reporters had the chance to acquire on the campaign trail.

Indeed, as Bradley stumped for votes, reporters found him not only not very amusing but also not particularly interesting—almost as dull as, well, say, Gore, only in a different way. To reporters, and also to voters, Bradley seemed more concerned with relishing his own thoughts and protecting his own privacy than gaining support for his candidacy. "My abilities match the national moment," Bradley was fond of telling voters in Iowa and New Hampshire, and he seemed to rest his chances on the hope that the nation would be astute enough to recognize the truth of that proposition.

In his self-absorption Bradley at times ignored the legitimate needs of the press assigned to cover his candidacy and thus caused himself damage. In December 1999 he had revealed that he occasionally suffered a form of arrhythmia, a chronic irregular heartbeat. Although the problem was not life threatening, it raised questions about whether this condition might interfere with his performance as a candidate or a president, questions that Bradley was unwilling to discuss. In January it took a pointed question from a perceptive reporter, Jackie Judd of ABC News, to get Bradley to acknowledge that four episodes of arrhythmia had forced him to curtail his campaign schedule in Iowa as election day in that state approached. His heart had "flipped out" of its natural rhythm and then "flipped back in," as Bradley explained it.

But if Bradley's health was unimpaired, the same could not be said for his candidacy. Stories about his failure to be more forthcoming about symptoms of his heart condition, even when they affected his ability to stump for votes, overshadowed his message in the climactic days of the Iowa campaign and probably contributed to his winning barely more than a third of the vote.

While both Democratic candidates seemed bogged down by the character issue, on the Republican side Senator John McCain of Arizona was using the appeal of his character to vault into the pantheon of media heroes. The media infatuation with McCain, which altered the nature of the early GOP competition, owed much to the contrivances of one of the Republican party's most imaginative strategists, Mike Murphy. In 1996 Murphy had taken former Tennessee governor Lamar Alexander, a notably drab personality with little national experience, and transformed him into a potential threat to Bob Dole by revitalizing his image. The changeover was symbolized by the plaid shirts that Alexander habitually wore and handed out to his supporters. When Alexander tried another run for the presidency in 2000, he discarded both Murphy and the plaid shirt. He never made it past the Iowa straw poll in August 1999.

In McCain, Murphy had a much more marketable product, a man possessed of one of the most dramatic biographies and most appealing personalities in politics. The son and grandson of admirals, and a bona fide war hero from his long imprisonment by the North Vietnamese, his support of campaign finance reform—almost alone among Republicans—had given him the reputation as that rare politician willing to place principle above party. What's more, McCain was a naturally gregarious man whose flamboyance was tempered by humor and who seemed to have an almost unrestrained impulse to candor. That was a lot to work with, and Murphy wasted none of it.

The Murphy-McCain strategy was shaped by the nature of the candidate and the one-sidedness of the Republican campaign dominated from the start by Bush. "You have to start with an inventory of what your strengths are—money, fame, performance, a certain base," Murphy told me. "In McCain's case we thought we could become the candidate of the media." Not that Murphy believed the media could serve as a substitute for a real political base; rather he counted on getting favorable treatment from the media to help Mc-Cain build such a base.

That view was based on a realistic understanding of how the press actually works, unencumbered by ideological baggage. "We thought McCain would get a lot of attention because he was interesting," Murphy said. "The media, if you're good copy, they're going to like you. Reporters think, 'It's easy to make a living with this guy, because I can write a story about him and get in the paper.' In the movies you always see the media running around with note pads trying to destroy you. In fact what reporters are looking for is a way to get in the paper, to beat out the crossword puzzle that day."

The strategy had remarkable strengths, but in the end a fatal limitation. The technique for executing Murphy's blueprint was relatively simple. "We would bring national reporters up and put them in a van with McCain," Murphy explained. "One day some advance guy just planted a sign on the van and it said 'Straight Talk Express.'" Thus a legend and a campaign credo were born.

"Before you know it," Murphy recalled, "we've got a big old customized bus, like a third-rate rock band would use on its tour, with a cheesy near-red velvet living room." The furnishings consisted of a large U-shaped couch and a couple of captain's chairs. McCain would take one of the captain's chairs and the reporters, up to a dozen or so, would gather around him. Clutching a Styrofoam cup of coffee, occasionally using his cell phone to reach one of his supporters, McCain spent hours each day fielding questions from reporters on his campaign bus and making phone calls to his supporters.

"Most campaigns limit the reporters to three or four minutes with the candidate," Murphy said. "But we let them talk to McCain as long as they liked." Meanwhile Bush was playing the role of the hard-to-get front-runner. The contrast between McCain and Bush was seductive."

The heart of the contrast as designed by Murphy was character: Bush, the cagey and slick front-runner, against McCain, the bold and candid underdog. Of course the substance of what McCain had to say mattered—his support for campaign finance reform, his opposition to Bush's tax cut. But what caught the attention of reporters, buried under these factual arguments, was McCain's willingness to take these positions in defiance of almost everyone else of importance in his own party. Reporters saw this as a mark of courage and conviction, and they conveyed this favorable impression to the electorate—or rather to the relatively minuscule portion of the electorate that was paying attention in the late fall and early winter.

Sure, Murphy and his cohorts knew all along they were running the risk that McCain might utter something he would later have reason to regret. "Normally Political Consulting 101 would say this is a nightmare, it will destroy us. Don't do it," Murphy conceded. He worried that "one day after three rallies and forty sugar donuts and nine cups of coffee, McCain is going to tell a joke about three rabbis and we're going to be in trouble. But because we were a long-shot candidacy, we were close to death anyway. We said, 'Let McCain be McCain.'" As McCain himself remarked to a reporter, "We're going to take some setbacks, particularly with my proclivity to put my foot in my mouth fairly frequently."

McCain did commit gaffes and he did pay a price for them, a higher price than he should have, according to Murphy who complained that reporters were overreacting to charges they were biased in McCain's favor. One notable example was when the *New York Times* seized upon what Murphy claimed was McCain's tongue-in-cheek reference to Pat Robertson and Jerry Falwell as wielding an "evil influence" over the GOP, and turned it into a headline that read: "McCain . . . Calls Leaders of Christian Right 'Evil'" McCain fumed but had no choice except to issue an apology.

McCain also found himself occasionally roasted for his conduct in Washington if it did not square with the lofty perception of himself he had forged. "When media had something on us they always did it 120 percent, because they were tired of hearing they were in the tank for us," Murphy said. In particular, reporters seized upon examples of McCain's fund-raising as demonstrating that he was a hypocrite when he called for campaign reform. "We would say he raised money like any politician," Murphy said, "but we were the only ones who were trying to change the law. But that did not stop the stories."

Still, by and large McCain's media strategy paid rich rewards—to the disgruntlement of Bush and his backers, notably Haley Barbour, former Republican National Committee chairman and an early endorser of Bush's candidacy, who complained on a television talk show that the press was "slobbering" over John McCain. "He is quite right. We are guilty as charged," confessed *Washington Post* columnist Mary McGrory. "The reason is simple: He talks to us, returns our calls, says things he shouldn't, takes them back, and doesn't blame anybody else. This is novel for us. Other Republicans prefer to bash the press, a longtime favorite activity. He woos us and wows us and seeks out our company. He jovially introduces some of us to local pols as 'old Trotskyites.'"

Clarence Page, a *Chicago Tribune* columnist, pointed out that McCain's appeal had little to do with ideology. "McCain is a good story because, for one thing, he is a maverick. He says things other candidates won't say on issues like taxes, campaign finance reform and saving Social Security. He also says them in a way that appeals less to passion or to pandering than to common sense."

McCain's success in using the media to exploit the importance of character was demonstrated in New Hampshire's first-in-the-nation primary, where he trounced Bush by eighteen percentage points. More than a third of voters in the Republican contest told the Voter News Service exit poll that the most important criteria in their deciding whom to support was whether a candidate "stands up for what he believes." And three of five of those voters cast their ballots for McCain. Poll responses to such subjective questions ought to be treated cautiously; but in this case, since the polls supported the story line, the press threw caution to the winds and embraced the polls. Or, as the *New York Times* put it: "Mr. McCain won because voters in the Republican contest said what mattered most was finding a man of unshakable character, willing to stand up for his convic-

tions." Other reporters explained the supposed enthusiasm for Mc-
Cain and his character as, in part, a delayed public reaction to President Clinton's behavior. The key to McCain's success explained the
Boston Globe, was "the ascendancy of character in voters' minds,
something that comes in no small part as a reaction to Bill Clinton's
presidency. The McCain phenomenon, so strong that it's reordering
party registrations, is all about biography and personal qualities and
almost completely divorced from ideology."

While the press did its job in explaining the reasons for McCain's
success, it went overboard in exaggerating its significance for the
race. What reporters overlooked was a lesson that should have been
learned from Bill Clinton's two presidential campaigns: as important
as character is, it is only one factor in the political mix. And the
longer the campaign went on, the more the novelty of McCain's personality lost its glow, overshadowed by other considerations. The
media mostly overlooked this reality, not because of ideological or
personal bias in favor of McCain but because of the inherent lust for
a dramatic story.

For example, the *New York Times* in its story on the New Hampshire results reported that "McCain's victory—not only the fact but
also the size of it, which staggered the Bush camp—dealt a painful
blow to Mr. Bush's principal stock in trade: the notion that his nomination is inevitable." But a closer look at the makeup of the New
Hampshire vote undercut such hyperbole. From the start of the
campaign it was always clear that if McCain was going to win anywhere, it would have to be in New Hampshire. Indeed if he had not
won there his candidacy would to all intents and purposes have been
finished.

The Granite State is traditionally hospitable to insurgent candidates—an attitude going back to Eugene McCarthy and George Mc-
Govern among the Democrats and revived as recently as 1996 by Pat
Buchanan on the Republican side. McCain had decided from the
first to concentrate on New Hampshire, skipping the Iowa caucus
and putting far more time and effort into the state than Bush or any
of the other Republican contenders. But probably McCain's biggest

asset in New Hampshire was the large number of registered independents who under state law can vote in either the Democratic or the Republican primary. McCain's candidacy, based on his strength of character and his zeal for campaign reform, was cut to order for independent voters. So it was only to be expected that they turned out en masse to vote in the Republican primary. The Independents were the key to McCain's victory. They made up more than 40 percent of the total vote on the Republican side. And they voted for McCain by a margin of better than three to one. Yet among Republican voters, Bush had the edge over McCain. That was the handwriting on the campaign wall, though few in the press bothered to read it or pass the word to their readers and viewers.

From the beginning, McCain and his advisers had recognized that the only way to defeat Bush was to win not only New Hampshire but also South Carolina, a conservative stronghold which had been a bastion for Governor Bush's father in the 1988 contest for the GOP nomination. "The tension in the campaign was to find a way to beat Bush in New Hampshire but do it in a way that would not cost us in South Carolina," Murphy said later.

But that was an almost impossible task. Because the very factors that made McCain appealing in New Hampshire—his strong character and maverick stand on the issues—made his candidacy anathema in South Carolina.

Murphy blamed the media for McCain's downfall there. "The media defined us in South Carolina. The media said we were McCain, the Independent candidate, running against Bush the Republican." But that was the way McCain had defined himself in New Hampshire, and that was the key to his success with the media and to his victory in that state. By winning that battle for the media, McCain lost the war. The flaw in Murphy's strategy was that the media could not lead McCain to the base he needed in the Republican party. Had the Independents had a party, McCain would have won their nomination hands down.

South Carolina defined the limits of the McCain candidacy. It was not just that Bush took more than half the vote and beat Mc-

Cain by more than ten percentage points. Even more important, Bush won nearly seven of every ten *Republican* voters while McCain won heavy majorities of Independent and Democratic voters. Once again character seemed to be McCain's strongest suit, with most of his supporters saying they backed him because "he stands up for what he believes."

Among the majority of voters, however, character was trumped by ideology and pragmatism—their belief that Bush best represented conservative values and had the best chance of winning the general election. Still, the media persisted in creating a sense of suspense about the election, an illusion that was reinforced a few days after the South Carolina contest when McCain won the Michigan primary and gained expected success in his home state of Arizona. McCain's victory in Michigan, according to Richard L. Berke in the *New York Times,* "threw the race wide open." But the really significant aspect of the election was carried in the deck of the headline to this story, which belied Berke's judgment: "Michigan GOP Voters Back Bush by 2-1 But Are Outnumbered." In Michigan as in New Hampshire, McCain had won because of the support of non-Republicans—Independents in both states, and in Michigan, Democrats too. In South Carolina he had lost the Republican primary because too many Republicans voted.

Yet the *New York Times* was not alone in promoting the notion of a closely fought Republican competition after Michigan. "McCain's Surge Shakes GOP," claimed the *Washington Post.* "McCain, Bush Ready for Long Battle," declared the *Los Angeles Times.* "Bush Seeks to Recover as Polls Show McCain Gaining Ground," said the *Boston Globe.*

Barely mentioned in most analyses of the Michigan result was the fact that the Michigan primary was no more typical of Republican primaries than New Hampshire had been. Not only were Democrats allowed to vote in Michigan's Republican primary, but resentment of the state's Republican governor, John Engler, an abrasive figure who was managing Bush's campaign, gave Democrats an incentive to vote for McCain as a way of punishing Engler. They did a good job of it too, good enough to bury Engler's long-cherished dream of being the vice presidential candidate on the Republican ticket.

This pattern suggested that in order to win the Republican nomination, McCain had to get enough Democrats and Independents to vote for him in Republican primaries. In other words, he could win only over the live bodies of the majority of Republican voters. This was not only unlikely but close to impossible because of the structure of the remaining primaries, few of which permitted Democrats to vote and many of which barred Independents.

It took Bush's overwhelming victory in the so-called Super Tuesday balloting on March 7, in which he captured nine states to four for McCain, finally to end McCain's candidacy and the media mirage of a contest. In truth the returns on Super Tuesday were not greatly different from the other results—there were just more of them. Exit polls in California and New York, the two largest states that balloted, showed Bush winning about 60 percent of the Republican vote, the same share he had received elsewhere.

McCain still captured most of the Independents and the majority of voters who most wanted a candidate "who stands up for what he believes." But they were outnumbered by the Bush voters who thought their man "best represents conservative values" and "has the best chance to win in November."

The same Super Tuesday returns that assured Bush's victory also sealed the Democratic nomination for Al Gore. With the identity of the standard-bearers for both parties clear by mid-March, the country, and the media, faced the longest general election campaign in memory.

E L E V E N

Ballots on Broadway

✍ OF ALL THE CHALLENGES facing the media in the spring of 2000, the most demanding and most fundamental was to find a way to cover the campaign between Bush and Gore that would command the attention of readers and viewers. This would have been a tough order in any event because election day was so far off. It was made even harder by the salubrious national condition. "It's not rocket science," Kentucky senator Mitch McConnell, the chairman of the Republican Senate campaign committee, told me. "The happier people are, the less likely they are to vote." Moreover these same circumstances seemed to bolster Vice President Gore's candidacy greatly, portending a one-sided race lacking suspense or any other element of drama.

Almost invariably when times are good, the annals of presidential politics show that voters do not turn an incumbent administration out of office. And certainly times were good in 2000 as the general election campaign began. While stock averages had been dropping during the year, this slippage represented merely a retreat from record levels which had brought paper wealth to millions of investors. Every other economic indicator of note—unemployment, inflation, productivity, gross domestic product, household income—was in a more favorable state than at any time in recent memory. Gauges of social conditions told a similar and not unrelated story. Among teens, the school dropout rate, the pregnancy rate, the suicide rate, and the use of alcohol was in decline; in the general population, the divorce rate was headed downward and violent crimes were at or near their lowest levels in twenty-five years. The sum total of such measurements, which had helped Clinton survive impeachment, now appeared strongly to favor Gore's succession and to drain the election of any sense of urgency.

Under these conditions, the media's difficulties in finding an audience for campaign coverage were manifest early on, once the flurry of interest stirred by the Republican primary contests subsided. Although both Bush and Gore stumped vigorously around the country as they positioned themselves for the climactic struggles of autumn, a survey conducted by Harvard's Shorenstein Center on the Press, for its Vanishing Voter Project, found that nearly five times as many Americans found the campaign "uninformative" as considered it "informative." What's more, nearly 70 percent regarded the campaign as "boring"; only 5 percent viewed it as "exciting." Not surprisingly then, the Center's surveys showed that seven of ten Americans were paying little or no attention to the campaign during those balmy late spring weeks when Gore and Bush staked out their ideological turf for the fall. "The presidential campaign has become a surreal abstraction for most Americans," said former network correspondent Marvin Kalb, co-director of the Vanishing Voter Project. "Uninformative, boring, disconnected from their daily lives, it hangs suspended—a crucial period of American politics, largely ignored by the American people."

Against this background the press sought a story line and found it in the rise in the polls of the Republican standard-bearer. In the wake of his triumph over John McCain, concern about Bush's youthful indiscretions and his lack of experience in international affairs and many areas of domestic policy were all but forgotten. He soon emerged—or so the spring opinion polls suggested—as that most appealing of American stereotypes, the underdog who had overtaken the front-runner.

Never mind the questionable import of polling data drawn from an apathetic and uninformed electorate. The *New York Times* and the *Washington Post,* the two dominant voices in political journalism, both pressed the theme of Bush's surging candidacy in May, nearly six months before election day. "Poll Shows Bush Ahead of Gore, with Leadership a Crucial Issue," proclaimed the *Times* over a page-one story by Richard L. Berke and Janet Elder. Along with news of Bush's advantage over Gore in a new poll—by a margin of 47 to 39 percent—the story introduced a subtext that would become one of the most enduring and prominent premises of political journalism throughout the 2000 campaign. "While many Americans find Vice President Al Gore's stands on issues more appealing," Berke and Elder wrote, "*he is not as well liked* or considered as commanding a leader as Gov. George Bush" (italics added). In the second paragraph of the story, for anyone who had missed the point, the authors added a reference to the vice president's "lackluster personal favorability ratings."

The *Times* provided the obligatory disclaimers—it was early in the game and Bush faced some potential "rough patches" of his own. But none of these parenthetical caveats were likely to offset the powerful influence of a page-one headline in the nation's leading newspaper just as the campaign was getting under way. Reinforcing that impact was a *Washington Post* story, also based on a poll, which might have been considered slightly better news for Gore since in this survey he trailed Bush by only five points, 49 to 44 percent, instead of eight as in the *Times* poll. But the *Post* stripped away that silver lining to reveal an ominous cloud: "White male voters are rejecting Vice President Gore in numbers reminiscent of the failed Democratic presidential campaigns of the 1980s, posing a serious threat to his hopes of gaining the White House." This article amounted to a double-barreled blast: not only was Gore losing, but he was losing the same way Democrats lost in the eighties, that wasteland of a decade when their party went down to defeat in three presidential elections behind Carter, Mondale, and Dukakis.

But why was Bush leading Gore by 23 points among white men, a margin about twice as large as the advantage that 1996 exit polls had given Bob Dole over Bill Clinton, whose policies Gore supported and mimicked? That big a defection among this particular demographic cohort suggested that white males had a significant objection to something in Gore's views on social or economic policy or perhaps civil rights. But no, it was just that old Gore bugaboo of character, or so the *Post* explained. "There is just nothing about the man that impresses me," Larry Griffies, an insurance agent from the Atlanta area, told the *Post*. "I couldn't put a finger on it if I had to. I couldn't tell you what. He just doesn't come across." Roger Johnson, a golf pro, was more blunt in his assessment of the vice president. "I just don't think he's got a lot of backbone," he said.

The *Boston Globe* found another way to describe Gore's problems by coining the term "marriage gap"—as in gender gap or credibility gap—to describe an antipathy toward Gore among married voters. "Something odd is happening to Gore, by all accounts a happily married and faithful husband, a devoted father and doting grandfather, and a conscientious advocate for families," wrote Mary Leonard in May, a month that was surely becoming Gore's cruelest month. "He has fallen into a yawning 'marriage gap' that is mostly about morality, somewhat about his masculinity, minimally about issues, and, if not reversed, could doom him on Election Day."

As proof, the story served up a supposedly prototypical quote. "No way will I vote for Al Gore, who stood there in Clinton's shadow, not if you paid me," said Valerie Gerheiser of Crofton, Maryland. Of course Gerheiser had voted for Bob Dole in 1996, and if she had ever voted for a Democrat for president, the *Globe* did not report that. But after all, it was easy to find plenty of polling data to support the theme. Bush led Gore by twenty-six percentage points among married men and fourteen points among married women in a *Los Angeles Times* poll. And Bush was ahead of Gore by thirty points among white married mothers in the Voter.com Battleground poll. What more proof was needed?

But wasn't the presidential election still quite a ways off? That made no difference, according to Ari Fleischer, Bush's press secretary, who offered the *Boston Globe* what political journalists dote on, a sports metaphor. "We look forward to going into the locker room at halftime with a healthy lead," he said. "It's early, but the points that are scored in the first and second quarters count as well."

Fleischer hardly qualified as a disinterested observer, and elections are not football games. And a campaign is not much of a campaign unless voters are paying attention, which they were not doing in the spring of 2000. "There's hardly a brain wave out there being applied to the campaign," said Thomas Patterson, co-director of Harvard's Vanishing Voter Project. Voters even appeared to have forgotten what they learned about candidates' positions during the height of the primary season. "People are losing information," Patterson said "They are kind of going backward in terms of how much they know." For instance, he said, fewer people could describe Bush's position on gun control or Gore's on school vouchers than could do so a couple of months earlier. "Some of this stuff is perishable."

It was not just the dubious validity of the early polling data that raised questions about stories hailing Bush's ascendancy in the campaign. It was also that Bush's rise to apparent dominance in the contest for the presidency seemed to be predicated not on any strength of his own, but simply that he was not Al Gore.

And what was the matter with Gore? Hard to say. Nothing you could put your finger on, as Larry Griffies had told the *Washington Post*. "Likability," or the lack of it, was the explanation offered by the *Boston Globe* reporter Scot Lehigh, who recalled the old quatrain, "I do not like thee, Dr. Fell. Why it is, I cannot tell." As both Ronald Reagan and Bill Clinton had demonstrated, Lehigh wrote, "if voters are naturally inclined to like a candidate, they are willing to overlook, or forgive, a multitude of sins. Which is a problem for Gore, who, more than Bush, has a personal style that too frequently comes across as patronizing and pedantic or apple-polishing and off-putting."

Of such stuff are presidential candidacies unmade.

At the end of May, Dan Balz summed up the conventional journalistic wisdom for the *Washington Post*: "The campaign of 2000 has settled into a familiar pattern. As George W. Bush cruises, Al Gore appears to flounder." Bush won kudos for "laying down markers on a series of Democratic issues, from education to health care to Social Security," thus casting himself as the candidate of "fresh ideas." Gore meanwhile was depicted as reacting as much to Bush's agenda as pursuing his own, and to putting most of his energies into attacking his rival. Remarkably, Balz did not mention the character and personality flaws that the *Post*, along with most other papers, had earlier established as Gore's main failing. But whatever Gore's defects, substantive and stylistic, his candidacy seemed stuck in a second-place rut. The condition prevailed through the spring and early summer, accentuated by the Republican convention in July.

The arrival of the conventions forced television to the center of the media stage. Except for the conventions, a strange division of labor between the print press and electronic journalism prevails in presidential competitions. The 2000 presidential campaign, like most campaigns in the preceding three decades, was designed for television. But for the most part television political journalism consists merely of serving as a conduit for the events planned by the competing campaigns, interspersed with brief sound bites from the candidates and their handlers. Television, as Tom Rosenstiel, director of the Project for Excellence in Journalism, points out, concentrates not on gathering information but on transmitting it.

Given the constraints and pressures that govern the medium, it is not surprising that television news has little time or inclination for exploring the meaning of campaigns. That was particularly true in 2000 due to the general perception by electronic and print journalists alike that the campaign was notably dull. "There hasn't been much interest in the race up to now," observed Bob Schiefer of CBS in midsummer. Conscious of past criticism of the superficiality of their coverage, the networks dutifully tried to cover issues that sprang up during the course of the campaign debate—soft money, Social Security, and prescription drugs, for example. But as Schiefer conceded, "We probably all could have done a few more stories on issues."

Occasionally, on the evening news programs, as the campaign ground on into the fall, the network correspondent on the scene would offer a few sentences of commentary—but nothing very long or very deep. The job of analysis—putting the political sights and sounds in perspective for the citizen—that burden is left mainly for Sunday morning interview shows and for the print press to bear, and is seriously attempted by only a score or so large publications.

As for the conventions, in bygone days they served as showcases for the broadcast networks, which paraded their top talent across the convention floors. But in 2000, accelerating a trend begun in recent quadrennials, the three major broadcast networks drastically cut back coverage. They contended that the conventions had little news value and that cable outlets such as CNN, MSNBC, and C-Span could provide for viewers interested in the gavel-to-gavel proceedings. For this the networks were criticized by some for disregarding the public interest. They deserved to be saluted for not insulting the intelligence of their audiences, which stayed away in droves even from what was televised. The fault lay not with the broadcasters but with the political parties, both of which have worked steadily and successfully to drain the conventions of any of the grit or spontaneity that comprises political reality and interests the public.

For the portions they did cover, the networks felt obliged to tackle the task of analysis more energetically than during the rest of the campaign. They brought in pundits from the print media and the world of politics itself, but the result too often ranged from vacuous superficiality to smug superciliousness. For these shortcomings some in television blamed the political process and its practitioners. The political parties had "succeeded in making us theater critics," Lawrence O'Donnell, a former liberal Capitol Hill aide, who during the campaign served as a pundit for MSNBC, told Howard Kurtz of the *Post*. "The consultants, the James Carville types, have gotten the press to agree that the issue here is how well these things are performed. You could look at hour after hour of TV analysis and notice that no one actually talked about the policy content of the speeches."

Along with avoiding policy, at the Republican convention in Philadelphia network correspondents seemed notably reticent in providing their own views on the image of diversity that the GOP was striving to get across. On the first night of their convention, the Republicans appeared determined to use those few televised hours to convince the viewing audience that despite all that had been said about their party, they were intensely tuned in to the needs of all Americans, regardless of race, creed, or national origin. The session started off with an African-American member of the Virginia legislature decrying racism, then a Native American giving the pledge of allegiance, followed by a Latina singing the national anthem. After her performance came a talk from the Latino deputy co-chairman of the party, followed by two African-American singers. Next were appearances by an African-American teacher who taught poor students in North Carolina; El Paso Mayor Carlos Ramirez, introducing a video about a program for minority children in his area run by a Latina; and another Latina educator who repeated Bush's promise that he "will leave no child behind."

But the GOP had still more diversity on tap. There was Oklahoma congressman J. C. Watts, Jr., an African American and deputy co-chairman of the convention, presenting a video about a black woman in Detroit who served as legal guardian of four needy children, followed by an Asian-American speaker, then an African-American preacher, and finally a swinging rendition from a hand-clapping African-American choir.

"It was amazing," wrote Howard Rosenberg, the *Los Angeles Times* television critic. "The GOP, known as the party of white males, in just four years had become the Grand Old Party of the Gospel Singers. Except for an occasional pan of the audience, you'd have thought there were no more whites in the party."

In fact there were fewer than one hundred black delegates among more than two thousand in the hall—about 5 percent, or about half the black presence in the electorate. But for the most part the networks treated this divergence between image and reality gingerly.

"Colin Powell challenged delegates to show a genuine commitment to minorities," said ABC anchorman Anderson Cooper, referring to the main speaker of the evening. But he did not mention that Powell had issued the same challenge four years earlier at the convention that nominated Bob Dole for president, with no visible impact on the party.

CBS offered only slightly more elaboration on the diversity during a somewhat skeptical feature on the GOP's attempt to present a new face. Two sentences' worth. "When you look at the makeup of this convention, it certainly doesn't match all the diversity rhetoric that you're hearing," said veteran correspondent Phil Jones. "But at least for now, they're all singing from George Bush's political hymnal." And that was that.

The most aggressive treatment of the Republican effort to make their party seem like an all-American rainbow was provided not on any of the main news shows covering the convention but on NBC's "Today Show," where the redoubtable Katie Couric grilled General Powell. She pointed out the discrepancy between the high visibility of blacks at the podium and their minuscule presence among the delegates. "Do you feel troubled by this?" she asked. "And do you feel used at all by your own party?"

Taken aback, Powell responded: "Of course I'm troubled by it. I'd like to see many more minorities represented at a convention such as this. But you have to start somewhere."

For the most part the network regulars and their guest pundits seemed much more comfortable analyzing what was generally described as masterly delivery of Bush's acceptance speech, in which he sought to ignore the nation's favorable condition by declaring, "This administration had its chance. They have not led. We will."

"George W. Bush was politician, preacher. But I think Democrats, Republicans, and Independents would all agree, he was also presidential," oohed NBC's Tim Russert after it was all over. "If this convention did not win the election for George Bush, I believe it came very close," aahed David Gergen on PBS.

In the wake of the Republicans' successful gathering, just as it appeared that Bush might be declared the winner before Labor Day, Gore acted dramatically to remedy what the press had labeled his biggest problem, character. One week before the Democratic convention was to begin in Los Angeles in mid-August, he announced his choice of a running mate—Senator Joseph Lieberman of Connecticut, who became the first Jew to run on the national ticket of a major political party. As striking as that fact was, the media found it more significant that Lieberman had been the first prominent Democrat to denounce President Clinton's conduct in the Lewinsky affair, calling Clinton's behavior "not just inappropriate" but "immoral."

As the *Washington Post* put it, "Lieberman offers Gore a partial solution to a dilemma that has hobbled his candidacy from the beginning, which is the question of how to escape the worst of Clinton's presidency while identifying with the best." The "best" part of the Clinton presidency, or so the *Post* judged it, was his departure from the traditional liberalism of the Democratic past, which Lieberman, as the head of the Democratic Leadership Council, the same group of self-described centrists that Clinton had led, certainly embodied. The "worst" of the Clinton era was of course the sex scandal, which Lieberman had so vehemently and conveniently condemned.

The press also reminded its readers that Lieberman's criticism of Clinton was consistent with the high moral tone he sought to establish for his public career. "Lieberman's culturally conservative streak—he has joined leading conservatives in criticizing the entertainment industry for excessive depictions of violence and sexuality—could strengthen Gore with morally traditional swing voters now flocking to Bush," pointed out Ronald Brownstein of the *Los Angeles Times.*

Now journalists concluded that Gore deserved extra points for boldness, for seeing what had to be done—severing his symbolic link to the Clinton scandals—and for doing what was necessary to accomplish it, even at the risk of bringing down the curse of anti-Semitism upon his candidacy. "Lieberman is a daring choice for Gore, in part because it is unclear how voters will react to having a

Jew on the ticket," wrote Naftali Bendavid of the *Chicago Tribune.* Gore's aides eagerly compared the significance of Lieberman's nomination to John F. Kennedy's campaign to become the first Roman Catholic president, Bendavid noted. And in case anyone missed the point, Bendavid quoted Lieberman himself as paying tribute to Gore's boldness, a word not previously associated with the vice president. "Let us be very clear about this: It isn't me, Joe Lieberman, who deserves the credit and congratulations for taking a bold step," Lieberman modestly declared. "It is Al Gore who broke this barrier."

By choosing Lieberman as the Democratic convention opened in Los Angeles, Gore seemed to have forced most of the media to change the subject, shifting to issues other than his alleged character failings. In covering the Democrats the networks were at least consistent, retaining their same commitment to politics as a diversion that they had demonstrated at the Republican conclave.

Before the convention opened in Los Angeles, Republicans made a point of publicly insisting that the networks give no greater coverage to the Democrats than they had offered two weeks earlier to Republicans meeting in Philadelphia. Broadcasters refused to take these admonitions to heart, though their position had less to do with ideology than with the cult of celebrity. On the second night of the convention the networks chose to telecast live basic stump speeches by both Senator Edward Kennedy and his niece, Caroline Kennedy. Neither address offered much in the way of content or substance, but both allowed television to exploit the apparently deathless legend of the Kennedy family in hopes of luring viewers.

Still, the convention provided a demonstration of the awesome power television wields. On Monday night when President Clinton addressed the delegates, a convention event second in significance only to Gore's acceptance speech, many delegates chose to watch the president on one of the huge screens inside the Staples Center, preferring the electronic magnification of the event to the reality of the flesh-and-blood president speaking to them from the podium.

Finally came Gore's speech, in which he exhibited the energy that he had previously been faulted for lacking in his public utterances. "I stand here tonight as my own man," he told the cheering delegates, "and I want you to know who I truly am." Style aside, on substantive grounds, the speech represented something of a gamble. Instead of resting on the laurels of the booming economy, which many believed was his greatest advantage in the election, Gore made clear he intended to extend the good times to those who had not thrived in the so-called new economy. "Let's make sure our prosperity enriches not just the few but all working families." To drive that point home, Gore infused his speech with a class-conscious rhetoric that portrayed him as the defender of "working families" against "powerful interests" such as "the big polluters," "the big drug companies," and "bean-counters at HMOs."

Gore's turn toward this populist appeal was all the more significant because of the decade-long argument among Democratic strategists over how to build a winning presidential coalition. Many of the centrist "New Democrats" around Clinton had favored concentrating on the upper middle class, with government playing the role of benign referee, while more liberal Democrats advocated aiming at downscale voters and stressing a more vigorous role for government. Surveying the political landscape at convention time, Gore concluded that many of the centrists Clinton had wooed were all too willing to defect to Bush and the GOP, who offered them a cut in their tax bill and a chance to make themselves even wealthier by partly privatizing Social Security. Gore's best chance of winning, he concluded, was to appeal to the less fortunate while trying to hold on to Clinton's centrists.

This decision was probably the most important of Gore's campaign. Yet television's analysts largely overlooked its significance. Comment on the vice president's emergence as a born-again populist was limited in the main to wondering aloud whether Gore's contentious rhetoric matched the national mood. "The populism really was pretty hard-edged," complained Norman Ornstein, a think-tank American Enterprise Institute fellow, on CNN.

But discussion of this issue had to compete against the charges levied by some commentators, true to their self-conceived role as theater critics, that Gore had been excessively vigorous in his presentation, hurrying through his address so rapidly that he rushed past his applause lines. "I didn't get it," complained Bill Schneider, a former Harvard professor who had morphed into one of the glibbest of CNN's political oracles. "I kept saying to him: 'Stop. You're stepping on all your applause lines. Pause.' It was very programmed and robotic."

"I thought the cadence was a little strange," chimed in Stuart Rothenberg, editor of a highly touted political newsletter. "The first five minutes, he seemed to remember that he had a train he had to catch. Then he slowed down, but he did step on some of his lines, and at the end, he—he must have thought, 'Oh, I looked at my watch. I've got to speed up here.' So it was a—it was a bit odd."

Also raising eyebrows among television pundits was the ardent kiss that Gore bestowed on his wife Tipper just before he took the podium. Osculatory interest was still rampant the next morning when Gore made the rounds of the television news shows. "You really planted one on Mrs. Gore," said Matt Lauer of NBC's "Today." "What were you thinking?"

Gore insisted that his embrace of his wife of thirty years had been "completely spontaneous."

Asked on CBS's "Early Show" if he was trying to "send a message," Gore replied, "Actually, I was trying to send a message to Tipper."

Whatever television analysts thought about Gore's kiss and speech, both seemed to go over well with the voters, as measured by opinion surveys. And as Gore soared in the polls, campaign coverage went into a new phase, dramatically reversing the view fostered by the press all through the spring and early summer. Now suddenly it was Bush who was in trouble.

It didn't take the press long to jump on this new bandwagon. The Democratic convention ended on Thursday, August 17. Less than a week later, Mike Allen of the *Washington Post* was reporting that "after five months in firm command of the presidential race," Bush "suddenly finds himself on the defensive, behind in polls and struggling to fend off attacks on his policies." The *New York Times* was right behind with a story headlined "Bush Stumbles, and Questions Are Raised Anew," which described Bush "as defending his proposed tax cut in a manner that came across as reactive and not entirely coherent." As the days passed and Gore's lead in the polls lengthened, the coverage grew bleaker for Bush. "GOP Leaders Fret at Lapses in Bush's Race," the *New York Times* announced as the first week in September ended. A few days later the *Washington Post* reported that Republicans were "nervously asking a fundamental question about George W. Bush: Can he beat Al Gore on issues that failed repeatedly to work against Bill Clinton?"—the issues being character and credibility.

Now suddenly it seemed that Bush and his party could do nothing right, and could not help doing most things wrong. The Republican National Committee was forced to scrap a planned commercial that implied Gore was a liar, because the commercial itself was misleading. Democrats raised such a hubbub about a Bush commercial that did run, because it included a fleeting, barely detectable image of the word "rats," that it dominated the coverage of Bush's campaign for a couple of precious days.

And Bush created another unwanted furor for himself when, in what he thought was a private aside to his vice presidential candidate, Dick Cheney, he referred to *New York Times* reporter Adam Clymer (who had written some unflattering stories about Bush's stewardship of Texas) as "a major league asshole." Cheney, never one to quarrel with his running mate, enlarged the inglorious annals of the vice presidency by responding: "Oh yeah. He is. Big time." Unfortunately for Bush, the remark was picked up by a live microphone. According to a poll conducted by the Shorenstein Center for the Press, except for the news stories announcing Bush and Gore's running mates, no campaign story of the preceding four months had been as widely noted by the American public as Bush's crack about Clymer.

By now the media was in full cry, in large measure because Bush's gaffes seemed to take on greater significance in view of his sharp decline in the polls. "We all respond like Pavlov's dogs to polls," said Howard Fineman, *Newsweek*'s chief political correspondent. The reflexive salivating was evident in print and on television. "Humpty W: How Bad a Fall?" *Time* asked rhetorically. CBS's Dan Rather reported that Bush "brushed off talk today, some of it from top Republicans, that what he is doing is not working." On the "Today" show, Matt Lauer declared: "There's growing concern in Republican circles about a loss of momentum in the Bush campaign."

Bush meanwhile damaged himself further by his unwillingness to agree to the three debates with Gore proposed by the Presidential Debate Commission. Instead he proposed meeting the vice president in just one of the ninety-minute debates suggested by the commission, and staging two other sixty-minute debates sponsored by individual networks. When Gore turned down this idea, Bush accused the vice president of backing off his challenge to debate Bush any time, any place. "And now all of a sudden the words any time any place don't mean anything," Bush complained in his folksiest manner. He was trying, none too subtly, to revive questions about Gore's credibility and integrity, going back to the furor over the vice president's role in 1996 campaign fund-raising. "It's time to get some plain-spoken folks in Washington, D.C."

This ploy impressed no one outside of Bush's immediate family. Instead it allowed the press to portray Bush as fearful of open combat with his opponent and too devious to take his lumps.

Strangely enough, in the long run Bush's clumsy handling of the debate issue probably helped his cause. His evident reluctance to debate so lowered expectations for his performance that it paved the way for him to win, even when he lost. The pattern was established with the first debate, October 3, when, as most pundits agreed, Gore dominated the exchanges between the two men, seeming more confident and forceful, and better informed. A snap Gallup Poll taken the night of the debate showed Gore the winner by a 48 to 41 percent margin. And a poll commissioned by *Time* gave Gore the edge by an average margin of more than twenty points on having "more to say on the issues" and having better "command of the facts."

But that did not stunt the growing notion that Bush had somehow triumphed by merely surviving. The grading of the debate became a variation of the insidious expectations game so often applied to competition in presidential primaries. "Bush Wins by Not Losing," alleged the headline over the New York Times column written by William Safire, the erstwhile Nixon White House aide, a brilliant essayist whose normal skills at analysis were submerged during the campaign by his commitment to the success of the Republican candidate. But the same basic point was made by other purportedly neutral observers. "I think they held their own. They both did. And in the end, that has to favor Bush," contended CNN's Candy Crowley, who regularly covered the governor's campaign for her network, and who like some other beat reporters at times had difficulty separating her own judgments from the self-serving arguments of her sources.

Bush also benefited from the spread to print reporters of the concept, fostered by television, that the campaign was really a form of entertainment. Many of them responded to the Gore-Bush encounters as if they were theater critics reviewing a Broadway opening. In the New York Times, Safire's far more liberal columnist colleague, Bob Herbert, advanced the post-debate notion that while Gore "was better prepared, was more knowledgeable and had a greater command of the issues," he had a tendency "to pour it on—to offer not just his answer to a given question, but to show us everything he knows about the topic." This behavior Herbert would not forgive. "The vice president's boorishness gets in the way of his message," he wrote, "and almost certainly pushes some voters into a more favorable view of Mr. Bush, who benefits from a more conversational tone and the demeanor of an ordinary guy."

This was a theatrical point that conservatives eagerly exploited. "If you looked at Al Gore, you thought back to the smartest kid in class who was always raising his hand and sighing audibly when you made a mistake trying to answer the teacher's question, showboating a little, being a goody two shoes," remarked conservative intellectual and strategist Bill Kristol on Fox.

In fact Gore's mannerisms, his tendency to grimace and sometimes sigh in seeming impatience during Bush's answers, became a
major point of discussion during post-debate analysis. Not everyone
noticed this aspect of Gore's behavior because the networks varied in
the length of time they trained their cameras on the vice president
while his opponent had the floor. But for the benefit of those whose
home screens did not show much of Gore's quirky reactions, Judy
Woodruff, anchor for CNN's daily "Inside Politics," a show which is
closely watched by other reporters, made it a major item on her
agenda the day following the debate. After providing a couple of clips
of Gore reacting to Bush, she turned to one of her "talking heads,"
Time's Margaret Carlson, and demanded, "What of the sighing, Margaret?"

Carlson was well pepared for the question. "The sigh kept Gore
from winning the debate," she replied. Although Bush had answered
questions "in a faltering, hesitant way," Gore was denied victory,
Carlson contended, because "he has so many mannerisms—leading
with the sigh, the bridge of sighs, that make people unable to embrace him as the winner." Even the media was powerless to declare
that Gore had won, Carlson added. "When I read, this morning, all
the commentary, I was amazed to find out that our colleagues all
said that it was a draw."

This was a remarkable statement. First of all it wasn't true. Not
"all" members of the media said the debate was a draw by a long
shot; a fair number thought Gore had won. Second, it did not occur
to Carlson to point out that the verdict that should have mattered
most, if any verdict on this event mattered at all, was the judgment
of the voters, who by several different polls had counted Gore as the
winner.

But convinced they were on to something big, reporters swarmed
around Gore's bridge of sighs, making a point of demanding that the
candidate himself account for his conduct. "Even some of those who
thought you showed a real command of the issue felt that with some
of the audible sighs off camera and some of the chuckles, that you '

seemed, maybe even a little condescending towards Governor Bush," said CNN correspondent Jonathan Karl, sounding just a little condescending himself.

"I certainly did not feel that way," replied Gore, who pointed out that the Presidential Debate Commission rules banned coverage of a candidate's reactions when his opponent was speaking, rules which the networks chose to disregard. "I'll be much more careful not to give an audible reaction when he's talking," said Gore, adding, "I don't think that's a big deal, incidentally."

Which just went to show how much he had to learn about media politics. The media, particularly the television media, had seized upon Gore's assortment of facial tics and would not let go. A week after the first debate, as the second approached, Gore was grilled by Fox's Jim Angle on the issue. "You're saying that the eye-rolling and the sighing was a major league mistake?" Angle said with a playful allusion to Bush's aspersion of Adam Clymer.

Gore was quick to catch on and play the Dick Cheney role. "Big time," the vice president said with a laugh.

He soon discovered he had little to laugh about. His sighing revived the character issue, which quickly expanded beyond Gore's mannerisms into the broader and more sensitive area of his credibility. Gore's troubles started with the first question of the second debate from moderator Jim Lehrer, who asked what Gore meant when he questioned whether Bush had the experience to be president. "I have actually not questioned Governor Bush's experience, I have questioned his proposals," said Gore, who then launched into a critique of Bush's plans for cutting taxes and overhauling Social Security.

There was no reason why Gore should not question Bush's experience. Such doubts had been raised about Jimmy Carter, Ronald Reagan, Bill Clinton, and other governors who had sought the presidency. Unfortunately for Gore, he had forgotten, or chose to disregard the fact, that in a speech five months earlier, as quoted in the *New York Times*, he had charged that Bush's proposed tax cut "raises the question: Does he have the experience to be president?"

Gore's explanation sounded lame: "The point I was trying to make in that speech covered by the *Times* was that the tax-cut proposal raises that question." But as even he conceded: "Maybe that's a distinction without a difference."

That was only the beginning of the opportunities Gore gave to the nitpickers who vetted his utterances in the debate for days to come. They pointed out that he had falsely claimed accompanying James Lee Witt, head of the Federal Emergency Management Agency, to Texas on a post-disaster inspection trip. In fact Gore, who had often traveled with Witt to stricken areas, had on this occasion done an aerial inspection on his own and had been briefed on the damage by federal officials.

An honest and understandable error? Not to his opponent George Bush, who argued that what mattered in judging Gore's credibility were not the details but the big picture. "If there's a pattern of exaggeration and stretches to try to win votes, it says something about leadership as far as I'm concerned, because once you're the president, you can't stretch." This from the candidate whose father, the president, told the country to "read my lips."

But much of the media seemed to buy into Bush's argument, and their depiction of the vice president as a serial exaggerator gave Bush and his allies a character club with which they now regularly bashed Gore. In both these instances—questioning Bush's experience and claiming to have traveled to Texas with James Witt—Gore was guilty of nothing worse than carelessness, obviously not a desirable trait in a president but hardly unique to Gore. They seemed especially trivial because Gore had very little to gain by either mistaken utterance. He could have stuck to the truth without suffering any damage. But the press and the Republicans were not satisfied with such rationalizations. Instead they sought more evidence of Gore's Pinocchio streak.

During the debate, Gore, in urging the need for increasing spending on education, cited a note he had received from a Florida father, Randy Ellis, who had sent him a snapshot of his daughter Kailey, who was forced to stand in the rear of her overcrowded Sarasota High School science class.

That got the school principal's dander up. He complained that Gore had overstated the case. Kailey no longer had to stand, the principal contended, because another student was sharing his desk with her.

The media joined the outcry. The *Wall Street Journal* wrote an editorial denouncing the vice president for maligning this allegedly well-appointed high school. The *Journal* did not explain why Sarasota's all-Republican school board had pleaded for a tax increase that had been defeated the past summer, forcing a $17 million budget cut in the district. Fox's James Rosen declared: "Gore flunked his description of classroom conditions facing Florida schoolgirl Kailey Ellis." The Bush campaign cited the episode as another example of "a vice president who likes to play fast and loose with the truth."

But in fact students in several classes at Sarasota High did not have desks well into the first two weeks of school, and teachers said the overcrowding would certainly lead to a decline in the level of education they could provide. "We've been asked if Gore stretched the truth," said Randy Ellis, the father whose note triggered the furor. "In my view, he used it to drive home a point, and it was a good point. The funny thing is, it looks like I'm defending Al Gore, and I'm a Republican."

Meanwhile, though, Republicans continued to use the media to degrade Gore's character. Former Wyoming senator Alan Simpson, sounding as if he had been schooled in Vienna rather than Laramie, diagnosed Gore's misstatements as "not just slips of the tongue" but "disturbing traits of exaggeration and prevarication." Seemingly endowed with similar clinical expertise, Bush's running mate, Dick Cheney, declared that Gore had an "uncontrollable desire" to exaggerate.

If the Republicans were trying to encourage the media's near obsession with Gore's alleged mendacity, they succeeded. The *New York Times* gave the issue additional prominence and significance with a story headlined "Tendency to Embellish Fact Snags Gore." Its lead quote was cheerfully provided by Karl Rove, Bush's chief strategist, who displayed the same confidence in his psychiatric insights as

Cheney and Simpson had. "It's a weird pattern that has emerged," Rove remarked. "We have these episodes in which Gore is playing Forrest Gump or Zelig."

Of course Gore's misstatements should have been reported, because they suggested a tendency to improve on the truth to his own advantage. But the reporting needed perspective—such puffing is typical of the political trade, as demonstrated by our two most recent two-term presidents, Ronald Reagan and Bill Clinton, and Gore's remarks were of relatively little consequence. What made the media's coverage of Gore's gaffes egregious was not only that his mistakes were too slight to bear the burden of the judgments imposed upon them, but also that they were not the only questionable statements made in the presidential debates. For one thing, during the first debate Bush had claimed that Gore had outspent him in their contest for the White House, while as Gore pointed out later, Bush had spent twice as much as Gore.

On more substantive grounds, Bush had attacked Gore's domestic policy programs, saying, "We're talking about adding or increasing two hundred new programs, twenty thousand new bureaucrats." Bush did not pull this number out of the air. He got it from the Republican staff of the Senate budget committee, which based the estimate on another estimate—their reckoning of the total cost of Gore's proposals. Apart from the guesswork involved in costing out Gore's ideas—the basic premise was a stretch—increasing spending does not necessarily mean increasing the federal payroll. In the preceding decade, while federal spending had risen 40 percent, the number of federal employees had dropped by 15 percent.

Most fundamentally, Bush airily promoted his plan to partly privatize Social Security by diverting up to one trillion dollars in payroll tax revenues to private accounts as an all-gain, no-pain proposition. Scoffing at Gore's warnings that benefits could be threatened, Bush said, "A promise made will be a promise kept. The money stays within the Social Security system." The catch that Bush slid by was that the system would be different, and the money would be in a different place. Under Bush's system, the revenues would go into the new personal accounts of young workers instead of, as under the existing system, into the reserve fund where it would eventually be used to pay benefits pledged to currently middle-aged workers when they retired. Sooner or later that debt would come due, and then benefits would have to be cut or taxes raised because the necessary funds would no longer be in reserve. But this was a point the media mostly overlooked or failed to spell out.

These inconsistencies and contradictions were more technical than Gore's missteps. Moreover it was Gore's errant ways that had become the dominant story line. So the few mentions of Bush's dissembling were drowned out by the barrage directed at the vice president, which persisted through the entire two-week debate period.

Media commentary on the eve of the second debate was infused with ominous admonitions about Gore's need to wipe out the bad memories of his first performance. "In a bit of a role reversal, Al Gore heads into his second debate with George W. Bush tomorrow as the candidate who may have more to prove," reported CNN's Bernard Shaw on "Inside Politics." "Even Gore is acknowledging that he needs to watch his words or risk another bombardment by the Bush camp on his statements and his credibility." Gore should "talk less and provide fewer embellishments of his achievements," instructed the *Minneapolis Star Tribune.* Gore headed into the debate "badly needing a win, or at least a new image," reported the *Hartford Courant.* ABC's George Stephanopoulos, a onetime colleague of Gore in the Clinton White House, summed up what he thought the Gore debate strategy should be: "No more sighs, hold the lies." And the *New York Times* let the world know that Gore's aides had forced him to watch the "Saturday Night Live" lampoon of his first performance. "They wanted the message to sink in that he had better watch his performance in the debate tonight and not come on too strong." Gore "seemed to get the message."

Did he ever. Gore absorbed the message so faithfully that during the first half of the second debate he behaved as if he were drugged, rousing himself only near the end to launch a fierce attack on Bush's record on health care as governor of Texas. But the edge of that point was blunted when the vice president felt obliged to offer an apology for his "getting some of the details wrong" the previous week. "I am sorry about that, and I'm going to try to do better."

No wonder the polls showed that Gore took a shellacking. The pundits offered him no mercy, continuing to display their bent toward what the *New Yorker* called "ludicrous theater criticism." "He kept back that obnoxious side of himself," said historian Doris Kearns Goodwin on NBC, adding: "The problem for him was, when that is kept back, some of the energy and the passion that is naturally his is also lost." Said CBS's Bill Plante: "It was a very different, very subdued Al Gore that we saw last night. Gore was extremely careful to avoid exaggerations and interruptions. He did seem to be holding back. Constrained. On a leash, if you will."

As for Bush, the critical standards were much more relaxed. Bush "offered deeper and longer answers to complex public policy questions" than he had in the first encounter, reported the *Raleigh News and Observer*, as if Bush were competing against himself, not Gore. In fact on foreign policy, which took up most of the debate, Bush avoided comparison by simply agreeing with Gore on most points. Even this aided his cause, or so Tim Russert of NBC News maintained. NBC's Russert: "Blurring the differences is something that benefited Bush, because if people don't agree with him on the issues and they see that he is in sync with Al Gore, then they can say well, maybe it can be a personality race."

Just as Gore's effort to reform himself did not help him with the media critics, it did not benefit him in the post-debate surveys. The Gallup Poll showed that Gore, who had fallen eight points behind Bush after the first debate and then recovered to catch up just before the second debate, once again fell into a tailspin. He managed to recover some of that ground by the time of the third debate, in which he abandoned attempts to change his personality and went after Bush hammer and tongs. But the best Gore could get for his efforts was a draw in the snap polls immediately after the debate, and in the judgment of most pundits. "No bodyslams; both candidates are still in the ring and still standing," said NBC's Brokaw.

Once again the media stressed style. "The image burned into viewer's memories" was of Gore as a "fighter" and Bush as a "conciliator," concluded David Shribman of the *Boston Globe*. In "body language and verbal language alike, the two men described political positions that differed little but displayed political styles that couldn't have differed more." These styles were "evident in the way they occupied the space and, remarkably, even sparred for physical domination of the stage." Gore's steps in Bush's direction "showed Gore's determination to show an aggressive side." And Bush's posture—"standing at ease at a moment of high tension"—showed his "determination to display a personal sense of comfort."

As absorbed as reporters were with style, Gore's aberrations drew the most attention. The lower threshold for Bush's performance was illustrated at the final debate, which was held in St. Louis the day after Missouri's governor Mel Carnahan, who had been campaigning for a U.S. Senate seat, was killed along with a top aide in a plane crash. With the state in mourning, debate moderator Lehrer called for a moment of silence in Carnahan's memory, and Gore, who fielded the first question, made a point of calling the debate "a living tribute" to Carnahan. Up next, Bush sought to do the appropriate thing, but as soon became painfully obvious, he had forgotten Carnahan's name, even though both Gore and Lehrer had mentioned it. "I too want to extend my prayers to the . . ." he began, then, awkwardly stumbling ahead, added, "and blessings, God's blessings on the families whose lives were up—overturned yesterday, last night. It was a tragic moment."

For Bush himself it was an embarrassing moment, but one for which he paid no price because the press chose to ignore it. As far as such things can be measured and compared, Bush drawing a blank on the dead governor's name held roughly the same significance as Gore's overstatements. For Bush as for Gore, it was part of a pattern—as suggested previously by Bush's difficulty in trying to explain the workings of his own proposals for tax cuts and prescription drugs—from which could be inferred a lack of intellectual suppleness, a tendency toward mental gridlock under pressure. This shortcoming is not necessarily disqualifying. But for a presidential candidate it is a debility of which voters should be made aware, and which they can balance against the strengths of that candidate and the weaknesses of his opponent. It is one of many aspects of presidential character.

Gore meanwhile continued to struggle to pull himself out of the hole that the press had dug for him during the debates. "Debates have been good for Bush," the Gallup organization reported after the polling returns were in. And how! The pattern was similar with each debate—Bush got a "bounce," Gore recovered and almost caught up before the next debate, when the cycle started over again. Gore was still battling to catch up with the ground he had lost in the third debate when the clock ran out on him on election day.

"The media's approach to George Bush's misrepresentations, as opposed to those of Al Gore, has been notably *sotto voce*, even though it seems to me that Bush's have been a good deal more substantial then Gore's," wrote Charles Peters, editor of the *Washington Monthly*, in the campaign's closing days.

The one-sidedness of the coverage was underlined in the four days before the election when news surfaced that in 1976 Bush had been convicted of driving under the influence of alcohol. That had been twenty-four years earlier. But the more serious offense, to a press corps consumed by the character issue, would have seemed to be Bush's withholding of this information, even though he had been asked by reporters whether he had ever been guilty of such an offense. As an excuse for his silence, Bush explained that he wanted to protect his twin daughters from embarrassment. This echoed the claim of President Clinton's admirers that he had lied to the country and to a grand jury about his affair with Monica Lewinsky to spare his wife and daughter. But if the press noticed the similarity, no one called attention to it.

Instead reporters seemed thrown off balance by Bush's attempt to turn the finger of blame away from himself toward whomever it was who had leaked the truth about him. The story turned out to be a two-day wonder, petering out by the time of the Sunday morning talk shows. "Arguably the biggest hit to the Bush camp came Friday night on the late-night talk shows, when Jay Leno opened his monologue with this: 'What's new with George Anheuser Bush,'" reported *National Journal's* Vaughn Ververs.

But a late-night TV wisecrack was not what the situation demanded. As he campaigned on the Saturday before the election, his past transgression apparently forgotten, Bush trumpeted the importance of presidential character and integrity in what the *New York Times* called "a defiant rebuttal" of the past week's disclosures. This surely provided a context for stories pointing out that Bush's claim on the character issue was called into question not only by his failure to disclose his driving arrest but by his previous reticence to discuss his use of drugs.

Another character-related issue was Bush's apparently misleading description of his Vietnam-era service with the Texas Air National Guard, in which he had enlisted in 1970. Critics claimed he had joined up to avoid being shipped to combat duty in Vietnam; Bush said he wanted to be a fighter pilot like his dad, who won the Distinguished Flying Cross when the Japanese shot his plane down over the Pacific. But Bush's zeal to follow in his father's contrails was apparently limited. Although he insisted that he attended required drills in Alabama and Texas in 1972 and 1973, Walter Robinson of the *Boston Globe* uncovered documents that demonstrated he had stopped flying early in 1972, two years before his service commitment ended, thus in effect dropping out of the Guard. Robinson's story reporting Bush's "lackadaisical approach to his six-year obligation" ran the week before election day but was ignored by the rest of the media.

These acts of nonfeasance culminated probably the media's worst performance in presidential coverage since the emergence of the new political order four decades earlier. Partly as a result, the victor was a candidate whom most voters knew little about and cared less, a candidate who relied on his handlers and pollsters to craft an image of himself, of his views, his background, and, most significantly, his character, creating an effigy that had about as much resemblance to the man who would be president as a hologram does to human flesh. These words were written after the counting and recounting was done and George W. Bush had been declared the winner. But the same judgment, with only minor qualifications, would have applied to president-elect Al Gore if the long count in Florida had gone his way.

The press was not chiefly responsible for these lamentable results, but it bore part of the burden. Once again journalists played the role of enablers, allowing the political operatives on each side to practice their deceptions and distortions. Occasionally some journalists sounded a timely alarm to the electorate when one party or another had gone too far. But all too often reporters contributed to the confusion, not because they sought a particular outcome but rather because they were pursuing their own agendas, seeking to beat the next deadline and make the next headline, gaining short-term recognition without reckoning the cost to their profession and the public.

Their major sin of omission was not addressing the fundamental question that hung over the general election campaign. Here was the governor of Texas, possessed of slim credentials, a nondescript intellect, and an underwhelming persona running a nose ahead of the incumbent vice president of an administration that had presided over a time of unparalleled prosperity. What's wrong with this picture?

The media not only failed to resolve this enigma, they did not even try very hard. Various explanations were offered, none of which were satisfactory. It was said that voters had come to take prosperity for granted—but they certainly had not felt that way in 1988, the closest analog to this election, or at any other time in recent history. Another notion was that the electorate, for the first time in the modern era, had come to understand that the incumbent president and his administration did not really deserve the credit for keeping the economy humming. But whence came this newfound sophistication about economic policy? Still another explanation was that voters had decided they just could not trust Gore. But whatever the doubts about Gore's integrity, they were certainly molehills compared to the mountains of suspicion that had accumulated against Clinton, in the face of which he twice won the White House and got the public backing that helped him survive impeachment.

It may be that the only real answer to the mystery of why Gore did not run away with the election was comprised of bits and pieces of these explanations, or perhaps lay in some other area. Perhaps the economic indicators were somehow misleading, and many Americans were not really as satisfied as the experts believed they should be. Perhaps President Clinton's much-heralded shift to the center had so blurred his party's New Democrat identity that its ability to compete against the GOP was undermined. Certainly the question of why the 2000 election departed from past precedents favoring incumbents in good times was no easy question to answer. By addressing it more vigorously, though, the media might have helped the voters better understand the stakes in the campaign.

The press itself may have been part of the answer for Gore's failure to dominate the election. Its major sin of commission was its ill treatment of the vice president. Reporters were obligated to report Gore's misstatements and other shortcomings. But they had a responsibility to give equal time and space to the downside of George W. Bush. This did not happen. The press paid far more attention to things Gore did wrong and made far too much of them.

The media continued to embarrass themselves even after the ballots were cast, first by an election-night performance in which the pundits of television at their moment of maximum visibility succeeded mostly in befuddling the nation, and then by the often muddled and sometimes uneven coverage of the prolonged legal and political battle that followed the election-day photo finish. And there was reason to believe that the nation might never have been plunged into that bizarre political twilight zone except for the harsh treatment of Gore before the vote.

"The problem is not bias, it's intellectual shiftlessness—paying too little attention to the major but sometimes complex issues of the campaign and far too much attention to matters that are minor but easily susceptible to ridicule and to clever one-liners that get journalists booked on the talk shows," wrote Charles Peters in the *Wash-*

ington Monthly, explaining the negative coverage of Gore. "The unfortunate result of all this is that Gore's credibility rating in the polls has plummeted."

What the media did was of particular importance in the 2000 election because, as was often pointed out, with the nation enjoying peace and prosperity, no overriding issue controlled the agenda and influenced votes. So Gore, Bush, and the political press had a blank canvas on which to leave their imprints.

Did the press beat Al Gore? The very closeness of the election which makes that question pertinent also makes it difficult to answer. Given Bush's miniscule margin of victory, any one of a number of factors might be said to have contributed. What does seem clear is that on balance the press's coverage hurt Gore's cause more than it did Bush's. That impression is supported by a study of more than one thousand stories from seventeen news sources during the climactic weeks of the campaign, produced by the nonpartisan Project for Excellence in Journalism. It concluded that "Gore's coverage was decidedly more negative" than the treatment Bush received. Gore suffered, the study concluded, because coverage, particularly of the debates, concentrated on strategy and performance rather than on issue differences, which polls indicated favored Gore.

"If Bush wins, this could be the first election decided by the press," Charles Peters wrote as the election neared an end. "And the irony is that I'm sure most reporters will finally cast their own votes for Gore." That paradox points up the troubled condition of political journalism more than thirty years after the upheavals that established the press's new importance in making presidents.

T W E L V E

From Liebling's Law to Gresham's Law

✎ AFTER JOHN KENNEDY'S historic first debate against Richard Nixon, the first of four such encounters in that 1960 campaign, the candidate got a piece of advice from Clark Clifford, the canny Washington lawyer who had been a strategist for the last Democratic president, Harry Truman. "You clearly came out the winner," Clifford wrote. "You were clear, concise and very convincing. Unquestionably the appearance made you votes."

Looking ahead, though, Clifford offered a word of warning to his party's young standard-bearer. "Nixon is making a determined effort to convince the American people that your and his goals are the same. *This is false.* The goals are very different, and he must not be permitted to create the illusion that you and he are working toward the same end."

Clifford spelled out some suggestions: "Be prepared to point out specifically the positive differences that exist in goals, i.e., minimum wage, housing, etc.," he wrote. "If Nixon can convince the people that his and your philosophies are the same, then he will rob you of one of your greatest strengths."

Mindful of the demands on Kennedy's time, Clifford kept his memo brief. Still, he also wanted to make a point about style. "Attention must be given to adding greater warmth to your image," the

246

lawyer urged. "If you can retain the technical brilliance and obvious ability, but also project the element of warm, human understanding, you will possess an unbeatable combination."

Forty years later Clark Clifford's counsel, shaped by his role as adviser to Truman in 1948, reads like a bridge between the relatively solid values of past presidential campaigns and the chimera that in the fast-emerging future would cloak both presidential politics and political journalism.

His reference to style shows that he was not unaware of the appeal of imagery. But Clifford's main point, the concern he emphasized to Kennedy, had to do with substance. The "difference in philosophies" between him and Nixon was Kennedy's "greatest strength," he told the candidate. No one ever accused Clark Clifford of being a starry-eyed idealist. After winning the White House, Kennedy regaled a dinner audience with the story of how, after his victory, he had said to Clifford: "Now, Clark, you've done so much for me. What can I do for you?"

"You can't do anything for me," Clifford supposedly replied. "But if you insist, the only thing I would ask is to have the name of my law firm printed on the back of the one-dollar bill."

Clifford advised Kennedy to underline his ideological differences with Nixon because, as the ultimate pragmatist, he believed this was what mattered most in the election. That is what he had learned in 1948. Yet in retrospect it seems clear that the resourceful attorney was for once fighting a losing battle, bucking powerful cultural and technological trends. These changes, given impetus by the political upheavals of 1968 and the magnified role of the mass media would, over the next decades, transform the face of presidential politics.

Certain fundamentals about presidential elections continued in force. The national condition remained the great determinant, particularly in bad times. Economic distress paved Ronald Reagan's road to victory over Jimmy Carter in 1980 and enabled Bill Clinton to beat George Bush in 1992. But what changed, and for the worse, was the way Carter and Reagan, Clinton and Bush, and the other seekers after the presidency over the past generation described the national condition and their plans for dealing with it. Puffery and cant were always companions of American political discourse, yet substantive arguments were usually at its core. Under the new political order, political communication increasingly emerged as an art form designed to provide not information or ideas but illusions and impressions, not illumination but obfuscation.

Even at the time Clifford wrote his memo, his commitment to substance was not entirely shared by other Kennedy advisers or by the candidate himself, judging from the conduct of Kennedy's drive for the White House. As Theodore Sorenson, Kennedy's closest personal aide, later acknowledged, the Massachusetts senator's campaign for the presidency "raised no clear-cut, decisive issue, and except for the Peace Corps, no new proposals." In the haze of rhetoric that enveloped the campaign, voters and the press had trouble marking what Clifford believed to be the significant differences between Kennedy and Nixon. Shortly after the 1960 nominating conventions, in a newspaper column that attracted wide attention, the esteemed television commentator Eric Severeid complained that both candidates lacked strong convictions and described them as "completely packaged products" of "the managerial revolution."

Stung by this appraisal and fearful that Sevareid's feelings were widely held by liberal Democrats, Kennedy encouraged Arthur Schlesinger, Jr., who functioned as intellectual-in-residence to the Kennedy campaign, to dash off a slim book called *Kennedy or Nixon: Does It Make Any Difference?*, designed to quell such doubts. But what was most revealing about Schlesinger's tract was that two-thirds of it dwelled on the differences in style and personality between the candidates. Schlesinger berated Nixon for mentioning his wife in his speeches and concluded, "The hard fact is that Nixon lacks taste." By contrast, Schlesinger described Kennedy as "a bookish man," "an exceptionally cerebral figure," and added: "Kennedy is non-corny"—whatever that meant.

Kennedy's style, his charismatic persona, captured the imagination of the media, helped him win the White House, and became the hallmark of his presidency. He set the stage, following the upheavals of 1968, for the new political order in which heightened media influence and media manipulation confirmed Eric Sevareid's misgivings and led to all candidates becoming "packaged products."

Thus fifteen years after Clifford's debate memo, soon after the charismatically challenged Gerald Ford had replaced the disgraced Richard Nixon in the Oval Office, Ford's two top campaign strategists, Robert Teeter and Stuart Spencer, argued that Ford must adopt the proper style if he was to succeed in the 1976 presidential campaign. "The key to reenforcing and improving the President's perception [sic] over the next few months is the style in which he handles the job of being president," they argued in a memo written at the outset of the campaign to Dick Cheney, then Ford's White House chief of staff and political right-hand man. "He needs to appear more presidential. While his warm friendly manner has served him well, he does not have any of the aura of being president. Also, appearing more presidential should help to improve his perception as being knowledgeable and competent. . . . We need a little more 'Hail to the Chief.'"

This presidential image-building, and the considerable power and prestige of an incumbent president, helped Ford defeat Ronald Reagan in the struggle for the GOP presidential nomination. But when the general election campaign began and Ford found himself far behind his Democratic challenger, Jimmy Carter, in the polls, Ford adviser David Gergen, among others, fretted that style alone would not do the job. He was particularly concerned about what he labeled Ford's "non-debate" strategy for his three televised debates with Carter, the first such encounters since the Kennedy-Nixon debates of 1960. The blueprint for Ford, as Gergen described it, was for him to seem "presidential" at all costs, maintain a lofty, above-the-battle stance, and treat Carter as if he were of no more consequence than "a lighting technician."

Instead Gergen argued for substance and vigor. "A non-debate strategy will reinforce the President's worst attributes," Gergen warned. "The public questions whether the President is competent enough to run the country. We know better, but many Americans

don't. If the President stands there and responds with fluffy platitudes instead of hard, concise arguments he will come across as a
dummy." Ford's chances for success in the debate, and for holding
on to the White House, Gergen asserted, depended on his being
"very well prepared with sharp, well-honed arguments that keep him
strong, forceful, and on the offensive—on his achievements, on his
programs and on his philosophy."

And that's just what Ford did in the first debate. In rebutting
Carter's response to a question about what his economic policies
would be in the White House, Ford came out swinging. "I don't believe that Mr. Carter has been any more specific in this case than he
has been in many other instances," he declared. And then, while
Carter blinked with surprise, Ford poured it on, citing chapter and
verse on economic policy, his own efforts in the White House, and
Carter's record in Georgia.

"Ford shucked his bumbler's image, proved himself articulate
and not such a nice guy that he couldn't zing an opponent," *Newsweek* observed. Ford won the debate handily, most polls showed, and
his issue-laden performance narrowed the margin by which he
trailed his Democratic challenger. For the moment it appeared that
Ford and substance were riding high. But then came the second debate and Ford's infamous denial of Soviet hegemony in Eastern
Europe. The media forgot all about the holes Ford had poked in
Carter's economic proposals and instead returned to its stress on
Ford's "bumbler image." Ford never recovered from his Eastern Europe gaffe, and the media's absorption with trivia and tactics helped
elect Jimmy Carter.

This is the pattern of presidential campaigns for the past generation, with politicians and the media combining to diminish the importance of substance and policy while elevating superficiality and
spin as the defining factors in political communication. These
changes have not occurred in a vacuum. They reflect the pervasive
obsession of contemporary American society with merchandising
and promotion, with polling, focus groups, and the other tools of
salesmanship. As William Greider wrote after the 2000 election: "The

marketing culture has swallowed not just parties, politicians and voters but also a vast array of mediating institutions from TV and newspapers to most organizations that ostensibly speak to and for their members." The retrospective provided in these pages on the making of our chief executive offers a disheartening insight into this atrophy of democracy. From Carter's inflated hostage crisis of 1980 to Reagan's short-lived geriatric crisis of 1984; from Michael Dukakis's pardon of Willie Horton in 1988 to Bill Clinton's "comeback kid" myth of 1992; from the fizzled conservative revolution of 1996 to Al Gore's "uncontrollable" exaggerations of 2000, the media's devotion to simplistic slogans and the relentless manipulation of imagery and appeals to emotions by political operatives have defined presidential campaigns and determined their outcomes.

This steadily worsening situation appeared to reach its nadir in the media coverage of the 2000 campaign when, according to the Project for Excellence in Journalism's study of coverage, only about three of ten stories dealt with issues, such as the differences between the Gore and Bush proposals for cutting taxes and reforming health care.

The average sound bite accorded to a candidate to say his piece on network television continued its steady drop, from 9.8 seconds in 1988, to 8.2 seconds in 1996, to 7 seconds in 2000, according to research compiled by the Center for Media and Public Affairs. A Brookings Institution study showed that the time given to campaign coverage by the network news programs dropped 12 percent below 1996 and 53 percent below 1992.

Blame can be assigned to destabilizing trends in both journalism and politics. One salient development, which has been both cause and consequence of the deterioration of presidential campaigns, has been the rise of consultants, the hired political guns who now control most campaigns for elective office, including the nation's highest.

In the late summer of 1996, just as the presidential campaigns of the standard-bearers of the two major parties were toeing the mark for the final sprint for the White House, each was shaken by the resignation of a political consultant. The departure of Dick Morris, Clinton's chief strategist, on the climactic day of the Democratic convention, received more attention because it was triggered by news reports linking Morris to a call girl, to whom he supposedly divulged confidential matters about the inner workings of the White House. By contrast, Don Sipple, who was Bob Dole's chief media adviser and message formulator, resigned from the floundering GOP campaign along with his colleague, consultant Michael Murphy, on more mundane grounds—a policy disagreement.

But each of these episodes in its own way illustrated the dramatic and disturbing rise of outside consultants to power and influence in the modern American political system. Politicians, including presidents, have always had staff members to whom they have turned for advice or help, usually when some special skill was needed, such as speech writing or advertising. In the past these assistants had been longtime retainers, or as in the case of Jim Farley, Franklin Roosevelt's top political manager and Democratic national chairman during FDR's first two terms, leaders of the politician's party. But today's outside political consultants are motivated less by personal or party loyalty and ideological conviction than by their own ambitions. They generally provide their talents to whichever candidate offers the most in remuneration or prestige. Patrick Caddell, a consultant to George McGovern, Jimmy Carter, and numerous other Democrats, put the matter succinctly: "Consultants' obligation to the campaign is only short term. Their obligation to their careers is long term."

Morris, for example, though he had helped Clinton win his second term as Arkansas governor back in 1982, later left his service and had advised numerous Republicans, including Mississippi's Trent Lott, the GOP Senate leader, before being recalled to duty with Clinton after the Republican midterm election victories in 1994. And Sipple had worked for a Dole rival for the GOP nomination, California governor Pete Wilson, until Wilson dropped out of the race late in 1995. Murphy had been the chief strategist for another unsuccessful GOP candidate, former Tennessee governor Lamar Alexander.

None of these three men has ever held a position in either political party. Indeed, it is the steady decline of political parties in the postwar era that has cleared the way for the emergence of consultants. The parties, whatever their faults, at least had served as institutional mechanisms for linking the promises of politics to the performance of government, a role which the consultants, driven by their own personal agendas, are ill suited to fill.

Another factor contributing to the rise of consultants has been the increasing importance of technology in politics, notably in television and polling, which has stimulated the market for operatives with expertise in these areas. In recent years some consultants have outgrown the limited role of specialists to take overall charge of a campaign, as James Carville did with Clinton's 1992 candidacy, devising the theme that carried it to victory: "It's the economy, stupid."

Also helping to promote consultants are consultants—they never miss an opportunity to command attention. Dick Morris had the rare distinction in 1996 of being on *Time*'s cover two weeks in a row. On the first occasion he was taking bows for shaping the Democratic convention. The way Morris told it, he was at least partly responsible for the timing of a series of presidential bill signings and directives, the decision to feature nonpoliticians at the convention, the idea that Hillary Rodham Clinton should speak there, the timing of Vice President Al Gore's convention speech, and the content of President Clinton's acceptance address.

Morris's second appearance on *Time*'s cover was one he would rather have skipped. It was because of his dismissal by Clinton after disclosure of his lurid indiscretion.

In fairness to consultants, they are only partly culpable for the faults of the political system. Their role reflects the failings of the political process and of the candidates who hire them. Noting that Don Sipple was hired by the Dole campaign to help create a message that would spell out Dole's vision for America's future, David Keene, another veteran GOP consultant, asked, "Can you imagine Lincoln or Roosevelt hiring someone to give them a vision of the country?"

As the emphasis on style and tactics has drained presidential campaigns of much of their potential importance, partisan forces and interest groups seeking advantage have resorted to what amounts to political guerrilla warfare. In what political scientists Benjamin Ginsberg and Martin Shefter have called "the post-electoral era," contending political forces rely more on congressional probes and media smears than on elections to advance their agendas. With divided government more the rule than the exception nowadays, the executive and legislative branches are frequently pitted against each other in unrelenting conflict. Presidential appointments, instead of sailing through the Senate as in the past, now often trigger confrontations which serve as surrogates for political campaigns. The Democratic-controlled Congress brought the Reagan presidency to its knees in the final two years of his tenure with its investigation of the Iran-*contra* scandal. One of the forces leading to Clinton's impeachment was the resentment of the Republican-controlled Congress at being used as a political whipping boy by the president. Guerilla warfare raged again during the unnerving postlude to the 2000 election.

The root causes for this acrimony and turbulence go back to the birth of the Republic and the success of the Founders in designing what amounted to a dysfunctional government. "Ambition must be made to counter-act ambition," Madison wrote of the checks-and-balances relationship between the branches. "The interests of the man must be connected with the Constitutional rights of the place." With that hamstrung structure the Republic managed to muddle through the first century and a half of its existence. But in the closing decades of the twentieth century, the frustrations imposed on contemporary political leaders by Madison's ingenuity have been vastly compounded by demands imposed on government beyond anything Madison or his colleagues ever imagined. On top of that, sweeping social and economic changes have undermined old allegiances and blurred traditional fault lines.

"Voters are not fools," the revered political scientist V. O. Key famously pointed out. Given the present environment, it is no wonder that citizens have been staying away from the polls in droves. A recent study by the Institute for Democracy and Electoral Assistance, an international think tank, found that in national elections since World War II the United States ranks 103rd in voter participation out of 131 democracies. In the 1996 presidential election, turnout, adjusted for the alien population, was barely above 50 percent of eligible citizens, the lowest level since Calvin Coolidge's election in 1924. And this figure rose only slightly in 2000, despite what was widely—and as it turned out correctly—heralded as one of the closest elections of modern times.

Even more disturbing: officeholders chosen in low-turnout elections are plainly not interested in changing the voting trend since many fear they have little to gain and much to lose from boosting turnout. After all, an expanded electorate might well include voters who would prefer a different set of officeholders. For incumbents in both parties, the status quo works. Despite the much ballyhooed struggle for control of the House of Representatives in 2000, the re-election rate for incumbents was 99 percent. Only eight incumbents were defeated, and more than half the House members in the new 107th Congress won by margins of 20 percent or more. Given this measure of job security, it's not surprising that, as Curtis Gans, head of the Committee for the Study of the American Electorate, complains, "Increasingly, parties and leaders are targeting likely voters and don't give a damn about the whole electorate." The upshot is a vicious cycle—voter apathy and cynicism yield more power to special interests, which in turn makes voters even more cynical and more apathetic while the political environment grows more poisonous. And so the guerrilla conflicts that are a by-product of the deterioration of presidential campaigns also contribute to that decline.

Meanwhile the media, while trying to define their increasingly prominent role in a constantly mutating political environment, are having to deal with their own set of altered states. One particularly troublesome circumstance is the proliferation of media. Half a century ago the legendary *New Yorker* writer A. J. Liebling, in his "Wayward Press" column, contended that the fundamental problem with daily newspapers is that they come out every day. The public would be better served, Liebling maintained, if newspapers published only when they actually had news to report. Liebling's tongue-in-cheek recommendation, which he refined as "Liebling's law," had a serious and indisputable point. The pressure of daily deadlines forces journalism into exaggeration. Events that don't really matter are reported and published as if they did, distorting reality and confusing the public.

Liebling would not have been surprised to see how much more distortion and confusion there is nowadays, when the staid journalistic world dominated by daily newspapers has been made over into a universe shaped by purveyors of information on television, radio, and the Internet, each constantly striving to meet a deadline not every day but every *moment*. The news cycle that never ends goes like this: Something that may be of political consequence happens, and it pops up on MSNBC, CNN, and countless radio stations and web sites; but whether it is of real importance or not, it is soon flushed out of the system by some new event. As the cycle goes round and round, the print media must rush to keep up or lose the interest of a public whose attention has been captured by the dizzying pace of the new media.

In their book *Warp Speed,* two veteran journalists, Bill Kovach and Tom Rosenstiel, explore the new "mixed-media culture" in which the competing information streams of tabloid journalism, both electronic and print, high- and low-level Internet sites, and radio and television talk shows mingle with the journalistic mainstream of traditional newspapers and television news. The Internet, as the authors point out, particularly through political gossip purveyor Matt Drudge's web site and *Newsweek*'s own web site, was the engine that drove the early coverage of the Lewinsky affair by mainstream journalists. The net result of all this interaction has too often been to subvert journalism's time-honored goals of providing relevant information objectively and accurately in favor of presentations designed to attract audiences seeking instant amusement and excitement.

The consequences of this Gresham's law of journalism—the bad media supplanting the good—were exhibited all too plainly on November 7, 2000, when more than 100 million Americans cast their ballots and sat back to watch the television networks tell them what they had wrought. The tip-off on what was to come was provided by Peter Jennings, anchor for ABC News, as he welcomed the audience to his network's coverage of the election and announced: "With an enormous team of people all over the country tonight, we're going to try to make it fun and exciting." As if a little uncomfortable with what he had just said, Jennings quickly added: "It is inherently exciting already, and we'll try to make it instructive as well."

As it turned out, during the course of the evening Jennings's ABC and the other networks gave the nation more excitement than anyone had bargained for. Relying on exit polls and tabulated voting data provided by the Voter News Service (VNS), a consortium of news organizations, the networks made two crucial and wrong decisions. First, they awarded the state of Florida and its twenty-five electoral votes to Gore, then later in the evening, after withdrawing their initial projection, they anointed Bush as the winner—not just of Florida but of the presidency.

The networks had plenty of warning, since mid-afternoon when the exit-poll returns began piling up, that the election would be extraordinarily close and the evening long and frustrating. It was about this time that John Ellis, head of the Fox News Channel desk team, received a phone call from his first cousin and old drinking buddy, George W. Bush, governor of Texas. "Bush here," the governor drawled. "Here we go again."

Indeed, Bush and Ellis had made a point of being in touch on election nights as far back as Bush's first campaign, his losing run for Congress in 1978. Ellis was glad to hear from him because, as he later acknowledged, "I suspected I would need his help as the night wore on." This was an extraordinary attitude, because it meant that Bush would become something like a collaborator with Ellis in Fox's decision-making process. Leaking election-night exit-poll results is common practice. And while frowned on officially by those with a proprietary interest in the data, leaking is regarded by most political journalists as a relatively harmless way of cementing relationships with news sources.

But giving politicians input into the decision-making process, by taking their advice and information, is a very different act, viewed by most practitioners as not only unprofessional but also reckless. It gives politicians another chance to manipulate the political process at a critical stage in that process. And it offers little benefit to journalists.

"They have nothing to tell us," Warren Mitofsky, regarded as the dean of television polling analysts, who called the shots for CNN and CBS on election night, told me after the election. "We are the ones with all the information. All the politicians have is their interpretation of bits and pieces of haphazard information within their states. That's the best way I know to get misled." The only exceptions he makes in seeking information from outside sources, Mitofsky said, is for officials involved in vote counting, and then only with specific questions about the vote or its reporting.

As it happened, in mid-afternoon Bush had no great information or wisdom to impart. "Looks tight, huh?" the governor, already armed with exit poll-data, told Ellis on their first call. But before he hung up he made sure to give Ellis his private number at the governor's mansion. "Call me back when you can," he said.

At 5:30 p.m. Ellis did as he had been bidden, and called his cousin, the candidate. "Is it really this close?" Bush asked. The governor by this time had even more exit-poll data, figures that seemed to belie the optimistic forecasts given to him by his own strategists, and he expressed some disbelief at what the exit numbers suggested. "Keep in touch," he told Ellis before ringing off.

Uncertainty about the outcome only heightened as the minutes ticked by, the final exit-poll ballots were tabulated, and around the country the polls began to close. Nevertheless the networks did not let the fog of doubt cloud their customary self-certitude. Soon after 7 p.m., a few minutes after Peter Jennings had promised ABC's viewers an evening of fun and excitement, Dan Rather made a pledge of his own to CBS's audience. "Let's get one thing straight right from

the get-go," Rather said, his slight Texas twang adding a note of authenticity to his voice. "We would rather be last in reporting returns
than to be wrong. And again, our record demonstrates that. If you
hear someplace else that somebody's carried a state and you're off, as
you shouldn't be, watching them, then come back here, because if
we say somebody's carried a state, you can pretty much take it to the
bank, book it, that's true."

Before the hour was out, about 7:45 p.m., that warranty would be
tested. From the moment the polls closed at 7 p.m. everywhere in
Florida except in the western panhandle, Warren Mitofsky had been
closely monitoring the returns from the 120 precincts that made
up the VNS sample for Florida, precincts selected at random to
give a cross section of the state. Mitofsky had good reason to
focus on Florida. If there was to be a second Bush presidency, if
George W. was to follow his father into the White House, nearly
everyone in politics and political journalism had agreed before election day that the Republican nominee would have to win Florida.
There were two other important so-called battleground states—
Michigan, with 18 electoral votes, and Pennsylvania, with 23—big
states which polls also showed to be too close to call. But Florida
was more important. Florida, with its 25 electoral votes, was as essential to Bush's chances as California with its 54 electoral votes was
to Gore's hopes.

Early in the campaign there had been good reason to think that
Bush would win the Sunshine State. For one thing, his brother Jeb
was its governor. For another, Florida was a conservative state. But
in the days before the election it became clear that Gore was making
a stronger showing in Florida than most people had expected, strong
enough to cause Democrats to hope he could win the state and thus
likely guarantee his own victory. Sure enough, in the hours before
the polls closed, the exit survey results from forty-five precincts that
had been selected as a subsample of the larger state sample showed
Gore to be running very well indeed. And once the polls did close,
and the real returns flowed in from the entire sample, Mitofsky
could tell—as could his counterparts at the other networks, at NBC,

ABC, and at Fox, where John Ellis was making the decisions—that the vote from the sample was confirming the exit-poll indications.

Mitofsky had been in the business of making election-night projections—or refusing to make them—since he left the Census Bureau to work for CBS as director of its election and survey unit in 1967. In 1990, while he was still at CBS, he helped launch what was originally called the Voter Research and Surveys and eventually became the Voter News Service. Mitofsky had left CBS to become a consultant, but because of his experience and skill, CBS and CNN had hired him to make the projections for them on this election night. In all these years he had by his own reckoning made only five mistakes, all painful to him and much regretted, but none memorable.

Now, as he examined the Florida sample, which had served him well in 1996 and 1998, and which showed Gore winning Florida, he was confident he was not looking at a mistake. Pre-election polls typically claim that the results based on their samples are within plus or minus 3 percent of the true value 95 percent of the time. This means that the other 5 percent of the time the results are off by more than 3 percent. "The risk in the Florida sample was a lot smaller than that 5 percent figure for a pre-election poll," Mitofsky said. Based on his evaluation of the sample, CNN and CBS projected Gore as the victor in Florida, and the other networks followed in short order.

That forecast had tremendous implications, all the more so because within the next hour or so the networks also assigned Pennsylvania and Michigan to the Gore column. "We're building toward a Gore electoral victory," Ellis told his colleagues at Fox.

But the Bush campaign had other ideas. Soon after Florida registered in the Gore column, the GOP nominee and his brother Jeb began calling the networks to protest. Among other things, they pointed out that the polls in the Florida panhandle had not yet closed. They were told that given the strength of Gore's showing in the sample, the panhandle votes would not be enough to snatch the state for Bush.

That was true enough. What was false was the assumption of

260

Gore's victory based on VNS's 120-precinct sample, which turned out to be filled with wrong information. By 10 p.m., two hours after the original projection for Gore, the actual vote coming in from the embattled state made it all too clear to the networks that they had been misled by the sample. They pulled down the Gore prediction from their victory boards and set Florida and its 25 votes in limbo. The decision to reverse was unanimous among the networks, and so was the new category for Florida: "Too close to call."

With the election more in doubt than ever, Ellis put through a call to cousin George, who was more than glad to hear from him and more than glad to help. The candidate had been talking to GOP governors around the country, and his brother Jeb had been dialing his minions all around Florida. They had plenty to share with Ellis, particularly about Florida—which precincts had yet to report, and how those precincts had voted in the younger Bush's gubernatorial campaign. All of this, as Ellis later acknowledged, "helped me better understand the data that were appearing on our screens."

As midnight came and went, and the election became a two-day contest—two days that would ultimately become thirty-seven—the data seemed to look better and better for George W. Bush. His lead was increasing and so was the percentage of the remaining vote that Gore needed to win to catch up with Bush.

Looking at those numbers, Mitofsky was moving toward a decision. As 2 a.m. approached, VNS entered 10,000 votes in Bush's column from Volusia County, two-thirds of the way up the long coast between Miami and Jacksonville, not far from Daytona Beach. Volusia County is one of Florida's lesser-known sectors, but now it was to achieve historic importance. With the vote from Volusia, and 97 percent of the vote in, Bush seemed to have a lead of 51,000 votes.

Mitofsky did some calculating. Bush's lead would narrow, he knew, because most of the votes still out were from Broward and Palm Beach counties, both Democratic strongholds, as all America would learn before long. Even so, that would leave Bush with a lead of thirty thousand votes, wich Mitofsky judged to be sufficient to allay doubt.

At NBC the "Bush Elected" graphic was loaded into a video machine. "We were sort of on a hair trigger at that point," said NBC News Vice President Bill Wheatley. "The guy can't lose," thought Sheldon Gawiser, head of the NBC decision desk.

At CBS Mitofsky, wanting to be sure, tried to be patient. He had sat on two presidential calls in the past—in 1968 when Nixon edged out Humphrey, and in 1976 when Carter squeaked by Ford—even though other networks had gone on the air with forecasts that had ultimately turned out to be right. He had waited on those occasions because there were numbers he wanted to double-check, just as there were now in 2000. He decided to review the vote totals in each of Florida's sixty-seven counties, one by one.

Ellis at Fox was not that patient. He had been late in calling Florida for Gore the first time, and even though the call had to be retracted, that gave him small satisfaction. He had lagged on two other calls—Michigan and Pennsylvania. He did not care to be late in calling Florida for Bush. Still he hesitated. None of the other networks had yet made the call on Florida, though they all had the same numbers as Fox. Ellis figured that the decision-makers at the other networks were fearful, as he was himself, of calling the same state wrong twice in the same night. That, he noted later, would be "unacceptable."

Ellis waited for more numbers. Still no other network had made the call. Finally, after conferring with his Fox cohorts, Ellis decided to act. But first he called his cousins to break the news. "Our projection shows that it is statistically impossible for Gore to win Florida," he told them.

The brothers Bush rejoiced. "Their mood was up, big time," Ellis recalled. And Ellis himself savored the moment. "It was just the three of us guys handing the phone back and forth—me with the numbers, one of them a governor, the other the president-elect. Now, *that* was cool." At 2:16 a.m. Fox's anchor, Brit Hume, went on the air to call Florida and declare Bush the victor.

Soon thereafter CNN and CBS, under Mitofsky's stewardship,

matched Ellis's call, as did ABC and NBC. Within an hour Gore conceded.

Then, just before 3:30 on the morning after the presidential election, as Ellis put it, "the roof fell in." A message from VNS informed the networks of discrepancies between the VNS count and the tabulations of the Florida secretary of state. VNS did not know who was right. Shortly thereafter the networks again retracted their calls for Florida. "We had, in fact, done the impossible," Ellis said. "We had called the same state wrong twice in one evening."

Meanwhile Gore made a call of his own—on the phone to Bush, to retract his concession. And the nation plunged into a five-week polarizing marathon of lawsuits, counts, and recounts capped by a Supreme Court ruling that made Bush president but left the country deeply divided.

The key mistake in the network projections that set all this in motion was the Volusia County vote reported after 1 a.m. The 10,000 votes reported for Bush had been a mistake, taken from Gore's vote totals. That made for a net swing of 20,000 votes and meant that the 51,000-vote Bush lead, which Mitofsky had anticipated being whittled down to 30,000, would now be trimmed to 10,000—or, as it turned out, even less. "Without that 20,000 there is no call," said Mitofsky.

In the postmortems that followed, Fox was the most obvious target. Fox vice president John Moody insisted he had "no evidence" that cousin John had behaved improperly, though he did concede that the election-night intra-family chats "would cause concern." Howard Kurtz, the *Washington Post* media correspondent, reported that Fox was investigating Ellis's conduct and speculated that he might be dismissed. But if anything came of the investigation, Fox did not let the world in on it. Two months after the election, Ellis was still on duty at Fox—though he would not return my phone call. "Whatever I have to say I said in the article," he told the Associated Press.

In his article in *Inside* magazine describing his election-night actions, Ellis showed no sign of remorse, except that his forecast was wrong. As for his cousin, the president-elect, Ellis wrote, "Governor Bush was, as always, considerate of my position. He knew that I would be fried if I gave him anything that VNS deemed confidential, so he never asked for it."

But Bush did not need to ask; he already had plenty of exit-poll data. The point, which escaped Ellis, is that the opportunity he eagerly granted his cousin to influence his judgment was a manifest betrayal of those Americans who watched Fox on election night in the innocent belief that its projections would be made by someone who was not personally involved with one of the protagonists.

If Fox's insensitivity to standards of fairness and objectivity was the darkest blot on television's performance on the long night of November 7, what of the other networks? They surely knew of Ellis's relationship to Bush, and if because of competitive pressure they were (as some suspect) influenced by his call, they shared in Fox's culpability.

For his part, Mitofsky claims that what Ellis did had no influence on the decisions he made for CNN and CBS. "When Fox made the call, I had already decided to call the race," he said. And it would be hard to prove that the other networks, ABC and NBC, were guided by anything other than the VNS numbers which turned out to be so remarkably wrong. Given the numbers, NBC's Gawiser called the decision "an obvious no-brainer."

But it obviously was not a "no-brainer" or it would not have been wrong. Who or what was to blame? Various personages involved condemned the bad numbers, which have been attributed to penny-pinching or bad management, or both, at VNS.

But while these criticisms may have some merit, they gloss over the fundamental issue: the arrogance of the networks, their conviction that they not only had a right but an obligation to make a decision that in reality did not need to be made. This can be said without benefit of hindsight, without knowing that the returns from Volusia County were off base. Even if the figures had been right, the networks had no business calling the election.

Looking at Bush's supposed 51,000-vote lead early Wednesday morning, Mitofsky estimated it would drop to 30,000 votes and concluded that was sufficient to call the election. But 30,000 votes out of nearly six million cast in Florida is just about one-half of 1 percent. And that is not a safe margin when the presidency hangs in the balance.

What the networks should have done is simply report what they *knew*, not what they expected to happen—that Bush appeared to have a 51,000-vote lead with 97 percent of the vote in, but that the election was still too close to call. Had the networks done that, the public would have known as much as was knowable. And when the correct returns from Volusia County came in, the networks would have been spared their humiliation. More important, Gore would never have conceded to Bush, and the public would not have gained the belief, which would persist for the next five weeks and help shape history, that Bush had really won the election and that Gore was a sore loser.

"You can't do a story on election night without making projections," Mitofsky told me. But he also told me: "Sure, we want to get it on the air, but not at the risk of being wrong." But there is always a risk of being wrong in a close election unless you wait until 100 percent of the vote is in, not 97 percent. And the gain is not worth the risk, as November 7 demonstrated. Mitofsky, like most of his network colleagues, is a dedicated professional who hates making mistakes. But he cannot separate himself from the news culture of the networks, which he helped shape, a culture which believes it is smart enough to take the risk out of projections, which feels that the country looks to the networks to reveal the winners of elections, which is convinced that "you can't do a story on election night without making projections."

If there was a lesson in the election-night experience about the dangers of unnecessary haste, it had apparently been forgotten less than four weeks after election day when the U.S. Supreme Court handed down its ruling on the Bush campaign's appeal of the Florida Supreme Court decision that had allowed hand recounts of ballots in three Democratic counties to go forward. Every indication before-hand suggested that the federal tribunal was sharply divided on the issue and was unlikely to deliver a sweeping verdict for either side. Yet moments after the High Court acted on December 4, after appar-ently having looked at little more than an Associated Press bulletin, CBS's Dan Rather broke into regular programming about 11:45 a.m. to declare categorically: "The United States Supreme Court has struck down the Florida Supreme Court ruling in favor of Vice Pres-ident Gore. It's a Bush win." On NBC, Tom Brokaw said the ruling had possibly dealt "a crushing blow to the hopes" of Al Gore. On CNN, anchor Frank Sesno declared: "This sort of headline, I will tell you, for days now, has been what Democrats have said can be very injurious, politically, to Al Gore. That is to say, someone standing on the steps of the Supreme Court and saying, Al Gore lost it at the Supreme Court." All very dramatic and timely, but highly exagger-ated. On closer inspection, although the Supreme Court had set aside the Florida court decision, it had not overturned the lower court's ruling. Instead it had sent the case back to the Florida court for reconsideration, with suggestions that would allow the Florida court to take a different route to the same judgment. As Greta Van Susteren, CNN's legal specialist, ultimately told Sesno on the air: "You know what, Frank, having now looked at it, I think the best thing you could say is that it was a tie."

Less glaring but just as disturbing as the networks' tendency to rush to judgment was the pretentious self-importance displayed by members of both print and electronic media as they scolded the Democrats for challenging Bush's assertion that he had won the election. "This is a very treacherous path," warned Bill Schneider, CNN's chief political analyst, about Gore's refusal to accept Bush as the victor immediately after the vote. "The dangers are that the country will suddenly have doubts about the validity of the process," Schneider fretted two days after the election. "The dangers are that the candidates will look like they will do anything to win and ruin their own reputations and ability to lead the country by winning a disputed election." While these admonitions were ostensibly directed at both sides, it would be hard for viewers to conclude that the candidate who was really pursuing the "treacherous path" was anyone else but Al Gore.

In much the same vein was a *New York Times* article by R. W. Apple that appeared the Sunday following the election under the headline "The Limits of Patience." "Another week and no more," Apple wrote. "By next weekend, a group of scholars and senior politicians interviewed this weekend agreed the presidential race of 2000 must be resolved, without recourse to the courts. With remarkable unanimity they said that would be in the nation's best interest." At first glance it seemed as if Apple might have tapped into some variant of the trilateral commission. But on closer reading it turned out that this "group" became a group only when Apple interviewed them. As "remarkable" as their unanimity might have seemed to Apple, to others it might seem at least as remarkable that Apple had not contacted anyone who disagreed.

He would not have had to look hard or far. The same day Apple's story ran, warning that the recount battle "could drag on and on to the detriment of the political system," his own newspaper carried an op-ed piece by Harvard University law professor Lawrence Tribe warning that "the price of premature closure—of not giving the courts of Florida chance to apply their law to the present uncertainty—might be a cloud of illegitimacy we would long regret." And the day before, the *Washington Post* had carried an op-ed piece by another Harvard Law professor and former deputy attorney general, Philip B. Heyman, arguing the case for a court-ordered new election in Florida.

The weekend deadline set by Apple's group came and passed with no end in sight, and still the nation survived.

Not all members of the media were trained in the Chicken Little school of journalism. *Washington Post* columnist Mary McGrory for one saw a silver lining in the ominous clouds stirred over the recount. "The country has been transformed into a huge civics class with everyone, everywhere, talking about what they should have been talking about during the election," McGrory wrote. As for the warnings that Gore might be obstructing the important business of government and provoking a constitutional crisis, she pointed out: "But life goes on, there are no tanks in the streets and the telephones are working—while the country learns the hard way that every vote counts."

Nevertheless for some influential journalists the prolonged wrangle over the election seemed to be a crisis whose continuation they could barely tolerate. Within a week or so of the election they were warning gravely of the danger of exhausting the public's patience, when there was no evidence of that. To the contrary, public opinion surveys, for whatever they were worth, seemed to confound the pundits by suggesting that most Americans were willing to wait for a rational resolution to the deadlock. Even later the data were inconclusive, the results hinging on how the question was framed. About three weeks after the vote, a Gallup Poll showed that about 60 percent of those interviewed felt the "election situation had gone on too long." But a *New York Times* survey taken about the same time showed that a majority were opposed to Gore conceding, and that the public was divided closely along partisan lines.

Common sense should have made the press question whether polling data held much meaning. Public opinion was certainly not a determining factor in a controversy that was being resolved in the courts and was bound to change with developments. But whatever the public felt, some pundits behaved as if their own patience and attention spans had been consumed. No one was more emphatic in expressing this irritation than Tim Russert, the impresario of "Meet the Press," a relentless interrogator adept at bullying his guests. On the Sunday before the Florida Supreme Court handed down its decision to extend the deadline for hand recounting, Russert demanded that Senator Lieberman, whom the Gore campaign had dispatched as its agent to counter the barrage of Republican propaganda against the manual recount of ballots, announce that Gore would give up the fight and accept Bush as the winner if the Florida tribunal upheld an unfavorable lower-court decision against him.

Lieberman replied reasonably enough that this was an "open question." It was a complicated case, much was at stake, he explained, and they would wait to see exactly what the court decided.

But Russert could not understand why Lieberman, whose ticket had received more votes than any nominated by the Democrats in history, and ultimately half a million more than Bush and Cheney, would not stipulate to its defeat under the auspices of NBC News. "But, Senator," he protested, "if the [Florida] Supreme Court rules that the lower-court judge was correct and the hand recount should not be counted, it ends there. The Supreme Court has spoken. Why not accept that decision? Why keep dangling out there future litigation?"

Jim Baker, Bush's *consigliere* in Florida, could hardly have said it better. But of course the Florida Supreme Court did not rule the way Russert had suggested it would, and the struggle raged on.

Some journalists found a better outlet for their energies than pontification. John Mintz and Dan Keating of the *Washington Post* and Mireya Navarro and Somini Sengupta of the *New York Times* reported that thousands of black voters in Florida had been disfranchised by malfunctioning voter machines and sloppy record-keeping in their precincts. The *Miami Herald* conducted a study which showed that if the 185,000 uncounted ballots in Florida had been distributed according to the ratios Gore and Bush actually received in each of the state's 5,885 voting precincts, Gore would have won handily.

But another important story did not get the attention it deserved. This was the strange goings-on in heavily Democratic Miami–Dade County, where local officials started a hand recount and then abandoned it, a decision that ruined Gore's chances of overtaking Bush. Some stories suggested that the Dade election board had been intimidated by raucous Republican protests against their recount. A report in the *New York Times* indicated that Miami's Mayor Alex Penelas, a Democrat, might have influenced the decision to abandon the count in hopes of gaining Republican support for his own ambitions to run for Congress. But reports were inconclusive, leaving unsolved one of the most important riddles of the election.

The turmoil of the 2000 campaign underlined the lessons to be learned from the media's struggles to cover the eight previous contests for the presidency dating back to 1968. After each campaign journalists asked themselves how they might do a better job, and that same question was heard after election day 2000 with particular frequency because of the hairbreadth margin that separated the two presidential candidates. Hard and fast answers don't work for dealing with a process constantly in flux and where media outlets themselves are so variegated. But looking over these past nine campaigns, it is possible to delineate a few guidelines which can help the media fill their role of informing the public while helping their readers and viewers defend themselves against confusion and distortion.

Character counts, but the press needs to explain why and how. It is not enough to unearth examples of unsavory behavior from a candidate's past. Just as the media need to be certain they have the facts straight, they also have a large responsibility to explain to the public why it should care. Poll results, though they need to be weighed judiciously, do suggest that Americans are concerned with morality in politics and that a significant number view the role of the president as setting an example by his personal behavior. It is the media's job to link this respect for morality to whatever evidence it finds of the violation of such values.

Failure to make this connection clear in the cases of Gary Hart and Bill Clinton did not spare these politicians damage. But it left resentment among their supporters and confusion among everyone else. The press does not need to impose an absolutist standard of judgment on candidate behavior. Contrast and comparison better serve the purpose of explaining the meaning of character in a political context. Based on his campaign performance and his background, George W. Bush at times seemed careless to the point of recklessness. Al Gore's behavior suggested a smugness bordering on arrogance. The goal of the press should have been to help citizens balance these apparent flaws against the personal strengths of each man in casting their ballots.

Every negative episode from a candidate's biography is not equally relevant to presidential performance. The disclosure that Tom Eagleton, George McGovern's vice presidential choice, had received electroshock therapy and then concealed that information from McGovern raised legitimate questions about his fitness to serve as McGovern's backup. Much less significant was Dan Quayle, George Bush's running mate, using family influence to get into the National Guard at the height of the Vietnam War, because Quayle's past behavior had no direct connection to his future responsibilities as first understudy.

The media have an obligation to compare the candidate's rhetoric to actual behavior. Bill Clinton's womanizing and draft evasion took on political relevance because he campaigned as a champion of middle-class values. Vice President Gore wowed the 1996 Democratic convention with a gripping tale of the epiphany he supposedly experienced at his sister's deathbed in 1984 on the evils of tobacco. But the glow from that episode was soon clouded by the disclosure that Gore had received substantial financial support from the tobacco industry for years after her death. Similarly, George W. Bush's effort to present himself as an avatar of integrity was undercut by his unwillingness to disclose his arrest for driving under the influence.

The argument that voters don't care about character will still be made, of course, but there is an easy way to test that. Just wait for some future White House contender to say something along the following lines: "I'll do everything possible to promote prosperity and protect national security. But, just so you're not surprised, I want you to know that in my personal life I feel free to cheat and lie and enjoy whatever pleasures of the flesh are available." The first time a candidate makes such a statement journalists will know that presidential character no longer matters.

Meanwhile journalists should bear in mind that the presidency remains today as Franklin Roosevelt described it at the dawn of the media age, "preeminently a place of moral leadership." That concept, rooted in the very first presidency, is what makes the office unique and gives whoever holds the job a chance to win a place in history alongside the immortals on Mount Rushmore.

Polls can be either a useful tool or an instrument for sowing confusion, depending on how well they are explained. Data are more reliable when they concern simple, explicit questions such as voting choices, than more complex and abstract issues such as honor, betrayal, and the meaning of "high crimes and misdemeanors." Contradicting the notion that the public totally discounted the Lewinsky scandal were poll results that revealed a citizenry deeply conflicted about the affair. A majority of Americans, according to a Fox News survey taken in the midst of Clinton's Senate impeachment trial, believed the president had perjured himself before a federal grand jury the previous August. In a separate poll taken in January by John Zogby International, a majority also viewed perjury as an impeachable offense. Since most Americans according to other polling data opposed impeachment, the findings of the two surveys suggested that most Americans were against impeachment for acts they considered impeachable. If that proposition seems contradictory and confusing, it only illustrates the folly of relying too heavily on a few polling questions to understand a multi-faceted problem.

The pitfalls of polling on complex issues are many. "Whenever a question includes a benefit without a cost, or a cost without a benefit, the results are predictable and almost meaningless," points out former Clinton budget director Alice Rivlin. Then there's the loaded question, as in the survey on repeal of the estate tax which explained that "in order to pay for this tax bill, some sons and daughters have had to sell off the farms and small businesses they just inherited." No wonder about 70 percent of those surveyed favored repeal.

A good rule of thumb for evaluating the merit of a poll on thorny questions of public policy issues is to consider how many of those interviewed had ever thought about this issue even for a moment before the pollster popped the question. Simpler polls, like those which ask interviewees which candidate for president they prefer, have problems of their own. Unless such surveys are conducted close to election day, the opinions they solicit are likely to be no more firmly held than a teenager's feelings for his latest crush, a point demonstrated by the ups and downs for Bush and Gore during the 2000 campaign.

In mid-September a *Newsweek* poll of 580 likely voters gave Gore a fourteen-percentage-point lead over Bush, far greater than any other survey. Within a week a new *Newsweek* poll showed only a two-point lead for Gore. What went wrong? It could have been any one of a number of things, perhaps hard-to-detect flaws in the design or execution of the poll, such as subtle bias in the selection of the sample. Even the use of scientific sampling techniques cannot ensure that the correct population was surveyed.

Pollsters like to use impressive-sounding phrases like "margin of error" and "scientific sample" and "percentage of confidence." But what do they really mean? Not much, according to Harry O'Neill of the Roper Starch Worldwide polling organization. "God forbid the public should ever find out that all sampling error and its 95 percent confidence interval really say," O'Neill explains, "is that if you conduct the same biased survey among the same unrepresentative sample 100 times, you will get the same meaningless results 95 times within plus or minus some percentage points of the result of the particular survey being reported."

The press should cover the news, not predict it. The wisdom of this policy was demonstrated on election night 2000 by the errant forecasts of the networks. "We don't just have egg on our faces. We have an omelet," admitted NBC anchor Tom Brokaw. But such contrition did little to make up for the damage done by the networks double bobble on Florida. The initial declaration of Gore as the winner of the Sunshine State came early enough in the evening so that it gave the Bush campaign cause for complaint that its get-out-the-vote drive in the Western states had been dampened by this discouraging news. The subsequent declaration that Bush had won the state and the election, shortly after 2 a.m. Eastern time, led Gore to concede victory to Bush, then retract that concession. More important, it created the impression that Bush had really won the election, leaving the burden on Gore to prove otherwise, an advantage that Bush and his aides exploited to the fullest all through the chaotic days of the long recount and legal maneuvering that followed the election.

Of course the urge to predict the political future did not start with the television age. That same lamentable trait was prominently displayed in 1936, when the *Literary Digest* poll showed that Alf Landon would defeat Roosevelt; during the 1948 campaign by members of the pencil press who spent their days preparing the nation for the advent of the Thomas E. Dewey administration; and twenty years later when other journalists, both print and electronic, helped foster the myth of Lyndon Johnson's invincibility.

Why do journalists stick their necks out at the risk of looking like fools? Partly to keep from looking like fools. Once some members of the media pack have concluded that they know who the winner will be, competitive pressure makes it hard for others not to tag along. But predicting is a mug's game for political journalists to play—even when they turn out to be right. Once journalists guess how an election will come out, they have a vested interest in making that guess come true, leading them into closing their eyes to things they would rather not see. Thus in 1984 reporters, like myself, who were confident that Walter Mondale would win the Democratic nomination were unwilling to pay much attention to what Gary Hart was saying and doing as he whittled down Mondale's margin. And in 1991 when, following the Gulf War, political reporters were so certain in their belief that George Bush had a lock on the White House in the 1992 campaign, they forgot to consider what the troubled economy might do to hurt Bush's prospects and to put the Democratic party back on the presidential track. Besides, concentrating on who will win an election diverts time and energy from what journalists should be concentrating on, which is explaining what the election campaign is about.

Make no mistake, these precepts do not amount to a panacea for the shortcomings of political journalism. They might bring about some improvement and help make presidential campaigns more relevant and less insulting to the intelligence of the citizenry. But the amount of good that political journalists can do is limited by the drawbacks of the campaigns they cover, and ultimately of the nation's system of politics and government. At the end of the day, the coverage of presidential campaigns cannot rise above the level of the campaigns themselves.

Not surprisingly, because of its frustrating and chaotic conclusion, the 2000 campaign produced more than its share of proposals for reforming campaigns and the political system itself. But experience suggests that journalists should guard their objectivity against the enthusiasm of reformers. Claims are made that election holidays, weekend voting, and mail-in balloting—by making voting more convenient—will have a beneficial effect on voter turnout. But similar claims were made for motor-voter registration, enacted in 1993, which has had little effect on turnout. Even advocates of that change have come to realize that only making campaigns and politics more relevant to the lives of potential voters will get them to the polls.

When it comes to campaign financing, the most popular target for reform, it should be remembered that every financing reform has led to the creation of new loopholes, a tendency which is likely to continue as long as the Supreme Court insists on equating campaign spending with speech, thus restricting the reach of regulation. "You are not going to stop the flow of money in American politics," says University of Virginia government professor Larry Sabato, co-author of *Dirty Little Secrets*, a study of American political corruption. "So we should stop passing laws which encourage people and groups to use subterfuges."

As to other sorts of proposals, such as plans for shifting the schedule of presidential primaries or deconstructing the electoral college, most amount to little more than tinkering with the political machinery. Any effective change would have to be more fundamental and make politics something that matters. "You need issues that people care about," says City University of New York professor Frances Fox Piven, one of the original agitators for motor-voter registration. "But politicians have to be willing to provoke controversy, and that's what they try not to do."

The 2000 election underlined the enervated condition of the polity and assured the continuance of political stalemate. Even before the tussle over Florida's hand-counted ballots was settled, it was widely agreed that the winner, whoever he was, would have no mandate, nor for that matter would either party on Capitol Hill, where the GOP barely maintained control of both houses. Looking into the future, Curtis Gans of the Committee for the Study of the American Electorate foresaw, along with gridlock on major public policy issues, "further disaffection by the citizenry from the political process."

The revitalization of this political system cannot be accomplished with smoke, mirrors, or gimmicks. It would take a drastic remedy—nothing less than amending the Constitution to undo the Madisonian system of checks and balances with its institutionalized clash of ambitions. This would make it possible to inject cohesion and purpose into the political process and bring the political parties to life.

One approach, much pondered by scholars over the years, would combine presidential and congressional elections, placing candidates for chief executive, representative, and senator on the same slot in the ballot, and electing them all for the same four-year term. This would give legislators more incentive to cooperate with a president of the same party and make it easier for voters to hold them accountable. Another change would allow intraterm elections at the call of either the president or a majority of Congress, once during the regular four-year term, as a means of resolving deadlocks in government leadership, or to clear the air in the midst of some scandal such as Watergate or Iran-*contra*. The fact that by invoking this potent option both the president and the legislators would risk losing their offices would discourage its abuse.

But whatever the merits of these approaches to constitutional change, getting them enacted would demand vast resources—financial backing, intellectual energy, grass-roots organizing, and imaginative leadership—forces of which there is no evidence at present and little reason to believe they would develop in the foreseeable future. Nevertheless these proposals are worth examining if only because they help make clear the inadequacy of most of the half-measures that are now proposed as reforms.

Meanwhile the press can best meet its responsibilities by keeping a watchful and informed eye on the political system and its practitioners. With two wobbly parties in charge of the government, each avoiding its portion of responsibility while grasping for more than its share of credit, cynicism, while hard to resist, is counterproductive. But a vigorous skepticism can be a constructive force. In particular the members of the media should remind voters to be wary of blandishments tendered in exchange for their support. And reporters should remember themselves that politics is made up of choices and trade-offs, that everything of value carries a price, and that in this democracy the primary obligation of political journalism is to help arm the citizenry against self-delusion.

Notes

THESE NOTES provide the sources for most of the material in this book. The exceptions are information based on my own reporting, which I have indicated as such in the text, and events and statements that are a matter of public record and were widely reported and are readily accessible.

Abbreviations used in the notes:
NYT: *New York Times*
WP: *Washington Post*
LAT: *Los Angeles Times*

Chapter One. *The Enablers*

page
6 **Taken hold with scholars:** Thomas E. Patterson, *The Mass Media Election: How Americans Choose Their President* (New York: Praeger, 1980); Doris A. Graber, *Media Power in Politics* (Washington, D.C.: CQ Press, 1984); Austin Ranney, *Channels of Power: The Impact of Television on American Politics* (New York: Basic Books, 1983).

9 **Resisted concrete measures:** Michael Schudson, *The Good Citizen: A History of American Civic Life* (Cambridge, Mass: Harvard University Press), p. 76.

9 **"Depend on public opinion":** Roy R. Fairfield, ed., *The Federalist Papers*, 2nd ed. (Garden City, N.Y.: Anchor Books, 1966), No. 84, p. 262n.

10 **Washington's condemnation:** Richard Norton Smith, *Patriarch: George Washington and the New American Nation* (New York: Houghton Mifflin, 1993), p. 267.

10 **Hamilton on faction:** Fairfield, p. 34.

10 **Jefferson declared:** James MacGregor Burns, *The Deadlock of Democracy,* rev. ed. (Englewood Cliffs, N.J.: Prentice-Hall, 1963), p. 27n.

10 **Part of the bargain:** Joseph J. Ellis, *American Sphinx* (New York: Knopf, 1997), p. 220.

10 **Jefferson's nemesis:** Ellis, pp. 218–220; see also Fawn M. Brodie, *Thomas Jefferson* (New York: Norton, 1974), pp. 343–353.

11 **Newspapers in four sections:** Schudson, p. 75.

12 **Largest in the world:** Gordon S. Wood, "An Affair of Honor," *New York Review of Books,* April 13, 2000.

12 **Delaying publication:** Schudson, p. 126.

12 **Only eleven senators.** *Ibid.*

12 **Increase in papers.** *Ibid.,* p. 116.

12 **Tocqueville's axiom:** Alexis de Tocqueville, *Democracy in America* (New York: Oxford, 1947), p. 106.

13 **The rise of the penny press:** Michael Schudson, *Discovering the News: A Social History of American Newspapers* (New York: Basic Books, 1978), p. 65.

13 **A Marine Corps commission:** Schudson, *The Good Citizen,* p. 121.

13 **Lincoln blames the press:** Don E. Fehrenbacher, ed., *Lincoln: Speeches and Writings, 1859–1865,* vol. 2 (New York: Library of America, 1989), Letter to Carl Schurz, Nov. 10, 1962, p. 380.

13 **"I am used to it":** *Ibid.,* Letter to James H. Hackett, Nov. 2, 1863, p. 532.

14 **TR's trial balloons:** John Milton, *The Warrior and the Priest* (Cambridge, Mass.: Belknap Press, 1983), p. 70.

14 **"They'd never mention me":** Doris Kearns Goodwin, "Every Four Years: Presidential Campaigns and the Press, 1896–2000" (Arlington, Va.: Freedom Forum, 2000), p. 5n.

15 **A barrage of editorials:** W. A. Swanberg, *Citizen Hearst* (New York: Bantam, 1967), p. 516.

15 **Hearst's efforts in Georgia:** Franklin Delano Roosevelt Library, Democratic National Committee Files, Georgia, box 131n.

15 **A page-one editorial:** Frank Freidel, *FDR: The Triumph* (Boston: Little, Brown, 1956), p. 250.

16 **Not a straight line:** Ralph G. Martin, *Ballots and Bandwagons:*

Three Great Conventions (New York: New American Library, 1964), p. 138.

16 **Howe's inspection:** William Seale, *The President's House* (Washington, D.C.: White House Historical Association, 1986), p. 916.

16 **FDR's fall:** Hugh Gallagher, *FDR's Splendid Deception* (New York: Dodd, Mead, 1985), p. 103.

16 **The press did not notice:** Paul Taylor, *See How They Run: Electing the President in an Age of Mediaocracy* (New York: Knopf, 1990), p. 62.

17 **"To step aside":** Robert Shogan, "The 1948 Election," *American Heritage,* June 1968.

Chapter Two. *1968: The Omnipotent Eye*

20 **Truman's pointed question:** *Facts on File, 1960,* p. 230. Truman had his own favorite for the presidency, fellow Missourian Stuart Symington.

21 **"Some 50 to 100 men":** Richard Neustadt, *Presidential Power,* rev. ed. (New York: John Wiley, 1980), p. 175.

21 **A nation on the move:** Data are from U.S. Bureau of the Census, *Statistical Abstract of the United States* (Washington, D.C.: Government Printing Office, 1980).

21 **"Men still talk to each other":** Joseph Bensman and Bernard Rosenberg, "Mass Media and Mass Culture," in Phillip Olson, ed., *America as a Mass Society* (New York: Free Press, 1963).

23 **"They seethed with enthusiasm":** Theodore H. White, *The Making of the President 1960* (New York: Atheneum, 1961), p. 291.

23 **"We couldn't survive":** Theodore C. Sorensen, *Kennedy* (New York: Harper and Row, 1965), p. 325.

23 **"Social flattery":** Henry Fairlie, *The Kennedy Promise* (Garden City, N.Y.: Doubleday, 1973), p. 216.

24 **"A golden interlude":** Arthur M. Schlesinger, Jr., *A Thousand Days: John F. Kennedy in the White House* (Boston: Houghton Mifflin, 1965), p. 207.

24 **Johnson's insecurity:** Doris Kearns, *Lyndon Johnson and the American Dream* (New York: New American Library, 1976), p. 385; Robert Caro, *The Years of Lyndon Johnson: The Path to Power* (New York: Knopf, 1982), pp. 85–97.

25 **"He had to win"**: Caro, p. 72.

25 **"They're going to write history"**: Michael R. Beschloss, *Taking Charge: The Johnson White House Tapes, 1963–1964* (New York: Simon and Schuster, 1997), pp. 36–37.

25 **"What Asian boys ought to be doing"**: Rowland Evans and Robert Novak, *Lyndon Johnson: The Exercise of Power* (New York: New American Library, 1966), p. 532.

26 **"Better to fight in Vietnam"**: Hanson Baldwin, "We Must Choose," *New York Times Magazine*, Feb. 21, 1965, cited in Marvin E. Gettleman, ed., *Vietnam: History, Documents, and Opinions on a Major World Crisis* (New York: Fawcett, 1965).

27 **"Distrust, division and dissent"**: Walter Lippmann, "The Democrats in 1968," *Newsweek*, Jan. 1, 1968.

27 **GOP analysis:** "The Newsweek Delegate Count," *Newsweek*, Jan. 8, 1968.

28 **Tet offensive:** "Hanoi Attacks," *Newsweek*, Feb. 12, 1968.

29 **"Massively stirred"**: Harris Wofford, *Of Kennedys and Kings: Making Sense of the Sixties* (New York: Farrar, Straus, 1980), p. 236.

28 **"Naked in the streets"**: Theodore White, *In Search of History: A Personal Adventure* (New York: Warner Books, 1978), p. 506.

29 **Belie Washington's claims:** Kathleen Turner, *Lyndon Johnson's Dual War: Vietnam and the Press* (Chicago: University of Chicago Press, 1985), p. 118.

30 **Hawkish voters:** Todd Gitlin, *The Sixties: Years of Hope, Days of Rage* (New York: Bantam, 1993), p. 301n.

31 **"Five days last week"**: "The Fight to Dump LBJ," *Newsweek*, Mar. 25, 1968.

31 **"On a perilous course"**: *Ibid.*

31 **Johnson drops out:** Lyndon B. Johnson, *Vantage Point: Perspectives on the Presidency, 1963–1969* (New York: Holt, 1971), p. 435.

34 **"Militant nonviolence"**: Gitlin, pp. 320–322.

34 **Troops on standby:** *Ibid.*, p. 323.

35 **Bashing reporters:** *Ibid.*, p. 327.

35 **"The Iron Fist"**: "Sizing Up Chicago," *Newsweek*, Sept. 9, 1968.

35 **Humphrey fumed:** Theodore White, *The Making of the President 1968* (New York: Atheneum, 1969), p. 302.

36 **Pretentious phoneys:** "Reporting: Fear of Poisoned Wells," *Time*, Sept. 20, 1968.

36 **White scribbled:** White, p. 301.

37 **"Just let it lie":** William Safire, *Before the Fall: An Inside View of the Pre-Watergate White House* (New York: Doubleday, 1975), pp. 61–62.

41 **"The bad news business":** Chester Lewis, Godfrey Hodgson, and Bruce Page, *An American Melodrama: The Presidential Campaign of 1968* (New York: Viking, 1969), p. 293.

42 **"I called to kiss your ass":** Dan Carter, "Good Copy." *Media Studies Journal,* Fall, 1998.

42 **"The omnipotent eye":** Richard Nixon, *RN: The Memoirs of Richard Nixon* (New York: Grosset and Dunlap, 1978), p. 303.

43 **Mike Wallace's comment:** "He's More Fun," *Newsweek,* Mar. 18, 1968.

43 **"You must have peeked":** Jules Witcover, *The Resurrection of Richard Nixon* (New York: Putnam, 1970), p. 300.

44 **"What I want for America":** Joe McGinnis, *The Selling of the President: 1968* (New York: Trident, 1969), p. 71.

44 **Only the best:** *Ibid.,* p. 36.

Chapter Three. *1972: "The Greatest Goddam Change"*

46 **The new rules:** Commission on Party Structure and Delegate Selection, George McGovern, Chairman, "Mandate for Reform" (Washington, D.C.: Democratic National Committee, 1970).

46 **"The greatest goddam change":** Ernest R. May and Janet Fraser, eds., *Campaign '72: The Managers Speak* (Cambridge, Mass.: Harvard University Press, 1973), p. 4.

47 **"A sanity pill":** Richard Dougherty, *Goodbye, Mr. Christian: A Personal Account of McGovern's Rise and Fall* (New York: Doubleday, 1973), pp. 14–16.

48 **Muskie's speech:** Jules Witcover, *White Knight: The Rise of Spiro Agnew* (New York: Random House, 1972), p. 392.

49 **The press overlooked:** May and Fraser, pp. 44–45.

49 **"An air of uneasiness":** William Watts and Lloyd Free, *State of the Nation* (New York: Potomac Associates, Universe Books, 1973), p. 20.

50 **"In serious trouble":** May and Fraser, p. 47.

51 **"Muskie Campaign Lacks Spark":** *NYT,* Nov. 24, 1971.

51 **"A speedy response":** Dougherty, p. 41.

51 **Role of the *Times*:** Theodore H. White, *The Making of the President 1972* (New York: Atheneum, 1973), pp. 258–260.

52 **Muskie "choked up":** *Ibid.,* p. 82.

54 **"A vicious circle":** Gordon L. Weil, *The Long Shot: George McGovern Runs for President* (New York: Norton, 1973), p. 91.

55 **"We sweated blood":** Gary Hart, *Right from the Start: A Chronicle of the McGovern Campaign* (New York: Quadrangle, 1973), p. 115.

56 **"Unusual freshness":** Weil, p. 93.

56 **Press criticism of McGovern:** Hart, pp. 204–205; Weil, pp. 96–101.

57 **His advisers warned:** Weil, p. 77.

58 **"The goddam idea":** Hart, p. 190.

60 **Comments from Greider and *NYT*:** Quoted in Hunter S. Thompson, *Fear and Loathing on the Campaign Trail: '72* (San Francisco: Straight Arrow Books, 1973), pp. 330–336.

60 **Reston and Kraft's comments:** Quoted in *Newsweek,* Aug. 14, 1972.

61 **"This wouldn't have happened":** Arthur M. Schlesinger, Jr., *Robert Kennedy and His Times* (Boston: Houghton Mifflin, 1978), p. 210.

61 **"What's he done now?":** Dougherty, p. 213.

61 **Pack journalism:** Timothy Crouse, *The Boys on the Bus* (New York: Ballantine, 1980), p. 7.

64 **"We couldn't cover Nixon":** May and Fraser, p. 252.

65 **"Not a single reporter":** White, *Making of the President 1972,* p. 267.

65 **"A helluva press conference":** May and Fraser, p. 253.

66 **Parties in disrepute:** *Ibid.,* p. 219.

Chapter Four. *1976: The Talent Scouts*

69 **Jordan's advice:** Martin Schram, *Running for President 1976: The Carter Campaign* (New York: Stein and Day, 1977), pp. 56–57; Jules Witcover, *Marathon: The Pursuit of the Presidency, 1972–1976* (New York: New American Library, 1977), p. 326.

69 **Polsby's analysis:** Nelson Polsby, "The News Media as an Alternative to Party in the Presidential Election Process," in Robert A. Goldwin, ed., *Political Parties in the Eighties* (Washington, D.C.: American Enterprise Institute, 1980).

71 **"A little soul-searching":** David Gelman, "Covering the Campaign," *Newsweek,* Mar. 29, 1976.

73 **"At the pearly gates"**: James Fallows, "The Passionless Presidency," *Atlantic*, May 1989.

75 **Jordan's tactical advice**: Schram, pp. 375–380.

78 **One published analysis**: Pat Caddell and Robert Shrum, "Pale Horse, White Rider," *Rolling Stone*, Oct. 24, 1974.

80 **McGovern's questions**: George McGovern, *Grassroots: The Autobiography of George McGovern* (New York: Random House, 1977), pp. 263–264.

80 **"Ethnic purity"**: *New York Daily News*, Apr. 4, 1976.

80 **Stirred a storm**: Schram, p. 123.

81 **The forgiveness rally**: Witcover, *Marathon*, p. 326.

85 **"They'll remember the visual"**: *Ibid.*, p. 591.

85 **"A real plus"**: Jonathan Moore and Janet Fraser, eds., *Campaign for President: The Managers Look at '76* (Cambridge, Mass.: Ballinger, 1977), p. 134.

85 **Explaining Carter**: Witcover, *Marathon*, p. 622.

85 **Carter volunteered**: Robert Scheer and Barry Golson, "Jimmy Carter: A Candid Conversation," *Playboy*, November 1976.

88 **"Failure of communication"**: David Gelman, et al., "The Marathon Men," *Newsweek*, Nov. 1, 1976.

Chapter Five. *1980: Hostage to Crisis*

90 **Burnham's verdict**: Quoted in Haynes Johnson, "Media," in *The Pursuit of the Presidency, 1980* (New York: Berkley, 1980).

90 **Burnham later acknowledged**: Interview with the author, Jan. 28, 2000.

90 **"This year, by God"**: Arlie Schardt, et al., "Rating Campaign Coverage," *Newsweek*, Mar. 24, 1980.

92 **Wicker's critique**: *NYT*, May 21, 1978.

92 **Evans and Novak lamented**: *WP*, Sept. 30, 1977.

92 **"Like Elmer Gantry"**: George Will, "Lance, Carter, Babbitt and Gantry," *Newsweek*, Sept. 19, 1977.

92 **Safire's critique**: *NYT*, Apr. 20, 1978.

92 **"It's hard for me to describe"**: Robert Shogan, *Promises to Keep: Carter's First 100 Days* (New York: Crowell, 1977), pp. 276–281.

93 **"Carter's intent"**: Peter Goldman, et al., "Jimmy Carter's Cabinet Purge," *Newsweek*, July 30, 1979.

95 **Apprehension in the Carter camp:** Haynes Johnson, "Media," in *The Pursuit of the Presidency* (New York: Berkeley, 1980).

95 **"The sky is so blue":** Jack W. Germond and Jules Witcover, *Blue Smoke and Mirrors: How Reagan Won and Why Carter Lost the Election of 1980* (New York: Viking, 1981), pp. 70–71.

98 **"Patriotic fervor":** Johnson.

99 **Assault on Kennedy:** *LAT*, Dec. 4, 1979.

101 **Carter's use of incumbency:** *Wall Street Journal*, Jan. 11, 1980.

102 **"The best in history":** Patrick Caddell and Richard Wirthlin, "Face Off: A Conversation with the President's Pollsters," *Public Opinion*, December/January 1981.

103 **"Saber-rattling":** *LAT*, Aug. 15, 1980.

104 **"The worst thing":** Schardt.

106 **"There is no way":** quoted in Anthony King, "How Not to Select Presidential Candidates," in Austin Ranney, ed., *The American Elections of 1980* (Washington, D.C.: American Enterprise Institute, 1980).

106 **Carter or Reagan:** *NYT*, Oct. 26, 1980.

107 **The media's performance:** Jonathan Moore, ed., *The Campaign for President: 1980 in Retrospect* (Cambridge, Mass.: Ballinger, 1981), p. xv.

108 **"Utter malarkey":** Germond and Witcover, p. 264.

Chapter Six. *1984: "You Cover the News, We'll Stage It"*

113 **Campaign wasteland:** William Henry III, "The View from the Bus," *Time*, Feb. 13, 1984.

114 **Gatekeepers for celebrities:** Thomas Griffith, "When the Game Is Name," *Time*, Jan. 9, 1984.

115 **"Moment of brilliance":** David Broder, "Jane Byrne Reelected?," *WP*, Dec. 21, 1983.

116 **"Dares to be cautious":** *NYT*, Dec. 14, 1983.

118 **Changing chemistry:** Walter Shapiro, et al., "Gary Hart's Big Surge," *Newsweek*, Mar. 12, 1984.

119 **Pundits respond:** William A. Henry III, "Fast Freights and Side Rails," *Time*, Mar. 26, 1984.

123 **Jackson's slurs:** *WP*, Feb. 13, 1984.

123 **Farrakhan's reaction:** Charles Leehrsen, et al., "Special Coverage for Jesse?," *Newsweek*, Apr. 9, 1984.

123 **As the *Times* asked:** NYT, Mar. 8, 1984.

125 **The misery index:** Scott Keeter, "Public Opinion in 1984," in Gerald Pomper, ed., *The Election of 1984: Reports and Interpretations* (Chatham, N.J.: Chatham House, 1985).

126 **Reagan aides view the press:** Steven R. Weisman, "The President and the Press," NYT, Oct. 14, 1984.

126 **Stress on television:** Larry Speakes, *Speaking Out: The Reagan Presidency from Inside the White House* (New York: Avon, 1988), p. 271.

127 **Response to Gromyko meeting:** Weisman.

128 **Campaign plane atmosphere:** Jacob V. Lamar, Jr., "The View from 30,000 Ft," *Time*, Sept. 17, 1984.

129 **Dr. Ruge's response:** Peter Goldman, et al., "The Making of a Landslide," *Newsweek*, November/December 1984, election issue.

130 **Reston's response:** James Reston, "Reagan Beats the Press," NYT, Nov. 4, 1984.

Chapter Seven. *1988: Character Study*

132 **Hart's press conference:** LAT, Apr. 15, 1987.

133 **New Jersey wisecrack:** NYT, May 31, 1984.

133 **"Always in jeopardy":** Howard Fineman, "Gary Hart: A Candidate in Search of Himself," *Newsweek*, Apr. 13, 1987; Lois Romano, "The Unprivate Life of Gary Hart," WP, Apr. 13, 1987.

134 **Raskin's recollections:** Richard Harwood, "Who Sets Rules for the Press?," WP, Aug. 9, 1987.

134 **"No story there":** NYT, May 6, 1987.

135 **"A John Wayne straight shooter":** Stanley Greenberg, "Report on Democratic Defection," prepared for the Michigan House Democratic Campaign Committee, April 1985.

136 **"Like a Turkish pasha":** Martin Anderson, *Revolution* (New York: Harcourt Brace, 1988), pp. 289–295.

136 **"Who Gary Hart is":** Romano.

136 **"Not a traditional politician":** *Ibid.*

138 **"I was thirteen at the time":** E. J. Dionne, "Gary Hart: The Elusive Frontrunner," NYT, May 3, 1987.

138 **"Follow me around":** *Ibid.*

138   Tom Fiedler's sympathetic story: *Miami Herald,* Apr. 27, 1987.

138   "We don't need another president who lies": Jack Germond and Jules Witcover, *Whose Broad Stripes and Bright Stars: The Trivial Pursuit of the Presidency, 1988* (New York: Warner, 1989), p. 182.

139   Another affair: Taylor, pp. 48–52.

139   Reaction from politicians: *LAT,* May 9, 1987.

140   "Are there no limits?": Harwood.

141   Roehrich's warning: *LAT,* May 9, 1987.

142   No Major Legislation: Michael Barme and Grant Ugifusa, *The Almanac of American Politics 1988* (Washington: National Journal, 1988), p. 224.

142   Biden's Problems: LAT, Sept. 24, 1987.

143   "The camera is everywhere": Reuven Frank, "On Sound Bites, Strategizing and Free Media," *NYT,* Nov. 6, 1988.

145   Exposing the press to the public: *NYT,* Aug. 19, 1988.

146   "Symbolic of an approach": Germond and Witcover, *Whose Broad Stripes and Bright Stars,* p. 461.

146   Bush's focus group study: *WP,* Oct. 28, 1988.

146   Bush stress on values: *LAT,* Sept. 6, 1988; *LAT,* Oct. 17, 1988.

148   Bush at Newark Airport: *WP,* Sept. 21, 1988.

149   Justice Jackson's opinion: *West Virginia Board of Education v. Barnette* (1943), cited in Percival Jackson, *Dissent in the Supreme Court* (Norman: University of Oklahoma Press, 1969), pp. 207–208.

149   Lisa Myers comments: Quoted in *WP,* Sept. 21, 1988.

149   "No cost for ducking": *Ibid.*

150   "At least one hour a week": *WP,* Sept. 23, 1988.

150   Harwood's and Broder's views: Richard Harwood: "The Press Should Set the Agenda," *WP,* Sept. 25, 1988.

151   "Some smart politician": Walter Shapiro, "Why It Was So Sour," *Time,* Nov. 14, 1988.

Chapter Eight. *1992: Beat the Press*

153   Greenberg's thesis: Stanley B. Greenberg, "Reconstructing the Democratic Vision," *American Prospect,* Spring 1990. See also Greenberg's "The Democrats and the Middle Class," *American Prospect,* Fall 1991.

154 **"Nuclear war"**: Peter Goldman, et al., *Quest for the Presidency, 1992* (College Station, Tex.: Texas A&M Press, 1994), pp. 94–100.

155 **"Assure his re-election"**: *LAT*, Aug. 8, 1990.

155 **Clinton at press breakfast:** Jack Germond and Jules Witcover, *Mad as Hell: Revolt at the Ballot Box, 1992* (New York: Warner, 1993), pp. 169–170; David Maraniss, *First in His Class: A Biography of Bill Clinton* (New York: Simon and Schuster, 1995), p. 461.

157 **"A shabby accusation"**: Ellen Ladowsky, "Bill Clinton Is No Victim of the Press," *NYT*, Mar. 24, 1992.

157 **Comparison with Hart:** Jonathan Alter, "The Cycle of Sensationalism," *Newsweek*, Jan. 27, 1992.

158 **Grunwald vs. Koppel:** Goldman, et al., p. 95. Germond and Witcover, *Mad as Hell*, p. 182.

160 **Focus group views:** *LAT*, Feb. 2, 1992.

161 **Shore's couplet:** Goldman, et al., p. 138.

163 **Clinton vs. his stepfather:** *Chicago Tribune*, Mar. 13, 1992.

164 **Kerrey's reaction:** *Boston Globe*, Feb. 27, 1992.

164 **Clinton's response to Brown:** *NYT*, Mar. 16, 1992.

165 **"Damaged goods"**: Charles T. Royer, ed., *Campaign for President: The Managers Look at '92* (Hollis, N.H.: Hollis Publishing, 1994), p. 184.

165 **Clinton's "new media" campaign:** *NYT*, Nov. 8, 1992.

165 **Appearance on Arsenio:** *NYT*, June 5, 1992.

166 **"What I'm fighting for"**: Henry Muller and John Stacks, "An Interview with Bill Clinton," *Time*, July 20, 1992.

167 **Perot-King exchange:** *NYT*, May 8, 1992.

167 **"His New Hampshire"**: *WP*, May 5, 1992.

167 **Accepting Perot's image:** *LAT*, Apr. 19, 1992.

168 **Debunking Perot:** *WP*, May 5, 1992.

168 **"Media litmus tests"**: *NYT*, May 9, 1992.

170 **"A wounded president"**: *WP*, Feb. 20, 1992.

170 **The "excellent adventure"**: Walter Shapiro, "So Happy Together," *Time*, Sept. 7, 1992.

170 **Media coverage of Bush:** Howard Kurtz, "When the Media Are on a Roll": *WP*, July 25, 1992.

171 **"Annoy the media"**: *NYT*, Oct. 25, 1992.

172 **Perot's complaint:** *WP*, Oct. 31, 1992.

Chapter Nine. *1996: Not the Russian Revolution*

176 "A sharp turn": *LAT*, Nov. 9, 1994.

176 Living standard decline: Ruy A. Teixeira and Joel Rogers, "Who Deserted the Democrats in 1994," *American Prospect*, Fall 1995.

176 "Republicans Seek Changes": *NYT*, Dec. 8, 1994; "Gingrich Comes Out Slugging," *NYT*, Dec. 7, 1994; "GOP Blitzkrieg," *NYT*, Sept. 22, 1995; "Hill's GOP Freshmen," *WP*, July 10, 1995; "Democrats Seem Stuck," *NYT*, Feb. 22, 1995.

176 "A rout": *WP*, Sept. 20, 1995.

176 "They thought it was the Russian Revolution": *LAT*, Feb. 26, 1996.

177 No compromise: *LAT*, Nov. 12, 1994.

177 Exit poll findings: *LAT*, Feb. 26, 1996.

178 Signs of discontent: William Schneider, "The 'Uh-Oh' Factor," *LAT*, Mar. 26, 1995.

178 The Powell boom: Howard Kurtz, "Pressing for Powell," *WP*, Sept. 13, 1995.

180 Initial reaction to Forbes: *NYT*, Sept. 23, 1995; *WP*, Sept. 23, 1995.

180 Forbes's television blitz: *LAT*, Jan. 28, 1996; *NYT*, Jan. 27, 1996.

181 Coverage of Forbes's rise: *WP*, Jan. 22, 1996.

183 "Senator, you *beat* her": Author's interview with James Courtovich, Feb. 27, 1996.

184 Economic anguish: Reporters of *New York Times*, *The Downsizing of America* (New York: Times Books, 1996).

185 "I got three of them": *LAT*, Aug. 26, 1996.

186 "I didn't realize": *LAT*, Feb. 26, 1996.

187 "We didn't understand": *LAT*, Mar. 26, 1996.

187 Coverage of Buchanan: *LAT*, Feb. 28, 1996.

191 "Why let him off the hook?": Author's interview with Scott Reed, Jan. 16, 1997.

191 "I'm running mine": *NYT*, Aug. 3, 1996.

193 "Self-pitying terms": Elizabeth Drew, *On the Edge: The Clinton Presidency* (New York: Simon and Schuster, 1994), p. 182.

193 "A lot of drip-drip-drip": *LAT*, June 18, 1996.

193 Clinton over Dole: *WP*, Apr. 26, 1996.

194 Dole's old affair: Howard Kurtz provides the most complete account in *WP*, Nov. 13, 1996.

Chapter Ten. *2000: Seduction on the Straight-talk Express*

197   *Post* **sounds alarm**: *WP*, Jan. 10, 1999.

197   ***Boston Globe* story**: *Boston Globe*, Feb. 14, 1999.

199   **A "greater responsibility"**: David Broder and Richard Morin, "Struggle Over New Standards," *WP*, Dec. 27, 1998.

199   **"Responsibility era"**: "Hardball with Chris Matthews," MSNBC transcript, June 14, 1999.

199   **"Hand on the Bible"**: Ralph Z. Hallow, "Bush Bears Down . . ." *Washington Times*, June 15, 1999.

200   **"I refuse to play"**: *NYT*, Aug. 19, 1999.

201   **"A very good question"**: *NYT*, Aug. 20, 1999.

201   **Not since 1974**: *WP*, Aug. 20, 1999.

202   **"Opts for scamps"**: Frank Rich, "And the Winner Is," *NYT*, Aug. 28, 1999.

202   **Polls on asking about cocaine**: *WP*, Aug. 21, 1999.

203   **Gore seeks separation**: *NYT*, June 17, 1999.

204   **"Where was Al Gore?"**: *Washington Times*, June 17, 1999.

204   **Voters not convinced**: *WP*, Mar. 16, 1999.

205   **Gore's Internet role**: *WP*, Mar. 21, 1999.

205   **As model for *Love Story***: Margaret Carlson, "Stretches and Sighs," *Time*, Oct. 16, 2000.

205   **Clinton's concerns**: *NYT*, May 14, 1999.

207   **Will the new look work?**: Bill Turque, "Reinventing Gore," *Newsweek*, Oct. 4, 1999.

207   **More stumbles**: *WP*, Jan. 11, 2000.

208   **Bradley's limitations**: *WP*, Mar. 4, 2000.

208   **The arrhythmia incident**: Eric Pooley, "A Sense of Where You're Not," *Time*, Jan. 31, 2000.

209   **Murphy's strategy**: Author's interview, Apr. 14, 2000.

211   **"My foot in my mouth"**: *WP*, Dec. 8, 1999.

211   **"Evil influence"**: *NYT*, Feb. 29, 2000.

212   **"Guilty as Charged"**: Mary McGrory, "Anatomy of a Swoon," *WP*, Feb. 10, 2000.

212   **"A Good Story"**: Clarence Page, "New Hampshire and the Making of a Media Darling," *Chicago Tribune*, Feb. 6, 2000.

212   **"Unshakable character"**: *NYT*, Feb. 2, 2000.

213 **"Ascendancy of character"**: Scott Leigh, "The Most UnClinton Candidate Surges," *Boston Globe*, Feb. 27, 2000.

214 **Better than three to one**: *NYT*, Feb. 3, 2000.

215 **Headlines boosting McCain**: *WP*, Feb. 27, 2000; *LAT*, Feb. 24, 2000; *Boston Globe*, Feb. 26, 2000.

216 **Exit poll results**: *WP*, Mar. 8, 2000.

Chapter Eleven. *Ballots on Broadway*

217 **The healthy society**: Karl Zinsmeister, *et al.*, "Is America Turning a Corner?" *American Enterprise*, January 1999.

218 **Tuned-out voters**: Shorenstein Center on the Press, Politics, and Public Policy, Harvard University, Vanishing Voter Project, press release, June 1, 2000.

219 **Proclaimed the *Times***: *NYT*, May 16, 2000.

219 **An ominous cloud**: *WP*, May 12, 2000.

220 **"Marriage gap"**: *Boston Globe*, May 28, 2000.

220 **Fleischer's view**: *Chicago Tribune*, May 7, 2000.

221 **"Hardly a brain wave"**: *Ibid.*

222 **"A familiar pattern"**: *WP*, May 28, 2000.

222 **Not much interest**: Howard Kurtz, "Covering the Issues," *WP*, July 3, 2000.

223 **Cutting back coverage**: *WP*, Aug. 22, 2000.

223 **Stayed away in droves**: *NYT*, Aug. 14, 2000.

223 **"Making us theater critics"**: *WP*, Aug. 21, 2000.

224 **"It was amazing"**: Howard Rosenberg, "Waiting for Reality to Set In," *LAT*, Aug. 1, 2000.

225 **Powell's challenge**: "World News This Morning," ABC News, Aug. 1, 2000. Transcript, Burrelle's Information Services.

225 **Tongue in cheek**: "The Early Show," CBS News, Aug. 1, 2000. Transcript, Burrelle's Information Services.

225 **Kouric's interview**: "Today," NBC News, Aug. 1, 2000. NBC News transcript.

225 **Russert oohed**: *HOTLINE*, Aug. 4, 2000.

225 **Gergen aahed**: PBS transcript, Aug. 3, 2000.

226 **"A partial solution"**: *WP*, Aug. 8, 2000.

226 **Cultural conservatism**: *LAT*, Aug. 8, 2000.

226   **"A daring choice":** *Chicago Tribune*, Aug. 8, 2000.

228   **Democratic argument:** *LAT*, Aug. 20, 2000.

229   **"I didn't get it":** CNN transcript #00081801V23, Aug. 18, 2000.

229   **Ardent kiss:** *WP*, Aug. 22, 2000.

229   **On the defensive:** *WP*, Aug. 23, 2000.

230   **"Bush stumbles":** *NYT*, Aug. 24, 2000.

230   **"GOP Leaders Fret":** *NYT*, Sept. 7, 2000.

230   **"Can he beat Al Gore?":** *WP*, Sept. 10, 2000.

230   **Major league Clymer:** *WP*, Sept. 5, 2000.

230   **Drowning out Bush:** *WP*, Sept. 6, 2000.

230   **Widely noticed:** Vanishing Voter Project, press release, Sept. 13, 2000.

231   **"Like Pavlov's dogs":** Howard Kurtz, "Swinging with the Polls," *WP*, Sept. 12, 2000.

231   *Time*'s **debate poll:** Nancy Gibbs, "Where Is the Love," *Time*, Oct. 16, 2000.

232   **Safire's view:** *NYT*, Oct. 5, 2000.

232   **"They held their own":** *Hotline*, Oct. 4, 2000.

232   **Boorish to a fault:** Bob Herbert, "Gore Piles On," *NYT*, Oct. 5, 2000.

233   **A major item:** CNN transcript #00100400V15, Oct. 4, 2000.

233   **"Bridge of sighs":** *Ibid.*

235   **The inspection trip:** *Ibid.*

235   **"You can't stretch":** *Ibid.*

235   **The desk in Sarasota:** *NYT*, Oct. 16, 2000, *Sarasota Herald-Tribune*, Oct. 10, Oct. 8, 2000.

236   **Degrading Gore:** *WP*, Oct. 7, 2000.

237   **"Gump or Zelig":** *NYT*, Oct. 6, 2000.

237   **Bush spent twice as much:** *NYT*, Oct. 6, 2000.

237   **20,000 new bureaucrats:** *WP*, Oct. 6, 2000.

237   **Bush's Social Security plan:** *NYT*, Nov. 2, 2000; Paul Krugman, "Reckonings; No Good Deed," *NYT*, Nov. 5, 2000.

238   **"A bit of a role reversal":** *Hotline*, Oct. 11, 2000.

238   **Warnings to Gore:** *Minneapolis Star Tribune*, Oct. 11, 2000. *Hartford Courant*, Oct. 11, 2000.

238   **Saturday Night Live on debate:** *NYT*, Oct. 11, 2000.

239   **"Theater criticism":** David Remnick, "Good Days, Bad Days," *New Yorker*, Oct. 30, 2000.

239   **"Energy is lost":** *Hotline*, Oct. 12, 2000.

239 **"On a leash"**: *Ibid.*

239 **"Deeper and longer:"** *Raleigh News and Observer*, Oct. 12, 2000.

239 **"Blurring the differences"**: *Hotline*, Oct. 12, 2000.

239 **"No bodyslams"**: *Hotline*, Oct. 18, 2000.

240 **"Body language"**: *Boston Globe*, Oct. 18, 2000.

241 **"Debates good for Bush"**: David W. Moore and Frank Newport, "As Race Narrows Voters See Little Difference," Gallup Organization press release, Oct. 24, 2000.

241 **"Sotto voce"**: Charles Peters, "Tilting at Windmills," *Washington Monthly*, October 2000.

241 **A two-day wonder:** Vaughn Ververs, "Timing Is Everything," *National Journal*, Nov. 6, 2000.

242 **"A defiant rebuttal"**: *NYT*, Nov. 4, 2000.

242 **Bush's service record:** Walter Robinson, "Questions Remain on Bush's Service," *Boston Globe*, Oct. 31, 2000.

245 **"Decidedly more negative:"** Project for Excellence in Journalism, "The Last Lap: How the Press Covered the Final Stages of the Presidential Campaign," Oct. 31, 2000.

Chapter Twelve. *From Liebling's Law to Gresham's Law*

246 **Clifford's memo:** Clark Clifford, Memorandum on Television Debate, Sept. 27, 1960, Museum of Broadcasting Communications web site (mbcnet.org/debateweb/html/history).

247 **"The one-dollar bill"**: David Ignatius, "So Long, Super Lawyers," *WP*, June 11, 2000.

248 **"No clear-cut, decisive issue"**: Theodore C. Sorensen, *Kennedy* (New York: Harper & Row, 1965), p. 181.

248 **"Nixon lacks taste"**: Arthur M. Schlesinger, Jr., *Kennedy or Nixon: Does It Make Any Difference?* (New York: Macmillan, 1963), p. 13.

249 **Style is the key:** Robert Teeter and Stuart Spencer, "Analysis of Early Research," Nov. 12, 1975, Museum of Broadcasting Communications web site (mbcnet.org/debateweb/html/history).

249 **Gergen memo:** *Ibid.*

250 **Ford came out swinging:** Tom Mathews, "The First Round," *Newsweek*, Oct. 4, 1976.

250 **"Shucked his bumbler's image"**: David M. Alpern, "The Race: Stay Tuned," *Newsweek*, Oct. 4, 1976.

250 **"The marketing culture"**: William Greider, "Stupefied Democracy," *The Nation*, Dec. 4, 2000.

252 **"Only short term"**: James Bennett, "Consultants Steal Spotlight": *NYT*, Sept. 9, 1996.

253 **Morris on two covers**: *Time*, Sept. 2, and Sept. 9, 1996.

254 **"Post-electoral era"**: Benjamin Ginsberg and Martin Shefter, *Politics by Other Means: Politicians, Prosecutors and the Press from Watergate to Whitewater* (New York: Norton, 1999), p 16.

255 **Stagnant turnout**: Based on figures compiled by Prof. Walter Dean Burnham of the University of Texas.

256 **"Mixed media culture"**: Bill Kovach and Tom Rosenstiel, *Warp Speed: America in the Age of Mixed Media* (New York: Century Foundation Press, 1999), pp. 4–5.

257 **"Here we go again."** John Ellis, "A Hard Day's Night: John Ellis' Firsthand Account of Election Night," *Inside*, Dec. 26, 2000.

259 **"Take it to the bank"**: CBS News transcript, Nov. 7, 2000. Burrelle's Information Services.

262 **"The guy can't lose"**: Howard Kurtz, "Exit Wounds," *WP*, Nov. 9, 2000.

263 **"Whatever I have to say"**: *AP*, Dec. 12, 2000.

266 **Rather and Brokaw**: *NYT*, Dec. 5, 2000.

266 **The court decision**: *Ibid.*

266 **"It was a tie"**: CNN transcript # 00120401V00, Dec. 4, 2000.

266 **"A treacherous path"**: CNN transcript #00110914V09, Nov. 9, 2000.

267 **"The Limits of Patience"**: *NYT*, Nov. 12, 2000.

267 **"Price of premature closure"**: Lawrence H. Tribe, "Let the Courts Decide," *NYT*, Nov. 12, 2000.

267 **Arguing for a new election**: Philip B. Heymann, "The Case for a Do-Over," *WP*, Nov. 11, 2000.

268 **"Every vote counts"**: Mary McGrory, "Now They're Talking," *WP*, Nov. 12, 2000.

268 **Measuring patience**: Gallup Organization press release, Nov. 28, 2000; *NYT*, Nov. 30, 2000.

268 **Russert vs. Lieberman**: NBC News, "Meet the Press" transcript, Nov. 19, 2000.

269 **A better outlet**: *WP*, Dec. 3, 2000; *NYT*, Nov. 30, 2000.

269 **Miami Herald study**: *NYT*, Dec. 4, 2000.

269 **Miami mayor's role**: *NYT*, Dec. 1, 2000.

270 **Character counts:** See also Robert Shogan, "Covering Character," *Media Studies Journal*, Winter 2000.

272 **Conflicting poll data:** John J. Miller, "No Need to Hide," *NYT*, Feb. 18, 1999.

272 **Polling caveats:** Statistical Assessment Service (STATS), "Polls, Predictions and the Press," Washington, D. C., September 2000.

276 **"Further disaffection":** Committee for the Study of the American Electorate," press release, Nov. 10, 2000.

276 **Constitutional change:** See also Robert Shogan, *None of the Above: Why Presidents Fail and What Can Be Done About It* (New York: New American Library, 1982).

Index

Index

A NOTE ON THE AUTHOR

Robert Shogan was born in New York City and stud-
ied journalism at Syracuse University. After working
for the *Detroit Free Press* and the *Wall Street Journal*,
he reported on the political scene from Washington
for *Newsweek* and as national political correspondent
for the *Los Angeles Times* for more than thirty years
and over the course of seven presidencies. He has
been professional in residence at the Annenberg
School of Communications of the University of
Pennsylvania; a Robert R. McCormick fellow at the
Hoover Presidential Library; a fellow at the Freedom
Forum's Media Study Center; and, currently, adjunct
professor of political science at the Center for the
Study of American Government of Johns Hopkins
University. Among his several awards is one from the
American Political Science Association for distin-
guished reporting on public affairs. Mr. Shogan lives
in Chevy Chase, Maryland.